Where I Come From

Where I Come From

Vijay Agnew

Wilfrid Laurier University Press

We acknowledge the support of the Canada Council for the Arts for our publishing program. We acknowledge the financial support of the Government of Canada through the Book Publishing Industry Development Program for our publishing activities.

National Library of Canada Cataloguing in Publication Data

Agnew, Vijay, 1946-
  Where I come from / Vijay Agnew.

(Life writing series)
Includes bibliographical references.
ISBN 0-88920-414-4

  1. Agnew, Vijay, 1946-. 2. East Indian Canadians—Ethnic identity.
3. Immigrants—Canada—Biography. 4. College teachers—Canada—Biography.
5. East Indian Canadians—Biography. I. Title. II. Series.

FC106.E2Z7 2003   971'.00491411'0092   C2003-903591-3

© 2003 Wilfrid Laurier University Press
Waterloo, Ontario, Canada   N2L 3C5
www.wlupress.wlu.ca

Cover design by P.J. Woodland; interior design and layout by C. Bonas-Taylor.

To Nicole, who makes me proud.

We cannot control life, the joy and the sorrow of it, the achievement or otherwise, but one thing we ought to be able to control and that is our attitude to it. We can, I believe, make a work of art out of our lives, a song or a beautiful melody, even though that song may clutch at the throat and bring tears to the eyes. No one can deny us that artistry of living if we are ourselves capable of it—if we are capable, it is a big if! Not to reject life but to accept it in all its fullness, and yet to go through it finely and with light steps and refusing to allow it to besmirch us. That is a worthwhile ideal, a difficult undertaking, and the very few who may have the good fortune to approach it can never regret the choice. Success if it comes, comes worthily with no tinsel or vulgarity; failure itself approaches with noble and tragic mien.

> — Jawaharlal Nehru (from a letter written to his sister
> from Naini Central Prison, September 12, 1934)

Contents

Acknowledgements

A book of memories mines anecdotes about relatives, friends, neighbours, students, and colleagues, and as this book goes to press I am full of doubt and apprehension. I am concerned about retaining their and my reader's good opinion, and wonder if they will be disappointed in me for having revealed so much as I recall the feelings and emotions evoked in me by some incidents. I am indebted to all of them, and hope that they will not think I have unduly exploited my memories of them and of their role in shaping me. There will be differences of opinion and interpretations; this is just my experience of people and incidents and not, by any means, the "whole truth." Whenever possible, I have changed names and details of individuals to protect their privacy.

I spent a sabbatical writing the first draft of this book, and then finished it over the next couple of years. My previous books had explored how the intersection of race, class, and gender oppresses women from Asia, Africa, and the Caribbean; I felt talked out and wanted to move on to other, more cheerful subjects. That proved an illusory wish, however. I could not wipe the slate clean, and found myself coming back in this memoir to the concerns that have preoccupied most, if not all, of my academic work.

My writing career owes an immense debt to a friend who does not wish to be named. In the last ten years my friend has read and talked to me about everything I have written. Oftentimes when my mind was cluttered with fragmentary ideas, his patient listening and insightful questions helped me shape them into substantial arguments. Through the many drafts that each of my books and articles went through, he helped me hone my writing skills. I will always owe a debt of gratitude to this friend who has helped me to become a writer, an endeavour that brings me both satisfaction and pleasure.

I am grateful to the reviewers of this book—those I know and those who remain anonymous. Marlene Kadar and I had known each other as colleagues, but somehow it never "clicked" that she was the editor of the series in which this book is being published. Meanwhile, I agonized over whether I should ask her to read the manuscript and give me her suggestions. I thank her for her humour and patience in response to my many bumbling questions. I thank Alok Mukherjee for doing a superb job of reviewing the manuscript and catching the inaccuracies of Indian phenomena. He did this despite our different perspectives, though I think my interpretations must have tried his patience at times. Elin Edwards and Brian Henderson at Wilfrid Laurier University Press put up with my nagging, and I thank them both for soothing my anxieties when reviewers seemed to be taking, in my view, a long time to send in their comments. I think of Elin as a friend, and we have often swapped stories about daughters. I am grateful to Carol Pollock for editing the final draft of the manuscript and seeing it completed, much to my relief. A grant from the Social Science and Humanities Research Council and a one-year leave from York University helped to research and finish the book.

Since coming to Canada, my overriding concern has been with race and racism, and the powerful impact of each on the lives of immigrants and women such as myself. However, while writing this memoir I met Suzanne Sadler, a neighbour who suffers from multiple sclerosis. My own brush with serious illness drew us to each other, and we have become friends. Suzanne does not let her disease get her down, though it robs her of the energy to do the many things that interest her. She struggles to keep despairing thoughts at bay and courageously walks, talks, and parties. She is quick to laugh and always ready to share the latest witticism she has come across. In knowing her, I have learned a lesson in courage, and now I always think of her continuing struggle when a new incident of racism gets me down. Suzanne has shown me that although we all have our own burdens, what distinguishes us is how we bear our sorrows.

I am grateful to my next-door neighbour Nancy Nobrega, who unhesitatingly told me, when I wondered aloud at a book club meeting what I, as an immigrant, would do in a family emergency, "Vijay, just come to my door and knock." Her generosity of feeling helped allay my fears of being a "foreigner" and an "outsider." When I was laid up after an accident, she was there with food and comfort, and I knew that while I was alone and sick at home I could rely on her kindness. I also thank my other book club friends and colleagues from the university whose well-wishes and thoughtfulness, once again, shifted and changed the boundaries of my physical and emotional "home."

I am, as always, indebted to my husband Tom for not complaining as I remain absorbed with my writing for days at a time. I draw sustenance and comfort from him, as well as from the love of my sister Rita and her husband Pammi, and my brother Subash and his wife Linda. Ties of family, love and friendship bind us together, particularly now as our children go their own ways and we are confronted with the challenge of growing old gracefully in our chosen countries.

Ah well...what is life but a series of challenges?

Introduction

When I first immigrated to Canada, people used to ask me: "Where do you come from?" I thought it was a simple, straightforward question, and I used to answer, simply and straightforwardly, by reciting the names of the places of my birth and upbringing: "India...New Delhi...Bombay." Over the years, however, I learned that many "Third World" people resent being asked this question, because it implies that having a different skin colour (which is what usually prompts the question) makes a person an outsider and "not really Canadian."

Although I still don't mind being asked the question, these days I want to give a much longer and more complicated answer, listing all the communities in India and in Canada—both geographical and cultural—in which I have lived. All of these places represent "where I come from," and the values, norms, and attitudes that they have instilled in me are essential parts of who I am, in spite of a sense of loss for some of them after thirty-two years in Canada.

I grew up in India, spending my girlhood in Delhi and young adulthood in Bombay. Then I immigrated to Canada, where I was first a foreign student but eventually became a wife, a mother, and a professor. When I first arrived in Canada, I was unaware of my values and unconscious of their role in defining who I was, but being an immigrant compelled me to reflect upon and try to understand them. I realized that living in India with my aunt, and later with my father, I had taken for granted many class

Note to introduction is on p. 281.

1

privileges, hardly noticing the oppressions of gender, caste, and class all around me. I believed that the values by which I was raised were universal, rather than being upper-middle-class, Hindu values specific to my family, class, and culture. I also realized that if I wanted to be able to give an intelligent and coherent answer to the question of where I came from, I would have to learn much more about my Hindu-Indian heritage.

In graduate school at the universities of Waterloo and Toronto, where I studied Indian history and Imperialism, I tended to feel like an outsider: a student, like almost everyone I met, but like almost no one else, a non-white, "Indian" woman. Initially, I lacked confidence in myself, and I wanted to adopt the perspective of the white, mostly male professors whose classes I attended. Fortunately, and perhaps ironically, the analytical and critical skills that I learned from them—tempered with nostalgia for "home"—helped me to resist that urge. Eventually I realized that being an Indian woman made a difference in how I thought about things, and I came to see more clearly the limitations of their perspective.

At the University of Toronto I read about feminism and observed the then-popular feminist practices of some white Canadian students. "Patriarchy," "oppression," and "exploitation" entered my vocabulary, and I began to interpret my past and present through a feminist lens. What had seemed normal and natural before took on more ominous tones. However, the exclusion of race at that time from feminist analysis alienated me and led to my disenchantment with gender-centred, white feminism. I became an "Indian feminist." Now I am part of the academic feminist community in Canada, but sometimes I still feel like an outsider in it.

Teaching in Canadian universities has helped shape who I am now. At York University I have had an opportunity to meet many other immigrants, and their Canadian-born children, and gain insight into our shared experiences. My research came to focus on the study of immigrants from Asia, Africa, and the Caribbean. An unexpected side effect was that the more teaching and research I did, the more conscious I became of the race and gender discrimination I was encountering at the university as a non-white, "Third World" woman. Dismayed by the treatment I received from white professors (both male and female), I tried—being an academic—to assuage my hurt and pain by learning more about race, class, and gender discrimination in Canada and its impact on immigrants.

My research drew me to immigrant women's groups in Toronto. I derived some comfort from talking with them about racism and sexism, and from helping them set up government-funded social-service organizations to enable them to establish safe and dignified lives for themselves in Canada. However, my association with these organizations forced me to think again about where I came from. I had to confront the fact that certain sexist values and cultural norms of Hindus and Muslims in India were leading to horrendous consequences for some South Asian women in Canada.

As a wife and mother, however, I was being integrated at the same time into other neighbourhoods and "communities" in the city. Mutual interests and needs drew me to women who, like me, were mothers. Although some of us combined motherhood with paid work and others remained at home, we were all focused on our children's needs for playmates. We came together with little attention to race or ethnicity, fretting instead about the well-being of our offspring.

Memories of "home" and my old way of life still tied me to Bombay, and I used to return every couple of years to visit my father, but my experiences in Canada had changed me. I began to perceive familiar sights—especially the masses of people living in poverty and the untouchables excluded from mainstream Indian life—with Canadian eyes, and that put more distance between "home" and me. Relationships with friends and relatives lost their intensity as our lives took different paths. "Home"—and a sense of belonging there—became an illusion wrapped up in warm memories rather than a reflection of concrete reality.

On a recent visit to New Delhi with my sister, I was amazed when over and over again each of us was asked by waiters, store clerks, drivers, and hotel managers, "Madam, where do you come from?" We gave evasive answers, or said we were from Bombay. I encountered the same question when I visited the large, wooded campus of Jawaharlal Nehru University. I was by myself, dressed in a simple, cotton *salwar kamiz*—an outfit commonly worn by the people there and comprising a long, loose shirt and baggy pants—and a long, matching scarf, or *dupatta*. I stopped two young female students, ostensibly to ask for directions to the library, but really just to chat. One of the students had short hair and was dressed in jeans and a T-shirt; the other wore a salwar kamiz much like mine. After a minute or so of conversation, they asked, "Madam, what country are you from?"

I was not carrying a camera, a water bottle, or a campus map—things that might have identified me as a visitor. I touched my face and asked the students, "Can't you tell that I am an Indian?" They seemed doubtful. I asked them what set me apart from the local people. They replied vaguely that something about me was different, venturing that perhaps it was my hair (though it is black like that of most Indians), or my accent.

The students had verbalized what I felt but had difficulty acknowledging: that after living in Canada for over thirty years, albeit with frequent visits to India, I no longer seemed to be an insider in Indian society. I was more like an outsider, even in my community of origin.

Now I feel I am both an insider and an outsider—in Canadian and Indian society. Sometimes, despite my familiarity with them both, I feel I am mainly an outsider. However, I feel more like an insider than, say, Indian author Salman Rushdie, who lives in Britain. "I used to feel simultaneously on both sides," he says. "Now I've come down firmly on the side of those who by preference, nature or circumstance simply do not belong."[1]

When I arrived in Canada, I believed I had to choose between cultures. I dreaded hearing Indian friends say of a remark or deed of mine, "That is so Canadian!" I took this to mean that I had betrayed both them and my authentic Hindu-Indian self. Now, I have lived in Canada for many years; I am no longer the young woman I was when I first immigrated. I have discarded some of the values, norms, and attitudes with which I was raised in India, and exchanged others for "Canadian" ones. I have modified or become newly committed to still others.

Perhaps I should describe myself as belonging to the South Asian immigrant community in Canada. Yet, ties of love and friendship bind me to the white community as well—members of my husband's family, teachers and students at work, and neighbours among whom I have lived for many years. If I am an outsider, if I am "not really Canadian," I am still a relative, a friend, and a neighbour, and these too are parts of "where I come from."

1

Beginning in Canada

I came to Canada when I was twenty-four years old. Since I was born in India, I suppose people will call me an Indian-Canadian, but this suggests to me more than they may have in mind: that after going through a process of blending Indian—mainly Hindu—and Canadian—mainly Christian—values, I ended in a fixed state of being. I don't think this is true. Indeed, the more I think about what "Indian-Canadian" might mean, the less I think it describes who I am.

The question of who I am is important, not only because this is the story of how I became who I am, but also because I want readers to see the perspective from which it is written: the perspective of the *me* at the "end" of the story. It is important, too, because I am a woman with brown skin who has been perceived by other people almost exclusively in terms of gender and race, just two aspects of my identity. Yet, recognizing that who I am now is only one stage in a lifelong process of *becoming* (and an insignificant stage in a much longer process, according to Hindu religion), and that who I think I am and who other people think I am are different things, only raises additional doubts about trying to say who I am.

I have discussed these questions about identity with my daughter, Nicole. She says they are just symptoms of a mid-life crisis and that it is she, as the offspring of me and my husband, Tom, a white Canadian, who should be having the identity crisis. "Besides" she says, "what is all this about Hinduism? Aren't you a feminist? Hinduism encodes the subjuga-

---

Notes to chapter 1 are on p. 281.

tion of women." As an afterthought she adds, "I suppose that is also true of Christianity..." but this only provides me with another reason for not thinking of myself as an "Indian-Canadian."

Perhaps my daughter is right, and I am having a mid-life crisis.

The last few weeks have been full of preparations to send Nicole off to university in the United States. We have been debating what she should take with her and what she should leave at home. I tell her what to do when she is homesick and how to integrate into campus life, and she just nods indulgently. I share my experiences as a foreign student in Canada some thirty years ago, but I'm probably giving her outdated and not very useful advice.

When I left home to come to Canada, I had travelled nowhere outside India and only a little ways within. The little I knew about North America came from friends who had studied in the United States or from American novels and movies. I wouldn't have been able to say much about Canada as a distinct country, with its own history and culture. I hadn't read any Canadian novels or seen any Canadian movies, and knew nothing about its politics. Just before leaving Bombay, I did read a few books and brochures about the country, but the "facts" and statistics I gleaned from these texts meant little to me. I could not see through them to the everyday life of Canadian people.

I read, for instance, that winters in Canada were "very cold." My older brother Subash lived in Kingston, Ontario, having moved there to teach medicine after studying in the U.S. Although we were later to become close, we had grown up in different cities and households, and had little contact at that time. The occasional letters we did exchange contained news of people rather than details of life in Canada. I am not sure if weather ever came up for comment.

In Canada, where there are distinct seasons and extreme winter conditions, people are always discussing the weather. Bombay's climate, on the other hand, is generally warm and pleasant, except for some days in the monsoon season. Since a nice day was not exceptional, we seldom referred to it; I did not understand the difference between "cold" and "very cold." I later found out that what we considered cold weather in Bombay—a temperature of about sixty degrees Fahrenheit—might be a pleasant summer evening in Toronto. Since the radio (we had no television in India before the 1970s) did not bother to report temperatures, it meant nothing to me when I read that in Canada the thermometer often fell below thirty-two degrees Fahrenheit. I bought myself a couple of light sweaters and thought they would do me just fine.

The few books I did read about Canada provided little preparation for the social and cultural differences I discovered when I got here from India, but as the two countries are so vastly different, I wonder whether more reading would have helped me very much. I did not know about Native people or about the history of blacks and Asians in Canada. I took it as fact that all Canadians were white-skinned, and did not attach much significance to it. I was conscious of gradations of colour amongst people in India, from the dark-skinned people in the south to the very fair-skinned people of Kashmir. European colouring just seemed to be a part of this continuum. I had little or no consciousness of race.

I did know about technological progress in North America—the sophisticated telecommunication systems, the styles and varieties of automobiles, the household gadgetry, all considered highly desirable possessions by the Indians I knew—but I was more familiar with the glamorous images portrayed in movies and magazines that came from the West. I was savvy enough not to see all those images as real, but I had no sense of what North American affluence meant in contrast to what I was used to in India. I didn't think of it in terms of, for instance, waste and conservation, and many years would go by before I would understand the necessity of seeing things in context.

When I immigrated to Ontario in 1970 after completing undergraduate and law degrees at Bombay University, it was to study for a master's degree in history at the University of Waterloo. At that time, there were very few students at the university from Third World countries, and most of the ones who were there were enrolled in the department of mathematics and computer science; I was the only non-white student in the graduate history program. I was assigned an office with three other women, all Canadians. They were amazed that I had even heard of Waterloo in India and wondered why I had chosen to study there. In truth, I had wanted to study in the United States, but most of all I wanted to live and travel in the West. My decision to apply to universities in Ontario was part of a strategy meant to wear down my father's resistance to my leaving home. With a brother living in the province, I figured he would be less opposed to Ontario than someplace in the United States. I had come across the University of Waterloo's name in some brochures at the library in Bombay.

I must confess that my primary motivation for going to graduate school at all was to be free of the constraints of living at home. Leaving the country seemed like a good way to avoid having to continue school in Bombay; I could begin an independent life away from my father, sisters and remaining brother. My father was very reluctant to let me travel outside India to study, but I waged an unrelenting campaign for a year to be allowed to leave home. Finally, he said that if I could get admission and make all the arrangements without any help from him or any other relative, I could go.

I expect he thought I wouldn't be able to do all that. At the time I had only travelled within India, and always in the company of relatives. I had never had to make a reservation for an airplane or railway ticket. When I travelled to other cities, it was in the company of my two sisters, and we stayed with relatives who came to get us from the railway station, showed us around, made arrangements for us to visit other relatives, accompanied us shopping, and then took us back to the station for our journey home.

The university offered me a scholarship that covered tuition and some incidental expenses, and that clinched the argument with my father. He even agreed to pay for my books, travel expenses and room and board at an on-campus residence, as well as provide me with some spending money. First, though, I had to obtain a permit from the government that would enable me to exchange my rupees for dollars.

As anyone who has dealt with bureaucrats in India will testify, getting the simplest of tasks done requires enormous amounts of patience and time. Many signatures were required, and that meant I had to spend a lot of time lining up to obtain forms and have them signed by the right person (who might be away on a two-hour lunch break at any time during the day). I had to visit several government offices to find out about regulations on exchanging currency and whether I qualified for the permit to do so. It turned out it was only available to students who had received a "first class" in provincial examinations. Fortunately, I was among the qualified and, after making my way through the bureaucratic maze, was able to get the permit.

Although this enabled me to exchange some money, I did not know what this amount of money might or might not buy for me in Canada. I knew what the tuition and residence fees were, but I had no idea how much food, transportation, books and clothing might cost for one year's study, and the university hadn't provided any such estimate. Furthermore, I had no idea what it might mean to live within a budget. Up to this time, I had never been given a fixed allowance. I had taken spending money as and when I had needed it and my father had asked few questions. A budget was a new reality, particularly in the context of stringent currency-exchange regulations, and I just didn't absorb the fact that I would not be able to casually write home and ask for more money. When I got to Waterloo, the insecurity of being a newcomer in an alien environment and having limited funds made me extremely reluctant to spend any money, even to feed myself. For the first few weeks in Waterloo, I was hungry most of the time.

Other preparations were also difficult. One of the requirements for a passport—a birth certificate—presented a problem as I was born in a time when women delivered babies at home with the help of midwives; there had been no procedures for registering births. As a consequence, I had to find a lawyer who could provide an affidavit as to my birth that would enable me to apply for the passport.

Subash had sponsored me for immigration, and so I also had to obtain an immigrant visa, which meant travelling from Bombay to the Canadian consulate in New Delhi. My interview there with a Canadian immigration officer lasted only five minutes, and consisted of cursory questions about my father's economic situation. At the end of the interview, the officer remarked that my value in the marriage market had risen substantially by his granting me a visa. Happy to get my immigration papers, I paid little attention to the biases implicit in his comments.

As the time for my departure drew closer, my father encouraged me to go out and buy myself some appropriate clothing. My sister Rita and I decided to check out the stores in the major hotels where tourists shopped, hoping to guide my purchases by gaining some insight into what was appreciated in the West. We discovered that items made of silk and brocade were the most favoured in such places, so next we went to the bazaars, proudly telling the salesmen that we were buying clothes for me to take to Canada. This bit of information only encouraged them to bring out elaborately embroidered saris in vibrant colours while asserting knowledgeably that "foreigners" (a colloquial term for Western tourists) greatly admired such hues and craftsmanship, making them the most prudent purchases for me.

However, we thought we were smart shoppers, and insisted, as they continued to spread out sari after sari on the huge table in front of us, that they bring out simple, printed silk saris that I could wear to the university on a daily basis. It was obviously a case of the blind leading the blind. Rita and I had a great time shopping, but my purchases did not include a single item that would be useful or practical in Canada.

It was the beginning of September, and still no visa had come in the mail. Nonetheless, I packed and waited anxiously. The day it arrived, my father handed me the money he had promised. I went to the Thomas Cook travel agency, bought my air ticket, and was soon on my way to Canada.

When I think of my first few months at the university, I am reminded of the sitcom *Third Rock from the Sun*, where aliens from outer space come to live in the United States and are constantly amazed by the way people behave. My situation was somewhat like that. I had little or no knowledge of Canadian culture. I had never even met a Canadian. The other graduate students, for their part, knew little about India and had never met an Indian woman. Most of the students I met had not travelled outside Ontario, and I did not meet any who had made a journey to Asia, Africa, the Caribbean, or even to Europe. In fact, I was puzzled that the university had offered me the scholarship. Looking back, I think it was because they had recently hired a historian who specialized in British history and another who specialized even more narrowly in British imperialism; they may have wanted to have at least one graduate student in their areas of study. At that time there was little interest among Canadian students in the history of British involvement in either Asia or Africa.

The graduate program of the history department was small, as was the number of graduate students. The graduate women's residence, where I lived, housed eighty students, of which only two, besides me, were non-white—one a woman from Bombay who had come to study French, and the other a Chinese mathematics student. But being a rare species has its advantages. The professors and other students easily recognized me. They often introduced themselves to me and sought opportunities to engage me in conversation. At the graduate residence, women would strike up a conversation with me in the common room and in the kitchen. However, my three closest friends at Waterloo were Linda, Mary Jane, and Barbara, with whom I shared my assigned office. Mary Jane and Barbara were of British ancestry, and Linda was a French-Canadian from Sudbury who spoke little French. All three were studying Canadian history.

Linda was a pretty woman who was particular about her appearance and always dressed stylishly. Friendly and vivacious, she was quick to see the humour in any situation and laughed often and easily. Linda had left northern Ontario to experience an environment outside the one in which she had grown up. She was fascinated by me, so different from herself; and asked me many questions about India. Although I was fascinated by her as well, I felt much less comfortable asking her questions. Linda did not live at the residence, but in an off-campus apartment with her boyfriend. I made no judgement on this situation, not knowing at the time whether the arrangement was usual or unusual, right or wrong. I cannot say that I resisted the temptation to judge this behaviour by my Hindu-Indian norms; rather, such relationships were simply out of the orbit of my experience and so I accepted them without giving them much thought.

Mary Jane, a deeply religious Anglican who attended church every Sunday, had grown up in a middle-class family in Toronto. Tall and slim, with curly, shoulder-length hair, she wore little makeup and dressed simply and practically, in jeans and a sweater. Mary Jane had lived at home while attending university, but married soon after completing a bachelor's degree at York University. She and her husband had lived all their lives in Toronto, and coming to Waterloo was their first break away from home.

Barbara had been raised in Waterloo by a single mother, which was unusual in those days. Also tall and slim, with long, straight hair that fell below her shoulders, she liked to wear skirts, which made her stand out amongst the jeans-wearing university students. Barbara was supporting herself at the university by waitressing at a bar in a posh hotel in downtown Kitchener. Her work, which made her so different from anyone I had ever met before, placed me in awe of what I saw as her worldliness and sophistication but, in fact, Barbara had not travelled much farther than Toronto. The residence was her first venture into independent living. She too wanted to get to know people from outside her area. I suppose we were all aspiring to become educated, cosmopolitan women and were anxious to learn about each other as a first tentative step in that direction.

Linda, Mary Jane, and Barbara took it upon themselves to show me around the campus and explain things to me. I suppose I seemed exotic to them, and they were happy to introduce me to things I found fairly exotic as well. Even eating was a cultural adventure. I had never been to a cafeteria like the one on campus; I did not know how to ask for food or drinks or how to pay for them. I didn't understand the currency. I had never seen, let alone tasted, hamburgers, macaroni, mashed potatoes, or any of the food sold there. The aromas of the food were totally different from what I knew—not a hint of the cardamoms, cloves, and peppers that provide the flavour to Indian food. I felt little inclination to try any of it.

I did recognize French fries, and since they were the cheapest item available and I had limited money, I ate them every day. They were very popular with the other students too, but my friends noticed that they were just about all I ate. Finally, Barbara asked, "Why do you eat them every day? Don't you get French fries in India?" How funny to think I would want to eat food I had never seen in India! In fact, the reverse is the case for most immigrants, who often go to great lengths to find vegetables and spices that are familiar to them. Eating the foods one has grown up with provides psychological comfort in unfamiliar surroundings.

If the food was unappealing, I was entirely unprepared for the Canadian winter. I don't know how I would have survived without the help of Barbara, Linda, and Mary Jane. I had lots of silk saris, some dainty sandals, and those two light sweaters. No coat, hat, gloves, or socks. Relatives in Bombay had advised me that it would be best to buy a new wardrobe in Canada. That way, they said, I would be sure to get whatever the other students were wearing, which would put me at ease and prevent me from feeling out of place.

No one, however, had anticipated that I would not know what kinds of clothes I should buy, or where to buy them. In India, at that time, all clothing was custom-made, so the usual procedure was to buy fabric from a store, take it to a tailor, explain the design to him, and hope for the best. Of course, I should have asked someone at Waterloo where to buy clothes, but I was in such a state of shock and had so many new experiences crowding in upon me that I was finding it impossible even to think of simple things like that.

I was cold and miserable in my sari and sandals during my first Canadian September. Fortunately, Barbara realized that I desperately needed clothes—whether I knew it or not. She may have mentioned my plight to other students in the residence, for a number of them came knocking on my door, saying they had gloves, or socks, or pants, or sweaters they had no use for and that I could have them if I wanted. Within a few days I had accumulated a whole new wardrobe! I did not know when I needed to wear these things, though, so Barbara would explain all that when she came to walk with me to the department.

Seeing me bundled up in a newly acquired hat and scarf always made her smile broadly and made me feel self-conscious. Yet the clothes that were given to me were not only useful, but also helped me to make friends. When women came to give me a hat or a scarf, they stayed and talked to me. Some came back to chat and told me about their own lives. Some were quite uninhibited in confiding secrets, and I could not always tell what was truth and what fantasy. Nevertheless, I was fascinated and listened to their stories intently.

One day Barbara suggested we go shopping so I could get some boots and a winter coat. With my budget at the time, we should have gone straight to a bargain-basement store, but Barbara took me instead to some more expensive places. I suppose she figured I was middle-class, and I didn't think to ask to go to other, more suitable stores. With no advice to the contrary, I bought a bright-red, leather coat. A pair of brown woollen pants with a matching vest, shoes with high heels, and a pair of boots rounded out the ensemble. I was panic-stricken at having spent so much of my limited budget on clothing, and later, to my chagrin, I found that I had not made a very good selection. Brightly coloured clothing is common in India, but my red coat shocked the other students into smiles; the norm from what I came to observe of most Canadians was to prefer muted shades. The shoes and boots, although they had cost what seemed like a fortune at the time, were not waterproof, and since I was reluctant to spend any more money, I went around for the whole year with cold, soaking feet.

It was difficult for me to adjust to the weight of Canadian clothing, and the unfamiliar shoes and boots actually made it difficult for me to walk. The usual pace of walking in Bombay is fairly leisurely, but in Waterloo I slowed to a crawl. Sometimes, when I was inching along to the history department with Barbara, she would become very impatient and chide me. "Stop strolling," she'd say, "and walk!" Eventually I learned how to keep up with the Canadian pace. However, when, after four years, I went back to Bombay, relatives would say reprovingly, "Why are you running, Vijay? Walk slowly!"

That first year also marked my introduction to snow, something I had never seen before. Eager to see my reaction to it, Barbara, Linda, and Mary Jane took me outside on the day of the first big snowfall to have a look. They decided to show me how children play in the winter, demonstrating by making snowballs and throwing them at each other in fun.

However, the unfamiliarity of the scene made me apprehensive. I took little pleasure in watching their snowball fight or seeing the fresh snow on the ground and on the trees. I did *not* find it beautiful. After a few minutes of standing in the cold, white powder and nodding appreciatively, I was ready to go back inside. I found, unfortunately, that I couldn't walk through the snow: I slipped and fell down, and I kept on slipping and falling down as I tried to make my way home. This made Barbara and Mary Jane laugh, but I was soon in tears from embarrassment and hurt. Finally, they linked their arms with mine and walked me back to the residence.

This experience was very different from that of character Gibreel Farishta in Salman Rushdie's *The Satanic Verses,* who was quite delighted when he was first surrounded by snow: "He started capering about, saturnine and soggy, making snowballs and hurling them at his prone companion, envisioning a snowman, and singing a wild, swooping rendition of the carol 'Jingle-Bells.'"[1] Barbara and Mary Jane had acted like that, but I was just an onlooker, a (repeatedly prone) companion. This incident did, however, show my friends that snow made me nervous, and this insight saved me a few days later in the first big storm of the winter.

I had spent the evening of the big whiteout at the library, quite oblivious to the blizzard raging outside. Back in the residence, Barbara was on the phone with Linda, who asked in passing what I thought of the snowstorm. Concerned, Barbara ran down to my room and, not finding me there, assumed that I was probably at the library. She decided immediately to brave the storm and go look for me there, taking along an extra sweater, a scarf, and some snow pants. She found me, reading away, quite unaware of the dangerous weather conditions.

Half annoyed and half amused, Barbara told me what was happening outside and bundled me into the sweater, pants, and scarf. On the steps of the library, the cold, biting wind and snow hit us full in the face. It was all but impossible to see the street, and I couldn't even tell where we were headed. Luckily, Barbara was familiar with the campus and held my hand all the way to the residence. I felt lucky to get back at all that night, and in the privacy of my room I broke down and cried myself to sleep, thinking of Bombay.

I was still feeling insecure and self-conscious later that winter when Mary Jane and her husband Martin, also a graduate student at the university, invited me to a party in their home. I was pleased to be included in the party, along with Barbara and Linda and her boyfriend, but when the day arrived and I began to get ready to go to their apartment, I wondered what would make them—and me—feel more comfortable...a sari or pants? I began to have doubts about my ability to make conversation with them. Would I become tongue-tied and appear doltish? In spite of my fears, however, I was determined to go.

Mary Jane had taken care to inquire of me what kind of meat I ate; I guess she knew that strict Hindus do not eat meat (nor would they have it in their kitchen). As with any "rule," however, this ideal is seldom practised, and I told her that I had occasionally eaten chicken in restaurants, in spite of having grown up in a vegetarian household.

When I arrived at their apartment, Martin was cleaning chicken in the kitchen. Our conversation naturally turned to food preparation, although I did not know anything about Western cooking and they had no clue about Indian customs. I reassured them that I was familiar with some meats, adding, quite unselfconsciously, that I felt squeamish about touching it in its raw state, but could eat it quite well if it was cooked and disguised in some sauce. This must have been disconcerting for Mary Jane and Martin, who, I realized, had intended merely to grill the chicken: there was no sauce in sight.

When my friends asked what dishes would constitute an everyday meal in my family and I told them it was "lentils, vegetables, and plain yogurt," they were astounded that people could eat a meal without a main-course meat dish. (This was before the vegetarian fad came to North America.) Their amazed responses only heightened my consciousness of being different from them. However, they bravely asked that I prepare a typical Indian meal for them one day.

When I tried to do that a few weeks later, it was disastrous. I had no idea how to buy the groceries I needed, or how to cook in a Canadian kitchen, with its different layout, stove, and utensils. At home, we often cooked chickpeas with cumin, cilantro, ginger, garlic, turmeric, tamarind and black pepper, along with onions and tomatoes. In Waterloo, I used chickpeas from a can, which tasted quite different from the dried variety I was used to, and I had few spices to flavour them. I boiled up some rice to accompany the chickpeas. Unfamiliar with the taste and flavouring of the food, my friends had a hard time eating the pathetic meal that I prepared for them.

The day after the party at Mary Jane's house I was at the local super-market, marvelling as usual at the neat and clean packaging of the vegetables and at the huge varieties of items available on the shelves—which flummoxed me since I did not know what might approximate the kinds of foods I was used to eating. Completely absorbed in my own task, I paid little attention to the other shoppers. The following day, Mary Jane asked me with a puzzled look why I hadn't said hello to Martin at the supermarket. I apologized and explained that I had probably not recognized him. The split second's look of astonishment on Mary Jane's face stayed with me for a long time.

It was only many years later that I realized I had unknowingly reversed a situation that Mary Jane was familiar with in her own experience. White Canadians often find it hard to distinguish between "foreign" people. They find it difficult to distinguish between Chinese people, between blacks, and between South Asians. It is a matter of what are called "culturally conditioned reference points."

For example, white Canadians often describe an individual by referring to hair or eye colour. I can remember many small details of Barbara, Linda, and Mary Jane's appearance, but I cannot remember the colour of their hair or eyes. Since almost all South Asians have dark eyes and hair (except for gray hair), I often don't pay much attention to these characteristics. I may notice height, weight, or style of dress, but it's still easier for me to see gradations of skin colour, for instance, among South Asians, and to remember their regional identity, religion, or language. Martin was white, like nearly everyone else I saw in Waterloo, and dressed in jeans, like most of the other students. I had no mental reference points with which I could identify him. He looked like all the other white men to me.

Except for walks to the nearby supermarket, my life during that first year in Waterloo was confined primarily to the university campus. On occasion, one of my friends would take me into the city, but walking around in the cold on my own was simply too terrifying and uncomfortable. Besides, spending a quarter on bus fare seemed an unnecessary expense. Sometimes I walked long distances to save that quarter, but then the cold temperatures, my uncomfortable, wet shoes and heavy winter coat made me feel miserable. Usually, I opted to just stay inside the residence or go somewhere on campus.

One of the most difficult things for me to get used to was all the empty space around the campus and between the buildings on it. Large, mature trees surrounded the grounds of the university and a ravine on one side separated it from the main road. However, there were few trees between the buildings, and the landscape held no particular interest for me. What's more, there was a near absence of people on the sidewalks. This created in me the feeling of living in a deserted, desolate place. On the campus I saw plenty of cars, but I rarely encountered another person walking—no street vendors, no beggars, no stray dogs or goats wandering around. The streets were silent. There was no sound of people talking, no honking horns, and no loud music emanating from houses or corner stores. I missed the hustle and bustle of Bombay and its sidewalks and streets chock-full of people.

I saw Linda, Mary Jane, and Barbara every day, and it would be nice if I could say that we had intense discussions about cultural differences or similarities, but that was certainly not the case. All my energies were concentrated on trying to survive the ordinary routine of a student's life—eating, going to classes, and studying. I had little mental or emotional energy to reflect upon my situation as does Rosa Diamond, another character in *Satanic Verses* who is always asking herself, "Of what was she capable in all that space? What did she have the courage for, how could she expand?"[2] I wasn't setting any long-term goals for myself.

My three friends were as anxious to show me the sights around Kitchener-Waterloo as they were to learn about India. They, and other students I met through them, constantly mentioned two items of interest: the local farmers' market, which was held every Sunday, and the "quaint" Mennonite people who drove horse-drawn buggies to church on Sundays.

At the farmers' market, Barbara and Mary Jane showed me, with admiration, the handmade quilts made by the Mennonite women. I got a taste of some homemade jams and pickles. I could not figure out, though, what it was about these things that made them unique or interesting to my friends. In India, the only pickles and chutneys available were homemade, and hand-sewn and embroidered items were commonplace. But I was insecure in my new environment and hesitant to say anything, let alone voice an opinion or question what I was being told. I hoped that by keeping quiet I could hide my own ignorance, that by paying sufficient attention I could get a glimmer of understanding as to what I was expected to appreciate. So, I did not tell my friends that the local supermarkets, with their well-displayed shelves of food, fascinated me more, or that I was excited to try brand-name pickles, or that I wanted to go to the department stores and buy ready-to-wear clothing off the rack.

The farmers' market was a little like a bazaar in Bombay, but without its noise and commotion; it was clean and quiet. The prices of all items were clearly marked, and there was no haggling over prices. There were no beggars touching me on the arm and asking for money or pointing out their hungry children to me. There were no little boys trailing behind imploring me to hire them to carry my shopping. I liked the feeling of being free to spend money without a twinge of guilt, but I missed the kind of interaction one has with merchants in an Indian bazaar, the bargaining tactic of mentioning how so-and-so at a different bazaar sold better items at lower prices or had a better selection. I missed being recognized by the sellers.

One afternoon in early spring, Mary Jane and Martin took me to see the Mennonite community. We drove out to a country road and watched the horse-drawn buggies go by. I think we must have made a perfect picture of Canadian multiculturalism: I in a sari, Mary Jane and Martin in jeans and sneakers, the Mennonite women in black dresses and bonnets with white aprons, the men in long black coats and black hats. Mary Jane and Martin explained that the Mennonites, who were extremely religious, were most likely returning from church, but they assured me that this was their usual mode of dressing.

Multiculturalism didn't enter my mind at the time, however. Nor did I think it odd to take a person from one culture to stare at people from another culture. Now it seems to me that there was some racist thinking behind our trip, but I don't suppose that my friends had any particular prejudice against Mennonites.

My perception of the Mennonite mode of transportation was quite different from that of my friends. In Old Delhi I had sometimes gone with my aunt by horse and buggy to bazaars where the streets were too narrow for cars. In Bombay there were very few horse-drawn buggies, but I would have been acutely embarrassed if I had been compelled to ride in one of them. I wouldn't have wanted to show a horse and buggy to visitors from the West, who would infer that India was "backward" and not "modern." Only poor folks rode in such buggies, or people in villages and small towns. A few weeks later, a graduate student at the history department trying to make conversation with me asked, "Do you have elephants on the roads in India?" I felt humiliated by that question and started gushing about cars.

In fact, what I found interesting in Canada were all the different models, sizes, and makes of automobiles. That's what differed from my norm, not horse-and-buggy carriages. In India, at the time, we had two models of cars—a Fiat and an Ambassador. The same model was reproduced every year for twenty-odd years—all my life up to that time. The demand for these cars was so great that often the waiting period extended to several years. But I kept quiet that day, not wanting to disappoint my new friends, who were having such a good time showing me their sights.

———————————

In Bombay I had always worn a *bindi*, the red dot that women in India paint on their foreheads. Since it had always been a part of my makeup, I didn't expect that the other students or professors would find it very unusual. I also wore a sari, and other than complimenting me on its colour or texture, nobody said much about that. Yet almost every time I was introduced to other graduate students or to professors, after a few moments of conversation they would ask about the significance of the bindi. They would say, "What does this dot on your forehead mean?" Some professors asked whether it was a caste mark. Others thought they knew about it, but would ask questions like, "Isn't it supposed to be worn by married women? Why are you wearing it?" Or they would say that Hindus considered all psychic energy to be located at the centre of the forehead and ask if it that was what it marked. They were thinking of the popularized images of gurus and yogis, holy men who decorate their foreheads with saffron or red paint, but their questions made *me* feel ignorant.

I found I wasn't so sure about its significance myself. Had I been more confident, I could have said simply that it was part of my makeup, but I was less secure then about being so forthright. I began to think I had no idea of the right answer, so I actually adopted what some professors told me and passed that explanation along to other professors! Eventually I gave up wearing the bindi altogether. Now I would explain it by suggesting that different cultures have unique ways of decorating the body. I would give a few examples, citing some tribes in Africa and even North American bikers gangs, who decorate their bodies with tattoos.

Another thing that professors asked about was my caste identity. That is, *some* would ask what it was. Others would try to show off their "knowledge" saying, "You're a Brahman, aren't you?" Often these professors would go on to express some views about the plight of the untouchables as well. Although I am embarrassed to admit it, when I first came to Canada I really had no academic knowledge of the caste system, did not know what my caste was, and had no consciousness about its practice in India. The professors, however, seemed to consider this very important, so I wrote a frantic letter to my father to find out. He just responded that he supposed we were Kshatriyas.†

I do not know what my father's attitude to caste was, since the topic never came up for discussion when I lived at home; caste had no bearing on his work or on his social position. He was disdainful of social conventions, and his strategy seems to have been to ignore them. In large cities like Bombay, men were more interested in earning a living, particularly after the economic devastation brought upon many families by the partition of the subcontinent into India and Pakistan in 1947. They were not inclined to place much significance on traditional social distinctions.

My father was undoubtedly aware of caste politics during the nationalist movement, but he did not attempt to educate us either about its practice or about the need to resist such invidious distinctions among people. Although we often talked politics at home, I do not recall discussing caste or caste politics. Like other young people, I was absorbed in my world of family, friends, and studies, and had no occasion at that time to develop a consciousness about such things.

My admission that I did not know much about caste may make you think that I was an awfully ignorant person in 1970, and I'm not sure what I can say in my defence. I was a very good student and had received a first-class honours bachelor's degree in a statewide examination of several thousand students. In fact, I was ranked among the top six students that year in the entire state of Maharashtra, and first among students in history. However, I guess that just means I had learned what I was taught but hadn't been taught nearly all I needed to know.

I was a product of what we'd now call a "colonial education." It all but ignored discussion of the various regional cultures, social organizations, and religions, such as Hinduism and Islam. I attended, like other children from privileged families, what we called in India a "convent school," in my case a school run by Irish Catholic missionaries. The curriculum in the school

---

† According to a legend in the *Rig Veda*, the Brahmans and Kshatriyas emerged from the head and shoulders, respectively, of Purusa, the primeval being; hence their high-caste status.

did not include anything on India. We studied European history and English literature along with the other school subjects such as mathematics and biology. I remember we read Shakespeare, Charles Dickens and Thomas Hardy, but we were not assigned any readings by Indian authors, and none of the books we read had Indian themes. I memorized the gospels of Matthew, Mark, Luke and John, but nothing of the *Ramayana* or the *Mahabharata*, the classic Hindu religious epics. At the university I studied some Indian history, but the course did not include any discussion of caste, and just a little of religion. I had heard stories from the epics at home, but had read few Indian authors, not even Tagore or Narayan.

Although I spoke several Indian languages, I could read and write only a little Hindi. All of my education had been in English, which Salman Rushdie calls the "bastard child of India, sired on India by the departing British."[3] Although there were many eminent writers in Indian regional languages during colonial times, very few of them had been translated, and since I read only English fluently, I had no access to them.

Furthermore, the English that is used in India has acquired its own pronunciation and differs in many ways from British English—and American and Canadian and all the other kinds of English. My friends in Canada found my English different, and not just because I used terms like "lift" instead of elevator, or "postbox" instead of mailbox. My accent was different and I pronounced some vowels differently. Even today it is sometimes hard to distinguish between the v's and the w's in my speech: for example, "wavy." Or I say words that begin with "th" softly rather than with a hard emphasis, as in "Thailand."

I began, however, to think that my English was just wrong. Neither the professors, the other students, nor I had absorbed the idea, in 1970, that different Englishes reflect different locations and customs, and there is no one right way to speak or write the language.

My point here is that my education had effectively cut me off from Indian culture. I had to read up on caste. I found out the sociological explanation, that caste originally had the function of grouping people together according to their occupations. Occupations are often hereditary, so the caste label stuck from one generation to the next. There are four main castes—the Brahman, Kshatriya, Vaishya, and the Sudra. The four main castes are divided into several hundred sub-castes, and there are people who are considered to be outside the caste system, that is, the untouchables. Caste is still a significant factor in local and regional politics in India, and caste identity is an important consideration in arranging marriages in some communities. Some regions, like Bengal and southern India, are very caste-conscious, but the northwest part of India (and Pakistan), where my family originates, tends not to give caste any significance. Caste was not a topic that was discussed in my immediate family or amongst my relatives. Marriages were arranged in my family, but according to regional identity, language, and religion.

What provoked even more questions from the professors and students was untouchability. These questions gave me the impression that there was something terribly wrong and unjust with the system. My curiosity piqued, I decided to find out for myself about India's caste system. This led me to Mulk Raj Anand's 1935 novel *The Untouchable*, in which he describes the abject poverty of the untouchables in both urban and rural India, and the humiliation they experience every day. The jobs the untouchables do are considered dirty—sweeping the streets or cleaning public bathrooms—but that is not in itself exceptional, because people throughout the world who do such jobs may face some stigma. What makes their situation unjust is that their birth places them in the untouchable category.

Untouchables are not identified by any physical characteristics, so in large towns and cities it is possible for them to "pass." However, in the neighbourhoods where they work, they are easily identified because they carry a broom made of twigs and a ragged, dirty basket for garbage. They are not allowed into restaurants or temples. People avoid touching them or eating with them. Sometimes small towns and villages have special neighbourhoods and colonies where only untouchables live.

The questions put to me by individuals at Waterloo compelled me to think back to the everyday habits of my family. I realized that what had seemed most natural and normal while I was at home was part of the manifestation of caste biases such as untouchability. I remembered my house in Old Delhi and the *bhangan* (an untouchable woman) who used to come twice a day to pick up the garbage and clean the toilet. As the garbage was always kept in one corner of the house, she never went anywhere else in the house other than these two areas. That in itself was not exceptional, because the woman who came to wash the clothes went only to the bathroom to do her work and afterwards to the verandah to hang up the clothes; she did not go to the other parts of the house either, even though she was not a bhangan. But even as a small girl I had known the difference: I was not supposed to touch the bhangan, although it was okay to touch the washerwoman, who was only poor. The bhangan, likewise, stood out of the way if she saw me heading in her direction and refrained from touching anyone or anything in the house.

The bhangan would return in the afternoon, washed and wearing a clean, brightly coloured long skirt and a dupatta that covered her hair. She usually carried a basket under her arm, and when she knocked at the door, someone would go out and toss some food in her basket, a little extra she got from some families who also paid her cash for her work.

This routine was so much a part of the daily life of the household that there was no reason for me to pay any attention to it as a child or even as a young adult. After reading Anand, though, I realized that tossing the food allowed the household help and the family to avoid coming into any physical contact with the bhangan or her basket. As a child, though, I never asked why, when the bhangan was clean in the afternoon, we still did not go close to her.

In Bombay I lived in smaller accommodations. There the garbage was kept in the kitchen and the *bhangi*, a male untouchable who came to collect it, stood at the kitchen door and asked the cook to hand him the day's waste. Now I realized that it must have been because he had been asked not to go into the kitchen. We did not refer to him as bhangi, but by his name, Velu. However, he was "unclean," and religious Hindus would consider his presence in the kitchen polluting. I was mortified at the realization of the gap existing between what went on in our home and our pride in seeing ourselves as progressive human beings.

I learned much about India from the questions that were posed to me during my first few years in Canada. When I lived in India, I rarely gave any conscious thought to my everyday environment or questioned my values and norms. I accepted my situation as natural and normal. I gave no thought to people who were not like me or part of my small, tightly knit social circle of middle-class, educated, urbanized and Westernized friends. But in Waterloo I had to answer questions about my homeland. In a way, I discovered India only when I was in Canada.

Immigrants from Third World countries had only started coming to Canada in large numbers in 1967, and no well-established South Asian community existed in Kitchener-Waterloo, although there were some families living in the area. During my stay in Waterloo I came to know two Indian professors—both men—one in mathematics and another in biology. The wife of the biology professor was also a new immigrant, and she invited me to their home. I went a few times. They would come to get me at the residence and drive me back after the meal. Our similar situations created a slight bond, but we came from vastly different linguistic, cultural, and class backgrounds. Besides, I was single and a student, and did not fit into their social circle. Eventually I stopped visiting them.

My reservations about socializing with other Indians also created a barrier to my getting to know them. In Bombay I had heard tales about Indian students who had gone to Britain and spent all their time with other students from India. According to the stories, they cooked Indian food, listened to Indian music, and saw Indian movies. My friends said there was no point in going so far away if you were only going to immerse yourself in Indian culture while there. It was much more desirable to meet other people and get to know the culture of the West. It had been easy for us to make these judgements when we were comfortably ensconced in our homes and did not know what it was like to feel alone, different, and without any social and cultural moorings. Nevertheless, I held on to these notions; afraid to disappoint my friends in Bombay, I determined to make Canadian friends and get to know Kitchener-Waterloo.

Most of my friends at Waterloo were women. There were a few male graduate students from India and Pakistan on campus, but I did not get to know any of them during the school year. The week before I left Waterloo, however, I was sitting in a cafeteria by myself drinking coffee. A young Indian man sat down with me and started a conversation. I asked him why he had never spoken to me earlier, since we had both seen each other eating in the cafeteria that year. He said I had always been accompanied by my white Canadian friends and that had kept him from approaching me. I suppose I could have talked to him first. But I was a well-bred young woman, and the Indian (and Western) etiquette at the time was for males to initiate conversations. Good girls waited for the telephone to ring—and were sometimes disappointed.

My new Canadian friends had other ideas, however. Sometime during the winter, Barbara and Mary Jane decided that I needed some male company, and set about arranging a date for me. They obviously did not know anything about how Indian marriages are arranged or about cultural taboos regarding social interaction between men and women. They probably just assumed—correctly, as it so happened—that although dating was a very Western practice, it would be acceptable to me. They thought of the date as a way of providing "another new experience for Vijay," and within a short time they had picked out the man. I do not recall anyone asking me if I wanted to go on a date—or with whom—but I had no objections, and went along with their plans.

Barbara had gone to a high school with a Sikh boy who had grown up in the Kitchener-Waterloo area and was studying at one of the local community colleges. Barbara raved about this boy's looks and personality and said that he would be a perfect date for me. She set about trying to arrange a meeting between us. She invited him to a party on campus and introduced us to each other. We talked for a few awkward moments, but we had little in common other than the colour of our skin. He had spent his whole life in Canada, had never been to India and had little interest in talking about it—at least with me. His dress, manners, and speech were like those my white Canadian friends, and I did not feel any particular affinity with him. After a few moments he went off to talk to other people. He left the party early and I never saw him again.

As I write this, it seems to me that although Barbara had good intentions, she may have unwittingly hurt this man. In arranging a "date" for us, she presumed that our race would create a bond of commonality between us—which it didn't, given the more numerous differences that existed. At the time I did not mind, because I had little consciousness of the sort of thinking that underlay her scheme; I just felt confused and unsure of where and with whom I belonged.

I did make one Indian friend. The history department at the university hired a visiting professor from Oxford to teach a course on the Third World during the winter term. He turned out to be a Bengali Hindu from Bangladesh. He often invited me to his office to talk. We differed in age, experience and cultural background but, like me, he was feeling isolated in the history department and had very few friends on campus, so we kept each other company. He decided to act as my mentor for a few months. Since he had lived for several years in Britain, he knew how the "system" worked and how to cope with being a "foreigner." He later helped me with my most difficult decision that year—to find a summer job and stay for a while longer in Canada.

By March my funds were getting low, but I did not tell my father for fear that he would pressure me to return home. Since I had never worked before (not even at something like babysitting) I had no idea what kind of a job I could possibly get or how to go about finding one. I didn't have the confidence to apply for a job on campus, say, at the library or cafeteria, let alone attempt to find one in the city. Barbara, Linda, and Mary Jane were encouraging me. Their thinking was that it would be a "good experience" for me to have a job, that it would make me feel more like the other students on campus…"Canadianize" me a bit, perhaps.

My professor friend, sensing my insecurity, suggested that I try to find some work on a research project. Mary Jane asked an English professor she knew through her church if he needed any help, and he gave me a job on his research project! Several students had been hired for the project, which involved transferring some information to computer files. The work was not very interesting, but it gave me an opportunity to get to know some students from other departments.

Two young men from the English department, Andrew and Chris, took it upon themselves to make sure I understood the work. They included me when they went to get coffee or lunch. By that time quite comfortable at the university, one day I walked into the dimly lit common room. There were plenty of empty sofas and only two or three students, but the room had a smell I did not recognize. When I mentioned this to Andrew, he looked startled; he and Chris exchanged worried looks and told me sombrely not to go into the common room again. Now I know that what I had smelled was the lingering scent of marijuana and incense. Nobody had familiarized me with that aspect of Canadian university culture, something I was much too innocent to have known anything about, either here or in India.

The project team worked in a room reserved especially for it. Andrew brought in a tape recorder on which he played classical music while we all worked. "What do you think of it, Vijay?" he asked. It was all just unfamiliar sound to me, and I gave a noncommittal response. He then decided to bring in a tape of Ravi Shankar playing the sitar. The students asked me to explain its scales and rhythm, but I could offer nothing; I was not knowledgeable about classical Indian music, either. After they had all commented on its "different" rhythm and what they called its "lack of harmony," they stopped playing it and went back to listening to Beethoven and Mozart and the like.

Andrew, like my other friends, felt that since I was new to Canada I should see some of the countryside, and on weekends he drove me around to some of the small towns in the Waterloo area. It came out on these excursions that although I had read Shakespeare's plays, I had never seen them produced. One day he appeared, much to my surprise, with tickets to two performances and an invitation to see them with him. When I went back to the residence, I sought out Barbara and announced, "I'm going to Stratford with Andrew!" She laughed and said, "You're really getting around!" Although I don't remember what plays we saw, I recall being excited and getting dressed up in my sari to go to Stratford to see the plays. On the whole, it turned out to be a pleasant summer.

At the end of my first year at Waterloo, I was still lost and lonely, but I did not yet want to return to India. Barbara, Mary Jane, and Linda were all applying for a PhD program at the University of Toronto, and I decided to do the same. I think my different academic interests must have worked to my advantage. My three friends had to compete with many other students studying Canadian history, but there were few graduate students applying to study British Imperialism, and the department had three professors who may have had some interest in me as a graduate student. There was Milton Israel, whose specialty was Modern India, and Archie Thornton, who specialized in British Imperialism; between them they had less than a handful of graduate students. The third, Martin Kline, specialized in African history, but he needed teaching assistants for his course on the Third World.

The Indian professor guided me in filling out my application and recommended that I submit a dissertation proposal, although it was not required by the university. I had no special interests at the time, but he had heard of some students studying women's history in Britain. I could propose a study of the history of women in India, he suggested. He thought that a well-developed dissertation proposal in a new area of study might catch the interest of the admissions committee. Apparently, he was right, for the history department not only accepted me, but offered me a scholarship as well. That enabled me to stay in the country for what I thought at the time would be another year or two.

I had spent my first year in Canada having to explain to others "who I was," and it made me conscious of my own values. In trying to understand the responses to me of white Canadians, I had to learn about them and their values. Although my sense of self and my values were shaken a bit, I clung to them, as they were the only means I had of understanding my life at that time. Many years later when I was to read Peter Nadas's description of the past reverberating in the present, it reminded me of my feelings that first year in Waterloo. He writes:

"Experiences related to my past, hovering as rootlessly as any lived moment in what I might call the present: only memories of tastes and smells of a world to which I no longer belong, one I might call my abandoned homeland...[but] nothing bound me to the one I found myself in, either; I was a stranger."[4]

An Immigrant Student in Toronto

When I went to the University of Toronto in 1971 I had been in Canada for one year. Although I was over the initial shock of dislocation, I still felt skeptical of my ability to understand and cope with the cultural norms around me. I was pleased to be accepted by the university, and comforted that Linda and Barbara would also be coming to Toronto. However, outside the university, I knew little about the city. I was unaware that it had a long history of being home to many immigrant groups and that it had several ethnic communities and neighbourhoods. The ethnic identity of some of the white students provided clues, but there was no catalyst that might have provoked some reflection in me. I thought of myself simply as a foreign student who was in Canada temporarily, and I felt no need to situate myself in the larger context.

The University of Toronto, set in the heart of the downtown, brought me into closer contact with Canadian society. Hesitantly, I began to explore some of my surroundings, although without understanding much of their history. The university is located in a diverse part of the city. On its eastern and southern perimeters are government buildings, hospitals, corporate offices, and boutiques. Its north end is bordered by residential neighbourhoods, where in the 1970s huge rooming houses used by students were interspersed with many other homes being renovated and converted back into single-family dwellings. On its west end is Spadina Avenue, lined at the time with small stores and restaurants owned primarily by European immigrants, many of whom had come to Canada after World War II.

The Spadina Avenue area had attracted a number of immigrant groups upon their arrival in Canada. Immigrants from Europe had come here throughout the twentieth century to live and work, but as each wave prospered, people moved out of this downtown immigrant enclave and went to live in other parts of the city. In the 1970s the avenue had many Jewish garment wholesalers, but cheek by jowl to them some Chinese stores and restaurants were also opening up. In the early 1970s Eastern European immigrants were moving out of Kensington Market, and it had become predominantly Portuguese. Immigrants from the Caribbean were in turn joining these residents. However, in the first few years that I was in Toronto, I remained unappreciative of the ethnic diversity of the neighbourhood.

I had occasion as a student to go to Spadina Avenue. A Muslim Indian professor who taught Islam at the university, a very kind gentleman who was close to retirement, invited me to talk to him about my studies at his office on the corner of College Street and Spadina. The building's main floor was occupied by Tip Top Tailors, and on its upper floors were some university offices, all in a state of disrepair.

When I met with the professor on the appointed day, he seemed to regret having invited me to his office. As soon as I sat down, he apologized for the condition of the office and complained that it was a shame that a professor of his stature had been assigned an office in such a dismal place. He told me that when he entered the building he often encountered men in a debilitated state curled up in the corners and in the hallways. Sometimes, if he worked late in the evening in his office, he would encounter prostitutes hanging around the building. The professor chatted with me for over two hours and gave me tips on how to get along at the university. He made no mention, however, of the ethnicity of the neighbourhood we were in—the traditional signifier in the past of poverty—or of the history of immigrants to Toronto. Over the next two to three years I did get to know the Spadina area, but did not have the wherewithal to question, reflect upon, and come to conclusions about what I was witnessing.

One of the Indian women I knew from Waterloo had also come to Toronto and, like me, she was on a tight budget. She discovered Kensington Market, and sometimes when we cooked together we would walk down to the market to buy some vegetables. On one of the main streets of

Kensington were two or three big European-style meat stores, many small vegetable and fruit operations and a few cheese stores. The vegetables were displayed outside the store and we could pick and choose from the various baskets. At first, many of them looked unfamiliar, for broccoli, Brussels sprouts, leeks, celery and lettuce are not grown in India, but even when the vegetables were recognizable, they looked completely different from what we were used to. In India, vegetables are organically grown and are not as attractive looking as produce that comes from farms using chemical fertilizers. Getting to learn and like the taste of vegetables found at the market or in the superstores was an adjustment in itself. However, in Kensington Market, as in India, there was face-to-face interaction with the vendor and, if we chose, we could complain about the produce and haggle over the price.

The meat stores in Kensington were different from the large grocery store where we otherwise shopped. At the Dominion store, we had to take a number and explain what kind of meat we wanted, and how much. It was then cut to suit our preference and packaged in brown paper. We seldom shopped there, though; we were too poor to eat meat and had little taste for it anyway. In Kensington, the meat stores were crowded with women speaking to the butchers and to one another in languages I did not understand but assumed to be European. The atmosphere was less formal than in the superstores, and the verbal exchange was loud but friendly.

In India, where it is not usually part of the traditional diet in any region, only one kind of cheese was available, and it was very expensive. At Kensington Market we liked to go to a certain cheese store. It was small and cramped, but had an extensive selection—big slabs of cheese all piled up with no thought for aesthetic appeal. We were not going to the market in search of old world ambiance or the quaint and charming, however, but merely to save a dollar or two. Much the same applied to the stores that lined nearby Spadina Avenue and were also run by immigrants. Unfortunately, what we subconsciously imbibed from this experience was an equation of ethnicity with being poor and working class.

I lived at the graduate residence on Bloor Street. It was divided into a number of apartments, each of which accommodated four or five men or women. At Waterloo I had become accustomed to living with other women and I enjoyed talking, sharing food and watching television with them. The residence at Toronto was co-ed, and it took me a while to get used to having men walk into our apartment at all times of the day and night. I was unfamiliar with the logic of Canadian female students. Alison, a tall, blonde feminist with whom I shared a room for one term, complained that the separation between men and women in different apartments was artificial, antiquated, and unnecessary. She resented the implied authority of the university over her behaviour.

For me the issues were quite different. At first I felt shy and awkward when men suddenly appeared in our kitchen, and I would quickly go into my room and shut the door. But once I got to know the male friends of the women who shared my apartment, I would sit and talk to them in the kitchen or in the hallway. For me this casual talk had the feel of a dangerous and forbidden activity. Although I liked living in what I thought was a liberated way, I worried about what my father and sisters might think of my close proximity to young men. Would they think that this unconventional lifestyle jeopardized my reputation as a "nice girl" within our community in India?

The ethnic or national distinctions between white people were still too subtle for my untutored eyes and ears to perceive. I could not distinguish differences in physical characteristics between white Canadians or between white Canadians and newly arrived Europeans and Americans. There were very few blacks on campus, and none I can recall at the residence. There were some Chinese students; I got to know one of them who was studying at business school, but she was a "foreigner" much like myself. Although we sometimes talked of our common difficulties and shared impressions of Canadians, we had little confidence in each other's opinions since we were both new to Canadian society. Nevertheless, our desire to get to know Canadians and learn to interact with them appropriately drew us to each other, and I felt somewhat reassured that others were having much the same difficulties as I was.

The talk among students at the residence was mostly of studies, professors, clothes, and friends (or the lack of them, in the case of male friends). No explicit mention was made of the ethnic—let alone racial—differences among the students at the residence. In retrospect, I know that talk of ethnic differences would have been considered impolite and improper, and it would have made the other students uncomfortable. Although differences of origin and nationality did come up, the pretense was that such differences were inconsequential, and not to be dwelt upon. Perhaps the students had other, private opinions, but I can only go by what they said to me and the clear impression they conveyed to me, a new immigrant who was having some difficulty acculturating. Despite encountering such reticence, I did trade stories over the years with children of European immigrants about the experience of being "ethnic" and immigrant. Gradually I learned to distinguish between the different ethnicities of students, but it was not until many years later, when I started researching and studying immigrants, that I understood their significance.

My roommate Alison was of middle-class, British origin, but emphatically described herself as a Canadian. She was studying for a master's degree in psychology. She was friendly and went out of her way to be helpful. Taken up as she was by feminism, it was these new emerging ideas, both in the abstract and in day-to-day life, that we spent our time discussing.

Over the next four years I had occasion to live with some children of European immigrants. Maria, who was studying at the Faculty of Education, came from a working-class Italian background; her mother worked as a seamstress, and her father was a bricklayer. Anna's parents had come from Hungary, and her father was a blue-collar worker in Hamilton. She was studying speech therapy at the university and was being supported by her parents while she was there. Eva was the child of Czechoslovakian immigrants who had settled in Winnipeg. She had beautiful, long dark hair and was studying at the Conservatory of Music with the hope of becoming an opera singer. Her parents, skeptical of her goals, were constantly urging her to switch her field and get a teaching certificate instead. We were Anglican, Catholic, Jewish, and Hindu women, but religion was never discussed.

At the time I did not know enough to ask Anna if her Hungarian parents had come to Canada after the revolution in 1956, or to ask Maria if her parents formed part of the wave of immigrants from Italy after World War II. Eva's parents were not part of the large group of immigrants who came from Czechoslovakia after the 1968 revolution, but had I known about it, I could have asked her if any of her relatives had come at this time. Had the local church or the Czechoslovakian community helped in orienting the new immigrants? Perhaps her parents and their friends had helped the new immigrants locate classes to learn English, rooms to rent, jobs for the adults, and schools for their children. Now I would like to know if Winnipeg had neighbourhoods like Spadina Avenue and markets like Kensington, and if her parents shopped there.

Sometimes my presence evoked memories among the students of stories they had heard from their parents about the early years of their immigrant experience. They shared anecdotes of their families' histories and their own childhood memories. Anna described how as a child of Hungarian parents she had been mortified by her mother's insistence that she wear dresses and not jeans. Her mother was attempting to dress her like a middle-class girl in Hungary, but Anna wanted to follow the Canadian norm by wearing jeans and sneakers. She did not say, and I did not ask, whether this was simply a child's desire to fit in and be like everyone else or if there was an ethnic dimension to the difference she was hoping to overcome by wearing jeans. I do not know if Anna, like many immigrant children, felt self-conscious of her parents' accents. Now I wonder if Anna had been teased for being Hungarian, or worse, if other children in the playground had called her names.

Maria still felt self-conscious of being working class and Italian. She wanted some of her friends, most of whom came from middle-class backgrounds, to meet her parents, but was apprehensive about it. She explained to me that her parents talked loudly when they were excited, and used their hands to express themselves. She was worried about how some of her friends at the residence who came from staid, middle-class, British backgrounds would react. Would they think her parents were fighting? Would they consider them lacking in manners? She was always apologizing for talking loudly when she herself was excited and emotional. Maria and I became close over our shared feelings of being out of place and our desire to behave appropriately and to learn to "be Canadian."

The sentiments I was encountering in my friends were part of a long continuum of what immigrants have experienced in Toronto and elsewhere in Canada. Historian Robert Harney and other academics who study ethnicity write that attitudes to immigrants have evolved and changed in the last century. In the 1930s and 40s, Eastern European immigrants were often referred to derogatorily as "dangerous foreigners," and their communities and neighbourhoods as the "foreign presence." Long-term WASP residents of the city perceived these European immigrants as a "problem" and believed that it behooved the new immigrants to assimilate to Canadian norms. Children of immigrants learned not to "flaunt their difference" but to assimilate quietly and quickly into Canadian ways. Harney writes that the decision for an immigrant to retain his ethnicity or to "flee from painful consciousness into Anglo-conformity" was itself a response to "small but daily slights in his new country." After World War II, some perceptions changed and "dangerous foreigners" became "brave

allies" and "fellow victims." Social workers and other government personnel began to refer to immigrants more politely as "New Canadians."[1] But
these changes did not always find a response at the grassroots level of
neighbourhoods and school yards.

Ethnicity did come up in the residence through talk of food. One day,
Maria cooked spaghetti with meat sauce as a special treat for all of us. Our
comments about the food revealed our different cultural backgrounds. The
Canadian women commented at length on the spiciness of the sauce. I
found the garlic, sage, and rosemary flavours pleasant and different, but to
my taste the sauce was quite bland. Since I was only familiar with foods in
India, all of which have many different combinations of spices, it was hard
for me to comprehend how a little bit of garlic could be thought of as spicy
and hot. Luckily, there were no requests that I in turn provide an authentic Indian meal. I would have cooked what Westerners call a "curry dish,"
a term never used in India, where all food has curry—that is, spices.[†] My
friends would have had a hard time eating food laced with red pepper, ginger, cilantro, and a variety of other spices. That would have made me feel
even more self-conscious in that predominantly WASP environment.

Now that I am both more knowledgeable and assertive about the
rights of immigrants, if I happened to meet Alison at a party and in a
query about her ethnicity was still given her 1970s assertion about being
Canadian, I would seek an explanation as to what made Southern and
Eastern Europeans "ethnic" and her "Canadian." However, at the time I
did not know enough to even articulate such questions in my mind, let
alone voice them, and I was certainly not militant about the right of
European immigrants or of "visible minorities" like myself to be included
among "Canadians."

Since the Eastern and Southern European students had absorbed the
values of "Anglo-conformity" through their school experiences, entertainment, and friends, they saw their parents as immigrants and perceived
themselves as "Canadian." But even though they did not consciously
avow their ethnic and immigrant backgrounds, they were drawn nevertheless to other children of immigrants at the university. Friendships blos-
somed. Eva was attracted to Matt, who was also a child of immigrants from
Czechoslovakia. They both loved ballroom dancing and classical music.

---

† In India, dishes are named instead for their main ingredient, by region, such as Goan or Bengali, or by style of cooking. In the Muglai approach, for instance, food is simmered for hours in
  lots of oil, with tomatoes, onions, garlic and other spices.

Eva laughingly reported to us, "Mom is really thrilled about Matt." David, from a working-class Polish background, made overtures of friendship towards Sandy, also of Polish descent. Sandy constantly joked about how happy her mother was about her friendship with David. But if ethnicity was an attraction at a personal level, its public assertion carried risks. Such "flaunting of difference," it was felt, might potentially jeopardize job opportunities and become an obstacle to social mobility. Even at the university, discrimination against white ethnic groups because of accent, religion or other markers was not unknown, although it was not explicitly and openly discussed at the time.

I often had difficulty communicating with the other students because we lacked common interests. We didn't know how to make small talk with each other. Along with "Where do you come from?" people asked me: "Do you like it here?" "What do you think of our winter?" I gave dull, monosyllabic replies. One doesn't open one's heart to a stranger who is just being polite. I wonder if I would have scared them if I had told them the truth: I was in complete culture shock and petrified of being here. I could have said that when I was outside my room I was afraid I wouldn't be able to cope, and that in my room, loneliness and isolation overwhelmed me. I don't know how they would have reacted, since I never put them to the test.

Part of the difficulty I had in communicating with others was in not understanding non-verbal signs. In Bombay, if I met a stranger, I had some ready clues—dress or behaviour—that enabled me to form an idea of them. If I knew them, I could even anticipate how they might finish a sentence. Here, all the subtle reference points were gone, and the loss of them made me feel insecure and self-conscious—a bumbling fool, although if I made a misstep, people were usually polite and did not let on.

In India one can usually recognize the region people originate from by their dress. Even the sari, common to all Indians, is draped differently in various parts of India. Symbols of an individual's status are also regionally distinct. For instance, women wear gold chains to identify their status as married women. By looking at the design of a chain, I can identify the cultural and regional background of the woman wearing it. Some regions have particular biases. People from Bengal are proud of their knowledge of the arts and literature and perceive themselves as more "cultured" than people from Punjab. People from Punjab are proud of their martial traditions, their folk music and dances. People from southern India are proud of their traditions of classical dancing and consider Punjabis to be loud and ostentatious. Knowing these quirks of different regional groups made it easy not to ruffle their sensibilities. There are regional and cultural differences among Canadians, too, as well as variations in ethnicity and social background, but looking for certain kinds of differences in accordance with my Indian socialization left me truly clueless at first.

I spoke English fluently, so language as such was not a problem. However, some words had connotations that were lost on me, and even when I became familiar with their implied meaning, the values that underlay them were confusing. Alison often used the term "bourgeois" to express contempt for middle-class, North American social norms. She criticized hierarchical relations between people as being oppressive and exploitative, rejected symbols of status and success, such as academic or corporate positions, and swore not to exercise power, privilege, and authority over others. I remember the way a shrug of the shoulders, accompanied by the remark, "That is so bourgeois," expressed her scorn for middle-class values. As a relative newcomer to Canada, I was somewhat perplexed by this "anti-bourgeois" attitude. It was not clear to me what was so bad about being "bourgeois." I did not try to hide my own class identity, so I am afraid I was perceived, in her mind, as a bourgeois woman.

The women that I had first met at the University of Toronto were mostly from middle-class backgrounds. My experience up until then, in India and in Canada, had been with people who tended to boost their egos by exaggerating their wealth or insinuating that they were classier or more stylish than others. Now, some were expressing disdain towards all things middle class. I sensed a little reverse snobbery. Alison's feminist friends, whom I sometimes met with her, seemed to be competing with each other to demonstrate who was poorer or had struggled more than other women to get to university. Being poor had obviously become for them a way of showing commitment to feminism.

I had switched to wearing jeans and sweaters, but in a casual way and without giving it much thought. I didn't see my change in clothing as a rejection, however symbolic, of my culture and upbringing. It would have been more of a disavowal if I had switched to short skirts, because that would have contradicted the Hindu norm requiring women to cover their legs at all times. However, my friends saw my changed appearance as indicating that I wanted to become Canadian—that is, more like them. They would smile encouragingly and compliment me on my appearance. But although the jeans and sweaters were convenient—and warm—I felt drab

and unattractive in them and missed the feeling of elegance and sophistication that comes with wearing a sari.

Alison and her feminist friends were rebelling against societal norms,
and had taken to wearing loose-fitting T-shirts and sweaters and old,
worn-out jeans. They stopped using makeup, which they regarded as male-
imposed. They adopted a fresh, clean look—not as a fashion statement
(though it was soon treated that way by many advertisers) but as an ideological statement. I did not try to adopt Alison's way of dressing. Perhaps
it was because I couldn't overcome my class inhibitions and thus could not
feel comfortable in drab shirts or sweaters, with no makeup and no jewellery. Perhaps I had been too thoroughly socialized into the male standards of my culture and had not struggled hard enough to slay the dragons
that kept me hopelessly oppressed and enslaved. As a teenager, I had
avidly read Western magazines for their advertisements of clothes and
makeup, and still secretly longed to possess them. They were now available to me, but I had no money to buy them, so pretending to be disdainful of them would have seemed like sour grapes.

Furthermore, dress was only a part—and not a very significant part—
of my appearance. I felt that simple, inexpensive clothing would not signal my feminism, but rather my status as a poor immigrant. Fortunately
for me, the image of welfare-grubbing immigrants from Third World
countries was not prevalent during my first few years here, at least at the
university. Nevertheless, being a non-white woman did carry some negative connotations.

One Sunday morning, I went to a small grocery store to buy some
food. I was wearing a poncho that concealed my arms. I was looking
around for something cheap and appetizing to buy. Unbeknown to me, I
was being watched by the white male owner, who misinterpreted my indecisiveness as deviousness. He came toward me gesticulating and shouting
loudly that I was a thief. The noise attracted the attention of three or four
other shoppers—students, like me—and everyone stared at me. Nonplussed, I raised my arms to show him that I was not hiding anything.
Although I was too intimidated to defend myself, the other students in the
store, also white males, came to my rescue and shouted back at the owner.
They then unceremoniously dumped their baskets of groceries at the cash
register, loudly vowing never to shop there again, and walked out with me.

The subtle differences of dress, behaviour and language, and the values that they encoded, left me confused, insecure and adrift with no cul-

tural or social reference points. As a new immigrant, my psychological and emotional "home" for many years remained Bombay, and what mattered to me was what my family and friends there thought. What others thought was less important. Although, on the positive side, I did not have to put up with the restraints of family or community at the university, the new environment made me cautious. I had nothing to rebel against and little to conform to, and through force of habit stuck to my old ways.

For example, I did not adopt the graduate-student style of staying up most of the night and sleeping during the day. When I went out with friends in the evening, I returned to the residence at an early hour, abiding by the curfews I had lived with in Bombay. The need to feel secure made me cling to my Indian values and norms instead of rushing to adopt Canadian values or behavioural norms, of which I had little understanding anyway. Thus, my past dictated in many ways how I responded to my new environment.

I had been awarded a small scholarship by the history department. I worked hard, and my professors recommended me for an Ontario Graduate Fellowship and a teaching assistantship for the following year. I had similar support for the next four years. When I took my finished dissertation into the history office in my fifth year, the administrative assistant looked at me and asked, "Do you have a job lined up, Vijay?" "No," I replied. She said, "Take this thing home and sit on it. We have just awarded you another scholarship and it will be cancelled if you bring your dissertation in." Most students take five years and even much longer to finish their PhD program, so in a way I was rewarded for finishing my dissertation speedily. I spent that year doing all the reading I had wanted to do but had not had time for until then. These scholarships and assistantships enabled me to support myself without part-time jobs except for one in the summer of my first year.

Although we had not had frequent contact during the year, I had met occasionally with Barbara and Linda, and when they applied for summer jobs that year as guides for Parks Canada, I decided to do the same. One qualification for the job was a degree in history, and the advertisement for the opening had not specified any particular area of history. I was interviewed for the job, but while Linda and Barbara were both hired, I got turned down. The interviewer for the federal agency that did the hiring later sent an apology and an explanation through my friends. I had been an appropriate candidate, he said, but guides had to dress in period costumes suitable to the site where they worked. How, he asked, could he put an Indian woman in a period costume? It would simply ruin the effect they were trying to create. Linda and Barbara relayed the message to me, hoping it would make me feel better, and I accepted this explanation; at that time we had little consciousness of racial discrimination. Fortunately, I found a clerical job instead. A student friend in Archie Thornton's class heard that I was looking for a job and she prevailed upon her husband, a registrar at a community college, to give me a job.

The scholarships, assistantships, and job were important for me in more than one way. For the first time in my life, I was financially independent of my father, and that gave me a much-needed boost of confidence. Since my father was no longer supporting me, I could make my own choices. I could live as long as I liked in Canada as a landed immigrant. My father accepted this change and stopped suggesting that I return home. But when I told him of my plans to do a PhD, he gave me one last warning over the telephone. "Vijay," he said, "it is fine to study for a PhD, but remember you are burning all your bridges. Very few men want to marry such a well-educated woman." I paid little heed to his dire predictions, feeling liberated from convention and tradition.

Feeling free had its costs, particularly that first year in Toronto, when I had very little money and had to learn to watch my pennies carefully. I found myself in an ironic situation. In India I had plenty of money to spend, but the range of consumer goods was very limited, particularly items of interest to young people. There were no huge department stores with their typically wide varieties to choose from. There were no music systems, televisions, or transistor radios to buy. Tata, India's big industrial house, had only recently started manufacturing a few cosmetics and toiletries such as lipstick, nail polish, talcum powder and, as an alternative to the bar soaps and herbal mixtures used up to that time, shampoo (no hair conditioners, though).

In India I had plenty of silk saris and sandals and, like other Indian women from well-off families, a fairly large collection of gold jewellery as well. But there had been limited entertainment. We went to movies, which were cheap, and to restaurants. I visited my friends' homes frequently. There were no big theatre productions, although some Western-style plays were being staged in English.

In Toronto there were many things to buy and many places to go to, but I had no money for them. There were several department stores, but I could not purchase anything, determined as I was to maintain my financial independence from my father. I lived on a very tight budget. Tuition was five hundred dollars a year. The room at the residence cost ninety-six dollars a month and I paid an extra six dollars a month for a shared telephone line. I allocated twelve dollars a week for food. On this limited food budget I could eat only vegetarian food. Since I cooked for myself, my meals had a very limited repertoire and included only five items—green peas, chickpeas, yogurt, cabbage, and rice. Eating these items every day for a whole year got tedious, and the only break from them came when one of my friends at the residence invited me to share a meal. I allowed myself only one indulgence: every week I bought a small bag of cookies at the Laura Secord store for eighty cents.

The affluence of the West provided an obvious contrast to the poverty of India, where talk of ration cards and the various hassles associated with obtaining even basic items like wheat, rice, and sugar is commonplace in many homes. My family constantly worried about food adulteration, such as milk mixed with water to increase the quantity, or degraded cooking oil. In Canada the grocery stores were full of food, and finding all the ingredients carefully listed on the packages gave me confidence in its purity. (Much later, as a savvy Canadian, I would complain about the waxy shine given to apples.)

The contrasts between India and Canada were constantly highlighted for me by the questions I would be asked by other students. "What about beggars?" "Wouldn't it make sense to eat beef rather than starve?" I wish I could have answered with the equanimity of novelist R. K. Narayan, who, when asked a similar question in the United States, replied: "Cow is also scarce in India, and it's better they are not eaten off but allowed to provide the much-needed milk as long as they can, and when they go dry we like to leave them free to live an honourable, retired life instead of killing them—just as you treat old-age pensioners who may not be active now, but who are none the less treated considerately."[2] I was relieved that none of the students asked about caste.

Questions about India's poverty, overpopulation, or the prohibition against eating beef did not get under my skin, though they annoyed many of my friends from the subcontinent. Some of them adopted a defensive strategy and contrasted the spirituality and otherworldliness of the East with the crass materialism of the West. It was easy to do that in the 1970s, of course, when North America was just emerging from the counterculture led by hippies and (I thought) the Beatles. We came from the spiritual centre of the universe, where young North Americans were going to see the Maharishi or to live as ascetics in ashrams, following daily routines devoted to prayers, meditation, and spiritual learning. We had the secret of contentment and happiness that many young North Americans were seeking. Such arguments provided some solace and even nurtured the illusion of cultural superiority, but mainly they were much-needed buffers between nostalgia for home and a desire to project nationalist pride, which they felt was being attacked by such questions. But I did not use this crutch. I was too enamoured of Western consumer goods, and longed to possess them. I could not even superficially pretend to be high-minded, spiritual, or non-materialistic.

Recently I read Rabindranath Tagore's recollection of his journey to the United States in 1920. There was much about the United States that he disliked; he condemned "the country's soullessness and illusory ideals." Despite his misgivings, though, Tagore believed in the creative and enriching interaction of the East and West: "Whatever we understand and enjoy in human products instantly becomes ours wherever they might have their origin. I should feel proud of my humanity, when I can acknowledge the poets and artists of other countries as my own. Let me feel with unalloyed gladness that all the great glories of man are mine."[3]

I did not go to the pubs on campus since I did not drink beer—or any other alcohol. Come to think of it, I never spent any money on entertainment. Eva and Anna encouraged me to go to the campus pubs with them, but Alison disdainfully called them "meat markets." What could she possibly mean by that, I wondered. In my mental picture of a meat market in Bombay, there were several small cages, one on top of the other, in which live chickens were closely packed together waiting their turn to be bought and slaughtered, and animal carcasses hung from large iron hooks in front of dingy little shops. Storekeepers sat near blood-stained wooden boards stacked with chunks of meat while flies buzzed all around, loudly urging passersby to go into the shop. The filth and the smell of the meat market were revolting and nauseating. I didn't think that was what Alison meant, and so one day I asked her to explain. "Oh," she said disparagingly, "you'd only go there if you want to be picked up." Women who went to these pubs were just displaying themselves to the men. They were only interested in short-term physical relationships, not love or friendship.

On hearing that explanation, another picture flashed through my mind. To arrange a marriage in India, some parents of more assertive young people try to get the young man and woman to meet through the subterfuge of a family dinner party. Most of the people present know the intentions of the families, but they play along, trying to find ways to encourage the two young people to talk to one another. The relatives on the girl's side watch every move of the prospective groom and those on the boy's side watch the prospective bride's. Afterwards the families scrutinize every word for a clue to the psyche of the young person involved, and comment on his or her manners and behaviour, either in favour of the match or rejecting it. The young people have a veto, although they may not participate openly in the discussions. These dinner parties are the butts of jokes for weeks afterwards, and the two parties are mercilessly teased about their stilted conversation and self-conscious behaviour. But these occasions didn't seem to be so bad when I compared them with the "meat markets."

After hearing Alison's explanation, I was certainly not going to humiliate myself by going to the "meat markets." (In retrospect, I notice that Alison saw the men as making the selection while the women were in a passive role. Maybe, though, some of the women were there to "pick up" a male. My feminist consciousness had not yet evolved to the point of seeing that possibility.)

For entertainment, I usually went to the common room in the basement of the residence and watched television, played table tennis or watched other students playing pool. Since I often hung around the common room in the evenings, I got to meet many graduate students from other countries who were also living at the residence. Some of them invited me to parties in their apartments. Not surprisingly, there was much beer drinking on these occasions. The "pièces de résistance" at these parties were cherries soaked in pure alcohol brought in by some physics or chemistry students from their laboratories. For appearance's sake, I would hold a bottle of beer in my hand, but I never developed a taste for it. The other students smoked cigarettes, and some other things as well, familiar to me now from my experience in the common room in Waterloo.

I was often invited out to movies. We had coffee and dessert afterwards, but I ignored the practice of the "Dutch-treat" then. Some women, like Alison, said that paying one's own expenses was a way to assert equality in male-female relationships. Since a female on a date would not acquire any obligation to the male, she was free to assert her choice in how she wanted the relationship to proceed. Besides, if the expenses were going to be shared, a woman could initiate a date by inviting a man to a movie or dinner and not have to wait for the male to make the first move. No more waiting for the phone to ring! But although I heard a great deal about this idea from the other women at the residence, I did not try it myself. At the time I thought going on a date with a man was adventurous enough. I did not have the daring to pick up the phone and invite him to a movie.

The first few months that I was in Toronto flew by. I was getting to know many people and exploring the university. But just as I was beginning to feel confident, the Christmas season arrived—my first Christmas in Toronto, and I did not know what to expect. Some time in early December, Stephanie, a friend of Mary Jane's who was also active in her local church, telephoned and invited me to her home in Mississauga for dinner. She suggested that I go to the end of the subway line, where her brother would meet me with their car. I enquired innocently, "How will he recognize me?" She laughed and said enigmatically, "Don't worry, he'll find you." I dressed in a turquoise-blue, silk sari and chunky gold earrings; he had no difficulty picking me out from among the other passengers. In hindsight, I realize that I must have shone like a neon sign. And since Indians had only recently started coming to live in Toronto in any numbers, he would have spotted me regardless of what I was wearing.

At the dinner there were some other families from the local church. I had seldom been to a "Canadian" home, let alone during the Christmas season, so I had no way of knowing what to expect. Everyone else brought a gift for the hostess, but I came empty-handed. I felt tongue-tied and awkward. I did not know any of the people there. What was I doing there, I kept wondering to myself. At the dinner table one middle-aged man said to me, "Why do you keep fussing with your sari?" Mortified by this remark, from that moment on I just wanted the dinner to be over and to go home.

However, the evening was not over when the meal ended. Stephanie's family took me out to sing carols at their friends' homes in the neighbourhood. I was cold and miserable in my sari, and I did not know any of the carols. If anyone in that festive and happy group noticed my discomfort, though, they did not let on, and I tagged along with them from house to house. Fortunately, the neighbours invited us inside for coffee and cookies after we had sung a few carols. At least inside it was warm and I could thaw out a bit. It was a long and difficult night, and Stephanie probably realized that her kind gesture had not been well thought out: I never heard from her again.

The rest of December slowly deteriorated for me. Everyone else was talking about buying presents, but I had no money and, luckily, felt no compulsion to adopt this custom of exchanging gifts. By the middle of December, students started going home in a flurry of goodbyes and "happy holidays." The residence began to empty, and with each passing day, fewer and fewer of us remained behind. The security guard at the residence cautioned us to be extra careful about our personal safety, to lock the doors of our rooms at all times, and to report to him if we saw any strangers hanging around. My feeling of being alone and deserted deepened.

Just before Christmas the empty halls began to feel really eerie, and I was scared to be at the residence. However, loneliness drew the remaining few of us to one another. We decided that we would get together and spend Christmas day in my room. In the group were two Americans, draft evaders unable to go home to visit their families. One of them brought along his sister, who had travelled from New York to be with him. Along with them were two Indian men whom I had not known very well before, and a Chinese student from Hong Kong who was unable to go home to her family. As a Hindu, I had no particular sentiment for Christmas day or memories of other, happier Christmases with which to compare this one, but some of the others in that room probably did. Despite having no religious or emotional attachment to the day, I experienced an intense longing to be at home in India with my family. There was no turkey for Christmas dinner. We just sat around in my room eating snacks, listening to some non-Christmasy music and drinking beer—some of us, that is. We maintained a cheerful façade despite our inner turmoil. We were glad when the holidays ended, the other students came back, and we returned to our routines.

During my first few years in Toronto, I believed it was up to me to learn to be Canadian, and I tried hard to do so. Gloria-Wade Gayles, a black woman who travelled from the American South to live in a more integrated society in Boston, wrote about her feelings years after she had moved into a whole new world. She said: "What I see now, and could not and did not see then…is the extent to which…the cultural exchange taking place was a one-way street. I was eating their cuisine, studying their literature, listening to their music, admiring their art…immersing myself in their culture. And there was so much I could have taught them. So much they should have learned."[4]

Sentiments like these reverberate in discussions among my immigrant friends. Immigrants, particularly from non-Western countries, often express their resentment at having to bear the responsibility of learning the culture of "Canadians," their political heroes as well as their cultural icons...the Group of Seven, Robertson Davies, Gordon Lightfoot, and the like. In the 1980s, in a discussion with some of the faculty at York, I had to admit I didn't know anything about George Grant, a Canadian historian. A faculty colleague said haughtily, "Everyone ought to know who he is." I countered by asking her if she knew about Lal Bahadur Shastri, an Indian politician during the nationalist movement and prime minister of India for about a year after Jawaharlal Nehru's death. Although I had the satisfaction of challenging her perceptions, I had the distinct impression that she remained disdainful of me. But in the early 1970s I did not have the understanding or the courage to say more.

I was trying to become a Canadian.

3

Girlhood in Delhi

I was a "motherless girl." I dig deep into my memory, but I draw a blank about my mother and her death in a road accident when I was only three years old. I have no memory of her sound or smell or appearance. There was only one picture of her. It hung on the wall of my father's room. There were no family pictures, and none of my mother with my siblings and me. I felt completely detached from her while growing up, seeing no connection between me and the expressionless woman in the picture staring straight into the camera. I never heard anything from my father about my reaction to my mother's death.

I was always aware of her absence—not because I felt the lack of a mother's care or because I compared myself with other children who had a mother—but because throughout my childhood my aunts and uncles, on seeing me after a lapse of some time, would remark on my striking resemblance to her. But then they would stop short. Not knowing what to say next and fearful of upsetting me, they would either lapse into silence or try to distract me by talking about some unrelated subject.

My mother's death came three years after the partition of India, which had reduced my parents from affluent householders to refugees. My father had grown up in a small town—Quetta—in the North West Frontier Province of what was then India. He was happy not to have spent his life in Quetta, which had no industries and few schools. As a young man in the north in the 1910s, he had the choice of going to study either at

Lahore University or Khalsa College in Amritsar. He chose to go to Lahore, studying in English for his bachelor's degree.

My mother was the daughter of a school headmaster, and I assume she had some education, but I do not know how much. Like that of girls from well-to-do families in most parts of India at that time, her education probably came to an end when, as a teenager, she married.

After completing his education in Lahore, Pitaji ("pita" means father in Hindi, and "ji" is a term of respect) returned to Quetta, because, as he later recalled nostalgically, that was his home and he knew the people there well. He embarked on a teaching career, but soon got tired of that and, with the support of my grandfather, went into business. Lalaji owned property and had worked as a minor titled functionary (Diwan Sahib) in a state which, although nominally independent, was under the jurisdiction of the British. Successful in some of his early business ventures, Pitaji then invested in building the first and only movie theatre in town. My aunts and uncles fondly recalled the excitement generated by the opening of the cinema in the town, and how they got to see all the movies for free.

Quetta is located in a Muslim region, and the town's population is predominantly Muslim. Pitaji would reminisce about the close ties he had with other people in the town, and he was always telling us stories about a cousin or a cousin's cousin and so on. When I reflect on those stories, I realize that the family's closest social interactions were with other Hindus, particularly those who spoke Multani, their regional dialect. However, Pitaji could read, write, and speak Urdu, the language of the Muslims, and he and my aunts and uncles had cordial relations with their Muslim neighbours. Social events in this small town, however, revolved around religious rituals and festivities, and events such as births, naming ceremonies, weddings, and funerals at which their caste and social grouping, or biradari, gathered.

None of my aunts ever talked about having a Muslim woman friend. That was not unusual in itself; from what I gathered, the daily routine of my mother and aunts was lived within the purview of family and kinship, in which few outsiders were included. They never mentioned even peripheral interaction with the Muslim women who were their neighbours. In the 1950s, as political relations between India and Pakistan deteriorated, many adults in my community, as elsewhere in India, exaggerated the intimacy of Hindu-Muslim friendships. Over the years I have become skeptical of these stories because of what I know of the histories of the countries and the differing social norms of Hindus and Muslims.

Quetta was not located in a region as caste-conscious as Bengal or South India. But that is not to say that my extended family in their daily lives did not observe any caste rules. A fundamental principle of caste is the notion of purity, most strictly observed in the preparation of meals and sharing of food. My family socialized and ate only with their biradari. Later they disguised their reluctance to eat with others by imputing a certain lack of cleanliness to them.

Another significant barrier to social communication was the difference in diet observed by most Hindus and Muslims. My extended and immediate families were for the most part strict vegetarians. Muslims generally eat beef. When Pitaji was a university student, one of his adventures had been to eat meat with some Muslim friends, but other than that, he remained a strict vegetarian throughout his life. When I was a child growing up in Old Delhi, no meat was ever brought into our kitchen. On the very rare occasions when Pitaji entertained a Muslim business associate at home, the meat was cooked outside the kitchen with utensils kept aside specially for this purpose. On these occasions only the men ate together; the women did not join them. Although it became common for men of Pitaji's generation to eat meat, and at the present time meat-eating is more widespread in upper-middle-class Hindu households, where mutton and chicken are the usual alternatives to beef, most women of my extended family have nevertheless remained vegetarians.

Hindus and Muslims both believe in the segregation of sexes, although this is practised more stringently by the upper-middle classes. However, men and women of all classes often sit separately in temples and mosques. There are separate cars for women on trains, and separate schools and colleges for girls are preferred by most Hindu and Muslim families in India.

In 1999, I was visiting Khajuraho to see the tenth-century sculptures on the temples, some of which are known in the West as illustrations for the Kama Sutra. Khajuraho is also an important religious site for the devotees of the Hindu god Lord Shiva. The day I was visiting was believed to be the anniversary of his birth, and to mark the event, huge crowds of devotees had gathered to pray at the only temple open to the public for prayers. I watched from another temple on a small hill nearby. Thousands of people carrying flowers and offerings for the gods were straining at the gate, passing the time by heartily singing religious songs as they awaited

their turn to go in. The police controlling the crowds would open the gate
and summon in a group of women, whereupon a horde of them would rush
up the steps and into the temple before the entrance was closed again.
After ten minutes or so, the women would leave the temple through a different passage and the police would again open the gate, but this time they
would beckon in a group of men.

I saw a similar segregation of the sexes at another location during the
same visit. I had gone to Amritsar and from there onto the border of India
and Pakistan to watch the changing of the guard. A crowd of men,
women, and children had gathered at a makeshift barrier on the road,
patiently waiting to be allowed onto the grounds to watch the ceremony.
At the appointed time, a few of the guards lowered the barriers and
allowed the women and children to go in. We were asked to sit on bleach-
ers constructed for the viewing. Once we were seated, the men were
allowed to come in, but they had to assemble on the road, where no seat-
ing was provided. Some sat down on the ground while others stood and
jostled with each other. I noticed a young man standing next to me; taken
aback, I remonstrated with him for breaching the rules and coming into
the women's section. Apologizing politely, he defended himself by saying
that, like me, he wanted to get a good view. For the most part, though, no
one thought separating the women and the men was unusual, and they
accepted the situation cheerfully.

During the 1930s and '40s, in pre-partition days, only extended family members visited private homes. A family would not have liked a young
man, particularly one of another religion, to come to their homes.
Women's "virtue" brought prestige to the family, and it was ensured by the
segregation of the sexes. Pictures of women of my mother's generation
always show them with their head decorously covered by a dupatta to
connote their modesty, much like their Muslim counterparts.

The practice of sex segregation required a large home and paid household help. None of the women in my extended family did any paid work,
but as household tasks sometimes required interaction with male outsiders, domestic help was needed to carry out such chores. So the lives of
women from upper-middle-class families like mine were more circumscribed than those in less prosperous families. Men and women had separate rooms for entertaining their visitors. Women's rooms were located in
the inner recesses of the home, while the men used rooms on the perime-
ter of the house.

The partition of India in 1947 compelled my parents to uproot themselves. When Pitaji and my aunts and uncles talked of the partition, as they often did, they referred primarily to their loss of friends, relatives, community life, and possessions. They described the struggle that went into rebuilding their lives in Delhi and Bombay. They especially regretted the loss of their biradari. They said much less about the larger Muslim-Hindu conflicts that had ripped their lives asunder.

The struggle for Indian independence began in the early 1900s. It reached a critical stage during World War II, when the British government acceded to the demands of the nationalists and announced their intent to leave the country as soon as it was practical to do so. However, the two leading parties in India, the Indian National Congress and the Muslim League, had been unable to resolve their political differences. Muhammad Ali Jinnah, the leader of the Muslim League, had demanded a separate homeland for Muslims, arguing that an undivided India would only lead to a "Hindu Raj." Mahatma Gandhi, leader of the Indian National Congress, refused to countenance the division of the country on religious grounds, arguing that Hindus and Muslims were bhai-bhai, or brothers.

The British Viceroy, Lord Mountbatten, brokered a deal in 1947 that split the country into two sovereign nations: India and Pakistan. This did not satisfy either side, and the announcement unleashed riots, killing, and looting. Hindus in Muslim regions such as Quetta abandoned their businesses and homes and fled to central India, while Muslims in Hindu-dominated areas left for Pakistan. I do not know whether Pitaji discussed with the biradari the pros and cons of leaving his home, or consulted only my mother and immediate family members. I think he and his brother and sister panicked in the general hysteria surrounding the partition of the country, and became convinced that their lives were in danger. I never heard a single tale of anyone in the biradari who chose to stay behind.

At partition our family comprised Lalaji, Pitaji, four children, of which I was the youngest, and my mother, who was pregnant with another child. We joined the hordes of refugees pouring into the northern city of Delhi, bringing only clothing and my mother's gold jewellery with us. We avoided the refugee camps that sprang up throughout the city by selling bits and pieces of the jewellery. For a while we lived in the home of a distant relative, but eventually my parents decided to go to Bombay and try to start building a life there.

Throughout my life I have always wondered whether my parents' fears were well founded. What of all the Muslim friends they talked about in later life? Couldn't these Muslim friends have been relied upon to shelter and protect the family? My doubts about their fears were resolved to some extent when I read Urvashi Butalia's *The Other Side of Silence: Voices from the Partition of India*, but the book also increased my doubts about their claims of having close Muslim friends. Butalia is a Hindu, an activist feminist, and a journalist in India. She says that during the turbulent and unsettled partition days, Hindu men raped and killed Muslim women and that Muslim men did the same to Hindu women. Hundreds of women who were abducted and raped committed suicide. In rare cases when they escaped and returned to their communities, they were shunned and rejected, sometimes even by their families. A huge number of raped women and their children ended up in refugee camps.

A maternal uncle of Butalia who had not wanted to abandon his family property had stayed in Pakistan. He converted to Islam, married a Muslim woman, and had a family. He was despised by his family and taunted as a Hindu by his neighbours. In the late 1980s Butalia found her uncle living on the family property with his wife and children, and she reunited him with his brothers and sisters, all of whom had chosen to resettle in India. After a short time, however, he felt compelled to break off communication with his brothers and sisters in India, because the letters he received from them made the neighbours suspect he was a spy.

By the time we settled in Bombay, our family had grown to eight people with the birth of my sister Rita. Pitaji, however, had no income; everything had been left behind. Desperate, he returned to Quetta in 1948 to salvage some of his properties and businesses and obtain resources to provide for the family to start afresh. He arranged to swap his movie theatre in Quetta for one in Bombay, and obtained a refrigeration plant outside the city by selling some of his property to a Muslim family leaving for Pakistan. In Quetta, he found the family home broken into; a Muslim family had peremptorily claimed possession of it, and it was gone forever. We lived in a small rented apartment in Bombay, but the sale and exchange of properties provided a basis for our economic survival and raised hopes for better days ahead. But then my mother died, and the family was in crisis once again.

Indians of all religious affiliations tend to idealize the strong ties that characterize their family relations. Almost all my friends and acquaintances from the subcontinent proudly tell stories to demonstrate how individuals willingly make great personal sacrifices to secure the well-being of their brothers and sisters or even cousins, aunts, and uncles. Immigrants sometimes deny personal needs so that they can send money to help family members in India and Pakistan. This was true of my family during that crisis. Pitaji, Lalaji, Chachaji (my father's brother) and Bahenji (his sister) got together and decided how and where the children would be raised and who would be responsible for their well-being.

A collective decision was made that Pitaji would concentrate on getting his businesses established. Lalaji would be the primary caregiver to my teenaged brothers, Devinder and Subash, while Chachaji and his wife, themselves refugees and childless, took over the responsibility for Rita, the baby. Bahenji, a refugee and widow with three adult sons, assumed the care of my sister, Neena, and me, and we two moved to Delhi to live with her. There was an implicit understanding that my sisters and I would return to live with Pitaji when circumstances permitted. However, many years were to go by before we returned, and by then Lalaji had died, and Subash, ten years older than I, had already graduated from medical school and left home to pursue further studies in the United States.

My childhood was spent as a privileged girl in a relatively wealthy, old-money family. Bahenji (Pitaji called her "Sister," and so did I) had just turned forty when I went to live with her. She was tall, slim, and pretty, with an aristocratic mien. She had fine features, a "fair" complexion, and deep-set, dark eyes. Her hair was long and black, with a few flecks of gray, and she always wore it pulled back in a braid or a knot. Despite the severity of her hairstyle, however, she had a soft, gentle look. Temperamentally, she was kind, generous, and gracious. Bahenji's husband had owned considerable properties in the part of the country that had become Pakistan. These were inherited properties that belonged jointly, on his death, to my aunt and her brother-in-law. Like Pitaji, Bahenji and her in-laws had abandoned their home and properties to come to India, but they were able to trade these properties for some of nearly equal value in Delhi.

All of my aunt's possessions, except for gold jewellery and a few items of clothing, had been left behind. For many years after partition, a trivial or mundane event might provoke memories of things left behind. Recalling their colours, shapes, and textures in detail was perhaps one way of continuing to enjoy them. The sight of a rug on a visit to someone's house would elicit comparisons to the fine Persian rugs Lalaji had been forced to leave behind in Quetta. Talk of someone's dowry would bring out stories of her own, now irretrievably lost. From Lalaji, in keeping with the idea that a bestowal ending in the numeral one is considered auspicious, she had received a gift of fifty-one silk salwar kamiz and saris intricately embroidered with gold threads, but had to leave them behind for strangers to wear and enjoy. A shopping excursion to buy a wedding gift from the silver shops would bring out derisive comparisons of the merchandise we had seen with what she had lost. Heavy silver thalis and katoris (large dinner plates and bowls) and glasses received as dowry and wedding gifts were now all gone.

Bahenji had been able to save only a very few pictures of the family from the partition times or the early years in Delhi or Bombay. This seems strange when compared to the predilection of people of my generation, particularly in the affluent West, for collecting family photographs and albums. The handful of black-and-white portraits of Lalaji and of Bahenji's husband that remained were framed and placed on mantels. We all had the same picture of Lalaji: he is wearing a turban and what looks like a tweed coat; his hands are resting on a walking stick as he sits directly facing the camera. He is smiling a bit and looks warm and friendly.

We lived in a very large home that had originally belonged to a Muslim judge; it had been exchanged with him for my aunt's family home in a small town in the North West Frontier Province. Her new house was located in Old Delhi. Delhi, which dates back to the twelfth century, was built along the river Jumna, and had often been the capital of the Mughal, or Mogul emperors—Muslims who ruled large parts of India from the early-sixteenth century to the time of the arrival of the British in the seventeenth century. The Mughals built many splendid mausoleums, tombs, and mosques in Old Delhi. New Delhi refers to the part of the city dominated by buildings constructed for the British government during the late-nineteenth century. Many of them are within a short radius of Rashtrapati Bhavan, a grand palace built to house the British Viceroy.

Our house in Old Delhi was located close to the river in a neighbourhood walled off on one side by the remnants of an old fort; a stone archway stood at one end. The wall of the fort extended for about a mile before abruptly stopping. Parts of it had crumbled over the years, leaving some rather large holes. The fort divided the main city, with its heavy traffic along parks on one side, and our residential neighbourhood, a maze of narrow, winding lanes and byways that did not encourage much motor traffic.

The house was located on one of these narrow streets. It had been designed with high brick walls to protect the privacy of the family, and its only entrance was a huge gate, twelve feet high and made of solid steel. A small door in the gate was often used by the children and household help to come and go. There was a tiled courtyard at the centre of the house, and the building lay around it. There was no garden. The house was furnished in a simple, functional manner with a minimum of decoration, but the walls of the main rooms were lined with beautiful, hand-painted mosaic tiles. It was by far the biggest house in the neighbourhood. There was a three-storey apartment building with twenty units close by, but most of the homes in the neighbourhood were quite small. Bahenji owned the apartment building and several of the houses. I could not but be aware of the privileged economic status of our family.

Two of Bahenji's three sons had been compelled by the disruption that accompanied partition to abandon their college education and take over the family businesses. Her youngest son was an undergraduate at Delhi University. They were all much older than Neena and I, and they quickly adopted the conventional Indian role of protective and watchful big brothers towards sisters. Over the years they taught me how to play chess, and I spent many an evening in their company absorbed in the game. They would frequently drive us to school and to the homes of our maternal cousins, who were closer to us in age, for visits.

Once a week, usually on Sunday, I would go with some of these cousins to see a movie, frequently a Hollywood production but sometimes an Indian production, and to dinner afterwards in a restaurant. These were things we could not do with Bahenji, who felt that as a widow it was inappropriate for her to go to restaurants or movies. Outside the family circle, however, I had few companions. Sometimes I played hopscotch or skipped rope with some neighbourhood girls in our home, but only a very few times.

Bahenji was a devoutly religious woman who prayed daily and liked to study the religious epics herself, instead of going to a temple to hear a priest read like most women. Sometimes in the evenings, when the house was quiet, she would try to entertain Neena and me by telling us folk tales or stories from the Ramayan or Mahabharta. The storytelling usually occurred in the open courtyard as the daylight was fading, when our homework was done and there was time to while away, in those pre-television days, as dinner was being prepared. Sometimes on hot summer nights Bahenji would tell us stories on the terrace. The household help would put out a row of string cots with thin cotton mattresses, pillows and starched white sheets, and we would lie on them and gaze at the stars as we tried to cool down.

My aunt's storytelling always had a moral lesson. She would often change a familiar folk story to reflect some event of the previous day or two, along with a particular value or point of view favoured by her. This kind of storytelling is the staple formula of many Indian movies. A movie may begin in a lighthearted manner with lots of songs and dances, but after the intermission a moral or social problem is worked out—a conflict between duty and desire, the dilemma of falling in love and marrying outside one's social group, for instance. In the end tolerance always wins, and virtue and honesty are always rewarded. The first television program that I ever watched in Canada was a cop show. At the end, bewildered, I turned to my brother and asked, "What is the point?" He laughed loudly and said, "Nothing! It is just entertainment."

Many of my aunt's stories were about the courage and heroism of female characters in the epics. One of her favourites from the Mahabharta was about Draupadi and her fierce determination to protect her modesty. In the story, the Pandavs and the Kauravs fight a great war for the throne of Hastinapur. There is rivalry between them for the beautiful Princess Draupadi. King Draupd, her father, invites princes and kings from all the neighbouring lands to come to a Swayambar ceremony in which Draupadi is to be betrothed to one of the assembled guests. An archery contest is set up to see who can hit the eye of a goldfish revolving at high speed. One of the Pandav brothers wins the contest and marries Draupadi.

The victorious brothers return to their kingdom and go directly to their mother to show her their "prize." Saying she is busy, she refuses to come out of her room, instead merely instructing her sons that they should all share the prize equally, whatever it is. Thus Draupadi becomes the wife of all five Pandav brothers. The Kaurav brothers, smarting from their defeat, invite the Pandavs to their kingdom and entice them into a game of dice, in which they trick their unsuspecting guests into losing their entire kingdom. When there is nothing else left, the Pandavs stake Draupadi, and lose her as well.

When Draupadi hears of the game, she is furious, and refuses to come to the court when summoned by the Kauravs. They drag her in by the hair and decide to humiliate the Pandav brothers by stripping her of her sari in public. Draupadi is angry now at the Kauravs and the Pandavs, and is determined to save herself. She prays to Lord Krishna, and when the moment comes to disrobe her, they find that her sari has been transformed into an unending cloth. Her prayers have saved her.

The feminist in me is now appalled at the way Draupadi is depicted as an object, the property of her father and of the Pandavas, but there is also a lesson here of self-reliance, courage, and faith in God.

I was sent by my aunt to an all-girls convent school run by Irish Catholic nuns. The school was located in the heart of Old Delhi, a short distance from the Red Fort, built in the seventeenth century by the Emperor Shah Jehan, who also built the Taj Mahal. As a child I did not pay much attention to the fort, but it ran for several blocks, with a moat on one side and the river Jumna on the other. Much later I realized the significance of the site when I saw a documentary showing Jawaharlal Nehru proclaiming to the world from the Red Fort that India had become an independent nation. Politicians still use the grounds to hold enormous political rallies. Close to the fort are an Islamic mosque and an important gurudwara, or temple. The Jama Masjid (literally, "the great mosque") was also built by Shah Jehan, and is the largest mosque in the Islamic world. The Sisganj Gurudwara, a Sikh temple also built in the seventeenth century, is one of the holiest places for Sikhs. Between these monuments are the bazaars selling food, spices, silver, gold ornaments and all manner of things.

As a schoolgirl I remained unaware of the historical significance of these places and of the irony of placing a Catholic school near a mosque and a gurudwara. I never visited either at that time. Sometimes I went to the bazaars for some shopping with Bahenji, but I was never allowed to explore the city on my own or in the company of girlfriends. I could have gone into the gurudwara, since Sikhism is widely believed to be an offshoot of Hinduism, but going to the mosque would have been an altogether different issue, though many years later I did go inside the Jama Masjid. The school never took us on any field trips to the Red Fort or made us conscious of the historical character of the neighbourhood—or of our heritage, our history, or ourselves. I remained ignorant of their significance until I was a young adult.

The school building was large, set in a walled compound with spacious playgrounds at the front and back. There were living quarters for the nuns clustered around a small garden. Behind the living quarters and the classroom building was a large church to which the students had free and easy access. We often ran into the church during our play, dipping our hands in the communion water at the entrance and crossing ourselves while muttering, "Father, Son, and the Holy Ghost." Right at the back, in one corner, were the living quarters of a few Indians who cleaned the school and did other menial tasks. As students we knew—perhaps because we had been told by our families at home—that these people were untouch-ables who had converted to Christianity, perhaps to obtain employment and accommodation from the school. I remember seeing some children near those houses who did not attend classes with us. They, and we, took their exclusion as normal and routine. Probably the nuns did not include them as it would have caused great consternation to the parents of their existing students, and might even have led to the students' withdrawal. Poverty and untouchability were so integral a part of my daily routine and environment as a young girl that I had no reason to think of them as exceptional phenomena, let alone think about their social, ethical, and moral dimensions.

All the teachers, with some very few exceptions, were Irish nuns who dressed in black habits during the winter and white habits in the summer months. There was one Hindu teacher who wore a sari and taught us Hindi. During my high school years there was also one young Indian-Catholic woman who dressed in a sari; she taught the younger kids. The students wore blue tunics with white shirts and white shoes. The language of instruction at the school was English. The school day began and ended with Christian prayers, and Christian doctrine was emphasized. The teaching consisted of memorization and regurgitation of facts. Knowledge of the Bible and familiarity with Christian doctrine were to come in use-ful to me in later life when I read English literature and visited art galleries in Europe, but the intention of the school was simply to encourage belief in Catholicism and to praise the glory of the Lord Jesus Christ.

The decision to send my brothers, sisters, and me to convent schools and thus expose us to Christianity and possible conversion may seem sur-prising for a Hindu family. The decision had much to do with Bahenji's personal history and the availability of "good" education for girls. Bahenji had had an arranged marriage as a teenager, and that had brought an end to her schooling. She may have had a grade six or seven education. Later in life, when she became a widow and then a refugee, she would feel insecure not knowing how to manage her finances to protect her sons' inheritance. Although the management of the family properties and businesses had passed on to her brother-in-law, she still felt frustrated at always having to rely on the men of her family to ensure her own and her sons' well-being. She could not read English and thus had no way of reading business documents or supervising business accounts. She could not meet with lawyers or go to government offices to settle claims for property left in Pakistan. She trusted Pitaji to guide and help her take care of her affairs, but deeply felt and regretted her dependence on men and her lack of education.

The partition of the country had created a great deal of insecurity in Pitaji and Bahenji, and they always talked of the need to ensure against what they referred to as fate. Education, they said, was insurance against hard times. They made constant reference to their partition experiences to drive home the dangers of putting one's faith in material possessions. Property and inheritance could be easily lost, they said, and an individual's success and survival depended on ability and initiative. They were determined to inculcate self-reliance in both their male and female children. Social inhibitions and customs that conflicted with this goal were brushed aside.

Pitaji and Bahenji's faith in education has much in common with that of immigrants to North America. A history of persecution or displacement by war has prompted refugees to try to ensure the future of their children by emphasizing their education. In my family's case, besides my PhD, both of my sisters have BAs. One of my brothers became a physician, while the other, along with one of Bahenji's sons, graduated with law degrees.

According to Pitaji and Bahenji, the convent school provided the best education then available for girls from upper-middle-class families like ours. Even at the present time there's a certain cachet attached to convent education and knowledge of the English language. National Indian newspapers often include several pages of matrimonial advertisements; many of them include the phrase "convent-educated girl" along with her caste and class. My maternal cousins, whose families were middle-class, went to non-denominational schools, where the medium of instruction was Hindi. Although Pitaji and Bahenji admired nationalist leaders like Mahatma Gandhi, Motilal Nehru, Jawaharlal Nehru, and Sardar Vallabhai Patel, I never heard them express any anti-colonial sentiment regarding Western-style education. The British colonial government had introduced English education for the Indian middle classes, and missionaries, along with

Indian social reformers, had played a pioneering role in the education of women in the late-nineteenth and early-twentieth centuries. However, to counteract any religious influence that the nuns might have had, Bahenji took great pains to teach Neena and me Hindu doctrines, and discouraged us from bringing home any pictures of Jesus Christ given to us by the nuns.

I write this having lived in Canada for some thirty years, and I find that what seemed natural and normal when I was a girl now seems very strange or even incomprehensible. As a professor, I marvel that in my comfortable girlhood I never went to a library. There were no libraries in my neighbourhood or even in my school (and very few public libraries even today in India). I cannot recall having seen any encyclopedias or dictionaries around the house. I was a voracious reader of Enid Blyton mysteries, fascinated by the lives of the girls described in them, but also read comic books like Archie and Veronica, Jughead, and Tarzan. Later I subscribed to *Women's Weekly*, a British magazine, and avidly read the romances that were serialized in them. A Hindi and English newspaper came to the house, as did the English-language *Illustrated Weekly*, with a format much like that of *Life* magazine. There were the works of Hardy, Dickens and Shakespeare prescribed by the school, and my aunt had her collection of religious books in Hindi. She did not read or speak English, although over the years she came to understand conversations in English. I, however, did not read anything in Hindi other than some books prescribed by the school in a course on the language.

Bahenji was a strict disciplinarian who brooked no slacking off. Neena and I were expected to apply ourselves diligently to our school work. As there were few other distractions, I do not remember studying to have been a chore. The house had many rooms away from the main activity areas, and I was often content to hide in them and read my books, though Bahenji would scold me for being antisocial or for shirking some chore. Predictably, Neena and I brought home good report cards. Bahenji took great pride in them and would continually mention them during family gatherings. She always commended us for getting good grades, remarking that she never had to hire tutors for us, something many other families in our acquaintance did routinely.

In Bahenji's quest to make us what she characterized as "self-reliant," she insisted that we iron our school uniforms ourselves and polish our own shoes. Normally, paid help did the washing—by hand—and clothes were sent out to be ironed. In many neighbourhoods in Delhi, a man might

make his living ironing clothes: to make his services available, he simply
sets up a makeshift table and fills an iron with hot coals. I complained
about the ironing to my maternal aunts, who were sympathetic and grumbled that it was an unnecessary hardship for their motherless niece to bear
(although their own children did that and much more). But Bahenji did
not budge, and I went around for a while feeling very hard done by.

As a child and young adult, my attitude towards Bahenji's widowhood
mirrored her own. My aunt dressed austerely and simply; she always wore
plain white saris in public, although at home she sometimes wore pastel
shades. She used no makeup and wore only a couple of gold bangles and a
chain, although she owned a very substantial collection of jewels. I could
not help but notice that her appearance was very different from that of
other women, most of whom dressed in bright colours and wore many gold
bangles, big earrings, and thick, heavy chains. Sometimes I would ask her
to wear coloured saris, or at least have her white ones embroidered with
coloured thread, but she would explain in a matter-of-fact manner that it
would be inappropriate for her to dress in coloured clothes since she was
a widow. In these conversations, she displayed little rancour about her situation, so I too accepted it as just the way it was. Much later in life, when
I was introduced to feminism, I would remember her manner of dress and
her sad expression when discussing it with me, and I would be upset for
her and regret my own lack of sensitivity. However, at the time I did not
think much of it, and it evoked little sentiment in me about the injustices
of a patriarchal society.

Bahenji's daily routine was limited to the home and the satsang (literally a "truth association"), a religious group presided over by a guru.
Sometimes relatives or biradari families would come to visit, and she
attended celebrations of births, engagements, and weddings. But she spent
every afternoon at the satsang listening to scriptures being read by the
guru, who was called Mataji (literally, mother), and singing devotional
songs. My aunt had a strong, melodious voice and was always much in
demand to lead these sessions of devotional singing. Although the osten-
sible purpose of the satsang every afternoon was prayer, it was really a
place where the women could congregate and talk to one another. After
the singing, Bahenji and some other women would visit with Mataji in her
private living quarters. Their relationship was more akin to friendship
between equals than that of a guru and her disciple; Mataji's religious position and my aunt's social status seemed to balance. Mataji would some-

times come to spend the weekend at our house, and Bahenji would have elaborate food prepared for her. Then they would sit and chat together. Their talk was filled with mundane, everyday events rather than philosophy and religion. Sometimes I would be called to help serve them dinner, service being a mark of respect towards those with high religious status. I often hung around the house in my school tunic, but Mataji never said anything to me about my Catholic school.

As a Hindu, my aunt believed in karma—the idea that actions in previous incarnations dictate the circumstances of a person's present life— and so in her understanding, her situation was part of her fate. She tried to accommodate herself to her fate of becoming a widow—and a refugee—with dignity, rather than complaining about it. She did not describe having been born a woman as a matter of fate, however, because that would imply that she was somewhat discontent with her gender. As a woman, she had certain rights and responsibilities, none of which she considered to be unjust or oppressive. She accepted the gender roles of her class and community, and according to her, a "good" woman sought to live up conscientiously to these ideals. By example and through direct advice, she tried to inculcate these attitudes towards self, other women, and society in my sister and me.

Nevertheless, Bahenji recognized that her choices and options were limited, even though she was a wealthy woman. She had little education, and there were three sons who had to be helped to establish themselves in life. Most of her wealth was part of jointly owned family property governed by the Hindu Family Code (which exists alongside secular civil legislation), and legally she was not entitled to sell it or obtain an independent share of it. Her rights and inheritance, along with those of her sons, were integrally tied to those of her in-laws. Besides, as a dignified widow who observed the norms of her culture, my aunt was a well-respected member of the community, and her place in it was secured. Failure to conform would have jeopardized her economic and social survival. I cannot even fathom what shape her life might otherwise have taken. Bahenji's philosophy about a woman's life nevertheless conveyed some resentment. She would continually warn me that life was tough, and a woman's life tougher, and I had therefore to acquire a habit of hard work and discipline. This would help me negotiate the difficulties inherent in being a woman.

Bahenji was a conscientious and efficient homemaker who managed her house and family with a firm hand. The paid help who cooked and cleaned the house were supervised closely. If she was dissatisfied with their work, she would do it herself. Mano-ki-ma (literally, "the mother of Mano," a traditional way of referring to a woman by her child's name) came to the house daily to perform household chores. She had an animated face and an energetic and brisk gait. Although her clothes were often drab, they were seldom ragged or torn, and they were always clean. Her hair was covered tightly with a dupatta. She spent the whole morning sweeping the house and mopping the floors. Sometimes Bahenji would send her to buy vegetables or to take a special dish over to Mataji. Sometimes on holidays she brought her daughter Mano, two years older than I was, and we would play together.

Some evenings Bahenji would send me to Mano-ki-ma's house, around the corner from ours, to ask her to do some additional chores. Mano-ki-ma lived in a building with about ten rooms laid out side by side, each one home to a poor family. When I knocked on the door, it would be opened by Mano or one of her two brothers, and I would enter a small, enclosed verandah attached to their room. There were no windows, and the only light came from a naked bulb that hung from the middle of the ceiling. I always hoped that Mano's father would not be there. He worked as a labourer, but was an alcoholic. Sometimes I would see him curled up on the floor along one wall of the room. Then Mano-ki-ma would quickly shoo me out, telling me she would come over in a few minutes.

Mano's family had few possessions. A few string cots were piled up in one corner, and some bedding rolls. Two steel trunks stacked one on top of the other alongside one wall held clothes for the entire family. While I wore dresses, Mano had two or three salwar kamiz. One side of the verandah was for cooking, and on the other side there were some large terra cotta jugs for drinking water. Some steel pails with stored water lay in one corner. There was no indoor plumbing, and a communal tap was used by all the families in the row of housing. I often saw women, girls, and boys standing around it and talking.

The contrast between our lives was enormous, yet it evoked little response from me. I might have asked for explanations from Bahenji or her eldest son Omji, who helped take care of the family business and to whom a great deal of privilege accrued. I might have asked, "Why do Mano and her family live in that one room? Why does she not have nice clothes?" They would have replied impatiently, "What is the matter with you? Can't you tell that they are poor?"

"Why are they poor?"

"Her father works as a labourer...when he is not drunk. The man has no sense—wasting all his money, with a daughter at home to be married. He should be saving for Mano's dowry. How much can Mano-ki-ma earn by cleaning houses and washing clothes for other people in their houses?"

"Why can't he get a better job?"

"Tobah [for heaven's sake]! Doesn't the school teach you anything? You tell me what can an uneducated man do?"

Bahenji would have bemoaned the kismet, or fate, of Mano and her mother. That made them poor. Everyone had his or her own kismet, and one had to accept it as an unalterable fate. I should be grateful to God for my own kismet, they would add, and show my gratitude by helping the poor with money, food, and clothing, as and when it was possible. More questions from me would have led to a discussion of karma. But there was no need to have this discussion, because we all—Bahenji, Omji, Mano, her mother, and I—accepted this "truth" of life in our culture and community. No one challenged kismet or karma.

Omji, twenty years my senior, would have teased me had I asked him these questions. He would have said, "You are not learning anything at that Catholic school...But that is okay. Girls don't need an education since they are going to spend their whole life at home cooking and taking care of children. We should take you out of that school, teach you housework, and then we can get you married too, and be done with it." That kind of comment did provoke me, but anyone who happened to be nearby would have just added more of the same for the fun of seeing how it excited me.

At first Mano went to a state-run public school where the family did not pay any tuition fees. By the time she was about ten, though, her attendance at school, which had been irregular up to then, became even more occasional. Mano-ki-ma needed her help with work in our house and others. When I was eight and Mano ten, she would seek me out in the house and sit on the floor in the room I was in, asking me questions about the books I was reading. I would find myself on the floor with her so I could show her my school work. When her mother called her, we would giggle and pretend for as long as we could that we had not heard. However, Mano found a job as a maid in a neighbouring family and dropped out of school altogether. She still came to the house with her mother in the evening, but she sought me out less and less and lost all interest in school.

Mano, at eleven, had become part of the adult world of work, responsibility and its attendant complaints. Childhood evaporated.

Sometimes after Mano-ki-ma had finished her chores, she would sit on the floor near Bahenji and talk to her. I would pepper my aunt with questions afterwards: Why had Mano-ki-ma been crying? What had they been whispering about? Bahenji would say, "Nothing. It's about that man. He came home drunk again." One day I was told Mano was being sent back to her village for a couple of years. She was now twelve, and her mother was concerned about finding a husband for her and putting together a dowry. Mano disappeared from our life altogether for a while.

One day she reappeared in our house giggling and laughing and clearly excited. She had just returned from the village and, at fourteen, was engaged to be married. Her mother had found a young man, a labourer a few years her senior who worked in Old Delhi, and had arranged a marriage between them through some members of her family in the village. Before the marriage could take place, however, there was the matter of putting together a dowry for her and paying for the wedding celebrations. The talk now consistently revolved around this topic. I was curious, but no longer felt a connection to Mano, since our lives had taken such different directions. I watched from a distance the excitement of Mano and the increasing grimness of her mother.

Now Mano-ki-ma appeared in the evenings on her own to see if Bahenji was free. She would sit at her feet, with her head in one hand, and seek her advice on the dowry and the wedding celebrations. Mano's dowry would comprise eleven new salwar kamiz and saris, a gold chain, a ring, and two bangles. The groom would get one set of new clothes, and his parents and siblings would also receive a set of new clothes each. The neighbours would be given the customary sweetmeats celebrating the wedding, and a wedding lunch would be provided for the groom and the guests. Mano would also have to get a red sari with gold-coloured sequins and ribbon in which to be married.

Bahenji contributed to the dowry and the celebrations, as did other families for whom Mano-ki-ma worked. Some of it, I suspect, must have been a loan. Mano seemed to be blissfully happy in anticipating her new life, but Bahenji only looked sad when I talked to her about these preparations. Her demeanour made me feel that something was amiss, so I asked, "Don't you like the boy?" To my surprise, she became angry. "Mano is a fool!" she declared. "What is there to be happy about? You wait and see, in a year's time there will be a child. And then more children. Mano will be working as a maid just like her mother to feed them and herself." Mano, oblivious to these realities, was clearly anticipating the thrill of new clothes, a husband, a new family, and having a little room of her own to begin an adult married life.

I, in the meantime, was playing basketball at school, pestering my cousins to take me to movies, fretting and fuming about my clothes and appearance, and writing letters to Pitaji asking him to send me boxes of candy. I was beginning to dream of becoming a "college girl" and anticipating with some excitement my impending move to Bombay to live with Pitaji and attend college there.

4

Bombay

At the age of fifteen, I moved from my aunt's care in Delhi to live with my father in Bombay. I had finished my schooling and was ready to enter university, so Bahenji and Pitaji thought it was the right time for me to make the transition to my father's home. I looked forward to the change, but was also a little sad to leave my cousins and aunt, with whom I had lived for so many years.

The change in the gender and temperament of my caregiver meant that somewhat different ideals and values would now guide my daily life. My businessman father was impatient with traditional values, and took pride in being an independently minded individual who did his own thing. He wanted my sisters and me to be "modern," educated women, rather than follow the behaviour and norms common to upper-middle-class women in Hindu families. Although the transition required some basic adjustments, it was easy for me, since living with my father meant greater freedom from restraints.

Bombay, the largest city in the state of Maharashtra, is vastly different from Delhi. While Delhi has ancient historical monuments dating back to the Mughal dynasty, Bombay's landmarks reflect a mix of European and Indian architectural styles. Delhi is a capital city and supports a vast government bureaucracy and diplomatic corps, whereas Bombay, a port city, is the commercial and industrial centre of India. The population of Delhi is predominantly Punjabi, and its people are popularly perceived as entrepreneurial, vivacious and ostentatious, with little interest in highbrow culture. Bombay is made up of indigenous Maharashtrians and Parsis. Maharashtrians have the reputation of being quiet, simple and unenterprising people who like classical music, dance, and drama. Parsis (also indigenous to Maharashtra, and particularly to Bombay) are the most Westernized people in India, especially in their tastes in music and dance. Followers of Zoroastrianism, they are thought to be honest, straightforward, and trustworthy in their business dealings, although somewhat eccentric. Tata, one of India's leading industrial conglomerates, is owned by Parsis, and its headquarters are in Bombay.

The languages of daily commerce in Delhi are Hindi and Punjabi; in Bombay they are Marathi, Gujarati, and English. The populations of both Delhi and Bombay are predominantly Hindu, but in Delhi the gods most worshipped are the lords Rama, Krishna, and Vishnu, whereas in Bombay the lords Shiva and Ganesha hold rank. The women dress differently in the two cities. In Bombay jeans and Western-style clothing are common, along with saris, but in Delhi women mostly wear salwar kamiz and saris. However, both cities provide striking contrasts between the lives of rich and poor and are equally plagued by many urban ills. Delhi people tend to follow conventional Punjabi norms, but Bombay is somewhat Westernized and cosmopolitan.

In the years since partition, Pitaji had become very successful. Indians tend to be avid moviegoers (this was especially true in the days before the introduction of television and video) and Pitaji's movie theatre turned out to be a "cash cow" that supported us in comfort. When my sisters and I came to live with my father, he left the day-to-day running of the movie theatre to a manager, going there himself only for an hour or two in the evening. He also gave up the management of his refrigeration plant to my brother. He remained mostly at home and was always available—like many mothers—to listen and talk to my sisters and me about our myriad day-to-day problems. His decision to become personally involved in raising us was unusual for the times in India.

Pitaji was temperamentally quite different from Bahenji, and their life experiences had, of course, also differed. Bahenji was religious, but Pitaji strongly discouraged my sisters and me from going to temples or observing religious rituals such as fasting. While Bahenji had emphasized the need to learn some domestic skills, Pitaji deplored seeing us doing any housework: that was done by paid help, he said. Bahenji had wanted us to conform to the norms of our culture and community; Pitaji was critical of them, although he stopped short of encouraging us to defy them. Contrary to conventional Indian norms, he encouraged me to stand up to my brother Devinder, eleven years older than I, when he tried to assert authority or boss me around. I was free to talk back to him, much to my brother's disgruntlement and despite his complaints. Pitaji particularly emphasized the need to be shrewd managers of personal finance. Never sign a document without reading it thoroughly, he told us, even if asked to do so by a male relative.

Pitaji's authority was seldom expressed outright; it was subtle and indirect. He did control us, but maintained an illusion of independence and autonomy for us. His system of giving an allowance was one example. My sisters and I were not given a fixed allowance. Instead, Pitaji kept a bag of money in a locked closet along with a diary. We each had a key to the closet and could take out whatever amount we needed. The only requirement was to record in the diary how much we had taken and for what purpose. Pitaji never asked any questions or complained about our expenses. He didn't have to, because my sisters and I kept a vigilant eye on each other's expenses and saved him the bother of keeping us in line.

Pitaji had lived in different parts of the city, but by the time my sisters and I came to Bombay, he was living in an apartment in Malabar Hill, an upper-middle-class neighbourhood that was the home of businessmen, senior corporate executives, and politicians. Sindhi, Gujarati, Punjabi, Parsi, and Maharashtrian families lived there. Pitaji encouraged us to make friends with people of our own age in the building and neighbourhood. He felt that by getting to know them and visiting with their families, I would pick up the attitudes and behaviour appropriate for educated, "modern" women. Some of the families that I got to know followed traditional norms particular to their culture, while others were more Westernized.

One of my close friends was Kunda, a Maharashtrian, and we spent a great deal of time together. Like me, Kunda was a newcomer to Bombay, having lived previously with her family in other parts of India as well as in Britain and North America. Her father was a senior economist with the Reserve Bank of India, and his previous posting had been in London. Kunda's family lived in an apartment given to him by the bank. It was large by Bombay standards, but the family had furnished it simply and sparsely.

Kunda's father was a quiet man, and when I visited her apartment, he was usually sitting in an armchair reading, but sometimes he could be found sitting on a mat on the floor and entertaining himself by playing a small set of drums called a *tabla*. At his insistence, Kunda was learning to play the sitar from a tutor who came to the house to give her lessons. Sometimes, when the family went to a musical recital, I tagged along with them. Kunda's mother, a homemaker, dressed simply in cotton saris, wore little jewellery, and used no makeup. She was a wiry, energetic woman who bustled around the house and continuously fretted about Kunda and her other children.

Kunda's family ate in the traditional Maharashtrian style. An elderly male cook who had been with the family for several years reigned over the kitchen. He dressed in a white *dhoti* (a cotton loincloth reaching below the knee) and a vest. As is usual in traditional Hindu homes, he cooked while sitting on the floor surrounded by his cooking implements and the ingredients for the meal. He sternly reprimanded us if we dared to enter his kitchen wearing shoes. Sometimes Kunda and I wanted to cook something on a small propane gas stove he used, but he would have none of that, and firmly kept us out of the kitchen.

Usually, Maharashtrian families—Tamils, Marwaris, and many others—take their meals in the kitchen, seated on mats or low stools and served either by the older women of the family or by the cook. Kunda's family, however, ate in a dining room and sat at a table. They used large, stainless-steel *thalis* and *katoris*, but had Western-style crockery for formal events with more Westernized, non-Maharashtrian guests. The family ate with their hands rather than with silverware, but when I was visiting, the cook routinely brought me a fork and spoon without my having to ask. The entire family was vegetarian, despite having lived in the West for several years.

The members of Kunda's family all spoke English fluently, but at home they always spoke to each other in Marathi, and I picked up some of the language by listening to them. In our house we intermingled English, Multani, and Hindi, with no set pattern for their use. Sometimes a conversation would begin in Multani, shift to Hindi, move to English, and then return to Multani. At other times a conversation might take place in Hindi, with a few English phrases thrown in to better express the sentiment of the moment, or it might be in English, with Hindi expressions liberally strewn about within it. This use of different languages in one conversation is common in Bombay, and Salman Rushdie satirically calls it "Hug-Me"[1] (Hindi, Urdu, Gujarati, Marathi and English).

On a recent visit to Central India, I noticed several billboards and store signs using Hindi words and expressions, but they were written in the English alphabet. National, English-language Indian newspapers frequently use Hindi words and expressions, and some of their stories in this "Hinglish" may be incomprehensible to a reader unfamiliar with Hindi. Amongst my friends I almost always spoke English, adding some popular Hindi colloquialisms. Since we often came from different regional backgrounds, it formed the only common language amongst us.

The bane of Kunda's family was the mediocre academic record of her brother, Jaya, a tall, good-looking guy three years her senior. The parents were convinced that a good education at the Indian Institute of Technology, preferably in engineering, was absolutely essential for his future well-being. However, the Institute had a considerable reputation, and admission to it was highly competitive. His parents hired tutors to help Jaya get through his undergraduate degree with good grades, but to little avail. His parents constantly nagged him and unfavourably compared him to Kunda and his other sister, Tai. Jaya wanted to do well and especially respected his sister Tai's academic success, but his heart was simply not in his studies.

Much of the tension in the family was rooted in their beliefs about gender roles. They assumed as an incontrovertible truth that Jaya would one day be responsible for providing for a family and thus needed professional credentials to lead a middle-class life. Tai's success was highly gratifying for the parents and they commended her for it but, in the larger scheme of things, it was not considered essential.

Jaya was friendly and talkative. Sometimes he would come into Kunda's room to chat with us; he would be irked if he found us studying or reading and would make disparaging comments about girls who had nowhere to go and nothing better to do than study. He would encourage us to give it up, and would even include us in the parties that he and his friends were organizing. His parents and my father took it for granted that the people at these parties would be much like ourselves, and that Jaya would act as a kind of chaperone and keep an eye on us. Including us in his parties earned Jaya some brownie points with them, but it did not ease the pressure on him to do well academically, which continued until he was able, eventually, to get admission to the Institute. He graduated from there as an engineer.

When I came to live with my father, I had already passed the Cambridge University "O" (Overseas) Level Examination and was ready to enter university. When I graduated, only "O" level, equivalent to grade ten, was offered in India. Subsequently an "A" level was introduced, which was equal to grade twelve. (This structure is one explanation why Canadian universities do not grant equivalent standing to degrees obtained outside Canada. Some count the number of years of schooling rather than the degrees obtained. Thus, after a four-year bachelor's degree and a law degree from Bombay, the University of Toronto offered me admission only as a fourth-year undergraduate student. I turned them down and went straight to a master's program at the University of Waterloo.)

At Bombay University, I enrolled in the non-denominational Elphinstone College—named after a British governor with the extraordinarily pretentious moniker Mountstuart Elphinstone—for an undergraduate arts degree in history. My other choices were St. Xavier's, a Jesuit-run college, and the all-girls Sophia College run by Christian missionaries. Elphinstone had been established by the British in the middle of the nineteenth century as one of three government colleges for the spread of Western education in India, the other two being in Madras and Calcutta. The college had received a generous endowment from Sir Cowasjee Jehangir, a leading Parsi industrialist. It had a good reputation and was thought to be superior to the others. It was originally only for men, but by the time I enrolled, it had become coeducational. Since I had the requisite grades, I went there, as my sister had done a year ahead of me, without giving much thought to my other choices.

Elphinstone College is located in an area that had originally formed the nucleus of the city. When the British took over Bombay in 1665, they built fortifications on the site, but as these fortifications eventually lost much of their utility, John Lord Elphinstone, governor of the city from 1853 to 1860, ordered them torn down. In their place, a row of magnificent public buildings was later erected on one side of Oval Maidan, a landscaped park "as if on parade before the spectator."[2] The college and its next-door neighbour, Bombay University, were part of this complex.

The college and university buildings were designed in the ornate Gothic Revival style so popular in Britain in the nineteenth century. The domination of Gothic Revival architecture in public buildings in Bombay symbolized the subordination of Indian culture to British power. Wealthy Indians failed to support Indian architecture, donating money instead to European-style buildings. Although Bombay has hundreds of temples, mosques, and Parsi fire temples, none was considered notable for its architecture. A Hindu businessman, Premchand Roychand, endowed the university library and dedicated its heavily ornamented and soaring clock tower to the memory of his mother, Rajabai, for whom it is named. A British critic writes that the Gothic style of the "University Hall...seems to have been meant for a western College Chapel, and is as exotic as the system of education which we have introduced into the land."[3]

Behind Elphinstone College was the Prince of Wales Museum, built in 1905 to house Indian art. Concern over the decline of Indian architectural styles had led to an amalgamation of Gothic Revival and Indian decorative elements in what was called Indo-Saracenic style. The museum therefore included a Mughal dome and ogee arches set with carved screens and Gothic Revival sculptural ornaments. While at the college, I took a course on the history of Indian art and religion, but my studies focused primarily on text work; I was not required to visit the museum, nor did I did take the initiative to see for myself some examples of Indian art. Several years later, on a visit to Bombay from Toronto, I finally visited the museum, but found the building—dusty, smelly and unused—in an advanced state of deterioration.

The area around Elphinstone College had architectural and historical significance, but when I attended university much of its beauty was obscured by a mélange of undistinguished, heavily weathered buildings. Crowding in on it were stores such as Rhythm House (the largest music store in the city), an art gallery or two, and any number of offices, stores, banks, restaurants and coffee shops. The buildings were separated by tiny parks and playing fields, around which traffic moved briskly.

The college was built in locally quarried stone that had aged over the years, and when I went there it just looked gray and gritty to me. A wide, cobblestoned arcade in front of the building led to a large gate and then into a wide hall with high ceilings and walls covered with brass plaques detailing the founding of the college and the names of some of its donors. Usually, an old male cobbler was sitting in the arcade bent over his few tools and repairing the sandals of women standing impatiently nearby. Sometimes vendors would put out displays of magazines in the arcade; another man sold roasted *channa* (chickpeas) and peanuts in cones made from scrap paper, but otherwise it was unoccupied. The arcade protected the front of the building from monsoon rain and direct sunlight, keeping the interior of the building cool and somewhat dark—just as well, because the building showed the wear and tear of thousands of students tramping through its hallways and up and down its stairs over a hundred years.

The college had a small library on the second floor with several doors, perhaps twelve feet high, which were usually kept wide open. Still, the library was not an inviting place. With a few dust-covered racks of books lined up at one end of the room and some tables and chairs scattered in the middle, it looked bare. In the summer, a high ceiling fan whirred constantly in the empty space. Whenever I passed by the library, I saw only a few clerks impassively bent over desks or walking desolately among the books. I never saw any students there. Some other rooms in the college, which students were prohibited from entering, had doors with metal bars on them. They housed the archives of Bombay University.

Since I was never required to do any research essays, I never used the library at the college or at the university next door. For the final examinations we were required to have more or less memorized a text and to regurgitate facts. My first research essay was written at the University of Toronto.

The teenage me who went to the college revelled in its daily routine, and found little to complain about. I usually left home in the morning dressed in a freshly starched and ironed cotton sari and carrying a couple of books in my hand. I was at the college by ten o'clock and immediately went in search of my friends to make plans for the day. Attending classes was a secondary consideration when compared to my social activities. Four or five of us walked down to the then-popular restaurant, Volga, around eleven. On some mornings the restaurant hosted a special music session with a band that played Western pop music. Hordes of students sat crammed together there in a little room listening to the music, gossiping, and drinking cold coffee with ice cream. When the music ended at one o'clock, we meandered back to the college without experiencing much guilt or remorse for having wasted the morning.

Some of us then drifted into class, or went to get notes from students who had attended the morning lectures; others regrouped in the college cafeteria. By three o'clock, classes were over and we went home or, sometimes, to a movie. Once I got home, though, my mood would shift, and I would diligently read my textbooks and copy notes from lectures I had missed that day. Having no television made it easy to work at home. Sometimes in the evening I would go visit my friends in their homes or stroll with them on Marine Drive, which ran alongside the Arabian Sea.

I was expected to be back home when it began to get dark, usually around eight o'clock. We had dinner at nine and sometimes I studied again or just read novels. I had no complaints with the college, the curriculum, the professors, or their methods of teaching. They suited me just fine.

Now, as I write this, I am a woman of fifty-five, a professor who has spent most of her adult life at universities in Canada. I look back at those years with "Canadian eyes" and feel unhappy and critical about the education I received in the 1960s. The curriculum that was offered at the university showed strong colonial biases. The range of subjects that I studied had broadened to include Indian history and religion along with the hardy perennials of British and European history. The literature courses covered only English—read British—literature; I do not remember reading any American authors for a course, but some may have been included under the general rubric. The present curriculum does include some Indian authors writing in English, but it was not so then. Thus, even though I was attending a secular Indian institution, and not a mission college, its curriculum was still dictated by its colonial heritage.

Perhaps even more surprising than the literature courses was the requirement to take a foreign language. The two choices were French and German. I studied German for two years with a Maharashtrian professor who had received his training in Germany, but I learned only enough to pass my examination. Kunda, on the other hand, was greatly interested in learning languages and decided to major in German. It would have been far more useful for me to study Marathi, the local language, or Telegu or Bengali, but consciousness of the need to learn about one's own country was still at an incipient stage at Elphinstone College, and it took second place to learning about the West. (In the 1970s the government, responding to Marathi nationalism, made the study of Marathi language a compulsory subject in all schools.)

Male and female professors lectured to us in large classrooms with a couple of hundred students in attendance, but no time was allocated for questions and answers. There were no small group discussions or tutorials. The format was not conducive to learning analytical skills, and the anonymity of the large classes did not encourage regular attendance. Some professors were rumored to have used the same notes for years. The faculty did not give the impression of being scholarly or learned; they seemed to be more like poorly paid, low-level bureaucrats. Few of them seemed to have much enthusiasm for teaching, and even fewer took any interest in us as individuals.

Since students had little personal contact with professors, there was no way for us to know or to understand the experiences of our female professors. They remained mysterious people, sometimes ridiculed for being schoolmarmish "spinsters." One, Miss Jassawalla, was a prim, middle-aged Parsi woman who wore drab cotton saris, flat sandals, and had her hair tightly pulled back in a bun. She sternly reprimanded students when she saw them "loitering" in the hallways. We tried to dodge her if we saw her coming, but sometimes she surprised us, coming upon us unaware. She thought I was a good student, and when she found me loitering, she would tell me off for missing one too many lectures. But I did not get to know her, or any of my other female professors, and did not adopt them as role models. Instead, I remained immersed in frivolous activities.

When I was in my fourth year of studies, the looming question, obviously, was what I would do next. Though my friends and I were expecting to graduate, we were still just nineteen or twenty, and very much under the tutelage of our parents. We were all living at home; none of us had yet earned any money, even at a part-time job. Most of us expected that our parents would continue to support us financially until we married. Our financial dependence on parents, in the absence of student loans, grants, or job opportunities, made us seek our parents' approval and support. Such dependence strengthened our parents' authority and inculcated in us a habit of obedience and conformity. Although it was easy enough to defy parents in small ways, we realized that they had the last word. Without their financial support, we could do nothing and get nowhere. Their approval was critical to the realization of our goals.

All of our parents strongly supported education for females, but they perceived it as preparing us to be "good citizens." Few of them thought of it as preparing their daughters for careers. They assumed marriage to be inevitable, and anticipated a life for their daughters as housewives and mothers, not as employed wives and mothers or as unmarried career women. They also had a vague idea that education might be a "good resource to fall back upon" if things did not work out as expected for us in later life.

There were essentially three choices: a job, graduate school, or marriage. My friends and I spent many hours discussing these alternatives, but our talk lacked the intensity and seriousness that you might expect for life-shaping decisions. We did not seriously consider the possibility of combining choices—going to graduate school and finding a part-time job, or going to graduate school and getting married. We considered our choices in the context of the norms of our class and culture. Later, many of us found ways of combining these choices.

No sense of urgency attended our discussion of career choices, perhaps because of a subconscious awareness that we had few skills and that the rate of unemployment, which is always high in India, meant that jobs were few and far between for women raised as we were. Salaries for "women's jobs"—for public-school teachers, clerks, secretaries and so on—were so pathetically low that none of us would have deigned even to think of them. There were strong cultural and social biases against service-related jobs, though some—like being a stewardess or a sales clerk in an exclusive boutique—had a cachet of glamour. "Female professions," such as librarian and social worker, were still in their infancy in India. Women in the sciences were in a better position, and the most popular choice then was medicine. Indian cultural inhibitions had worked to the advantage of women in this profession. Responding to the reluctance of women to visit male physicians, the British government had started a few medical schools exclusively for women.

Some of my friends and I decided to go on to graduate studies. Continuing with graduate studies while living at home presented no substantial financial burden, since the costs of tuition and books were nominal. The professor who taught German at the college had guided Kunda in applying for scholarships in Germany, and she was awarded one for a master's program in Heidelberg. She was enthusiastically preparing to go. Although she intended to come back to India after she finished her studies, she had given little thought as to what, if any, job they would prepare her for. Her parents had no objections, considering a stint abroad an educational experience in itself.

Ayesha, another friend, was preparing herself for a career as an academic. She was a strikingly beautiful girl, with a "fair" complexion, fine features, and long, black hair. She dressed in elegant saris and eschewed the latest fads, which made her seem somewhat older than she was. She thought many of our classmates were immature and juvenile. She came from an old-money Muslim family, and her father was a well-respected historian at Bombay University.

Ayesha and her family were trying to maintain a delicate balance between the Muslim cultural norms of her community and her desire to obtain an education. The women in Ayesha's family observed a modified form of *purdah*, or gender segregation, in private and public life, and she was one of the few going to university, and a coeducational one at that. Her family devised a way to enable her to attend college without breaking too openly with traditional norms. She came to college in a car driven by a middle-aged Muslim who had been with the family for several years. (A driver has a status slightly higher than domestic help, and most upper-middle-class homes have one.) The car and driver waited for her while she was at the college. He also served as a chaperone, watchdog, and errand-runner. Ayesha was free to mix with the other students at the college, but her interaction, particularly outside the college premises, was limited by the presence of the driver. Ayesha and I never visited each other's homes. Her brother, who was also a student, had no such luxury, and used public transportation or cabs, which were very cheap, like the rest of us.

Ayesha's family had supported her undergraduate studies, but when they were finished they wanted her to agree to an arranged marriage. She, however, wanted to follow in her father's footsteps and study in Britain. She would regale us daily with stories of the arguments in her family over her refusal even to contemplate an arranged marriage. Her parents' insistence made us indignant and we encouraged her to stand firm against them. "They cannot do anything to you," we confidently declared. Then she would describe the tantrums she threw at home to fend off her parents. Eventually, she made a truce with them. She would go to graduate school in Bombay and her parents would drop their insistence that she marry. Although I lost touch with her, whenever I returned to Bombay I got news about her. She eventually went on to study at Oxford and wrote a PhD dissertation on the history of Bombay University. She made her home in Britain and did not marry.

I felt little pressure at home. My older sister, Neena, had chosen to marry and it had been arranged for her. My younger sister, Rita, disliked going to college and got my father's approval for finding a job in an advertising agency as soon as she graduated. I wanted to study law, like my brother and cousin, and that too was acceptable to my father.

There was one hitch. Although he was amenable to my studying law, my father said that being a practising lawyer was "not for a girl like you." He knew that law was a male-dominated profession and that few legal firms would hire a woman. Law was generally a family practice in India, and one trained by becoming closely associated with a senior practising lawyer. Since neither my brother nor cousin practised law, having chosen to become businessmen, there was no one with whom I could train, and Pitaji did not care to see me work closely with male outsiders. Besides, the clients would almost always be males, and some would be criminals. He pointed out two Parsi lawyer-daughters of a family friend. Both were accomplished lawyers, he admitted, but they were in their late thirties, had not married, and continued to live at home. "Do you want to end up like that?" he would ask me, knowing that exorbitant rents made it impossible for a single woman to find an apartment of her own. One could live as a "paying guest" with another family, but that was not an enticing prospect. Nevertheless, I enrolled in law school the next year, imagining that I could wear down his resistance when the time came for me to find a job and to practise.

A few of my friends at college became engaged at this time. Most of these engagements had been arranged by their families, and the plans were for the weddings to take place soon after final examinations. Such matches evoked neither envy nor disappointment in us that a girl had agreed to her parents' wishes. We discussed, much as our families did at home, the "qualifications" of the boy: his education, job, class, caste, religion, lineage, and siblings. Now I am critical of the businesslike tone of much of the discussion, which treated marriage as just a contract, not the beginning of an intimate relationship.

Kunda's sister, Tai, had completed her medical degree in Britain and was returning to become a resident at a local hospital. With the help of family friends, her mother had lined up two or three men as prospective grooms for her. I looked forward to taking part in the wedding celebrations. But all the excitement surrounding her homecoming evaporated when she learned of her mother's plans for her marriage. Enraged, she refused outright to countenance any such arrangement.

At first the family thought that there must be a boyfriend in London to make Tai so resistant to her mother's plans. She insisted that was not the case, but this only made her mother redouble her efforts, and in a month she had worn down Tai's resolve and had her agreement to at least meet Dipak, the favoured candidate. Dipak and Tai's families were part of the same network of friends and associates. Like them, he was of Brahman caste, a Maharashtrian who had studied medicine in London and was now practising in Poona, a small town near Bombay. Both families thought it was a match made in heaven, and that Tai was foolish not to seriously consider marrying Dipak. At first the couple was very awkward, but they went out together a few times, and I began to see a gradual change in them. Slowly they became comfortable with each other; they seemed to like each other, and even to be in love. One day they announced, to the great happiness of Tai's parents, that they were engaged and would marry.

Now that I have assimilated some white-Canadian values, I wonder why Kunda and I, who were avid readers of romance novels, did not express, at least to each other, any disapproval of Tai's arranged marriage. The way the match had come about proved unimportant eventually, since Tai, once she had become engaged, seemed happy. Perhaps subconsciously Kunda and I had already absorbed the attitude of our families, who believed that if a couple's backgrounds were compatible, that was enough to allow love and happiness to grow over time. I am trying to understand the way we were from the perspective of the values and norms of present-day Canadian society, and they are quite different from the ones in our minds then.

Some students at the college fell in love and wanted to marry. When both of the young people came from similar social classes and religions, their parents usually accepted it without much ado. There were problems, however, if the couple were of different religions, particularly if they were Hindu and Muslim. These provided grist for our gossip mill.

Law school at the university seemed much like the college, and I lost my enthusiasm for that field of study, although I did finish the degree and graduate. My father then became more anxious for me to marry, but I wanted to travel to the West. I argued and argued, and finally wore him down. He agreed to let me go to Canada for a year to study.

5

History and Herstory

Many Indians, and particularly males, both of my generation and the present one, share the desire to travel and study in the West. Western education is considered by middle-class Indians as enhancing one's prospects for good employment, and the idea of studying in the West has a certain glamour that is attractive to young students. My friends and I, however, were largely ignorant of the educational systems in Canada or the United States, and had little knowledge of the relative strength of the academic programs in their universities. One negative effect of study in the West, as we saw it, was the tendency of some "foreign-educated" Indians to put on airs. We said they had a "superiority complex" and we joked about their "*sahib*," or white master, mentality. We resolved not to become like them if we had the opportunity to go to the West, but we gave no thought as to how much the coveted Western education might transform our perceptions of ourselves and of India.

When I arrived at the University of Toronto, my first priority was to decide on appropriate courses to take. The history department offered courses covering many different periods and countries; I had studied European and British history in college, but had no desire to continue in these areas. My new interests were imperialism, women's history, and Third World countries, areas in which the department offered very few courses. My first year in Canada had made me more conscious of myself, and now I wanted to find out, as an Indian woman, "who I was." There was a course on British imperialism at the university, and one on modern India. They seemed to be the most relevant to me, so I registered for those, along with an independent studies course on "Women" with Jill Conway. In a way, the limited number of alternatives made my choice easier; I did not have to try to guess which professors' styles of teaching I would be most comfortable with.

The course on British imperialism was taught by Archie Thornton, who was then the chairman of the department (the current practice is to refer to the head of a department as the chair). Professor Thornton held the class in his office, so I had to walk past two or three secretaries sitting in a larger room outside it. This arrangement created an aura of authority around the professor that made me somewhat nervous, but the secretaries were friendly and would smile encouragingly when they saw me come in.

The class consisted of only three students, and although it should have been a stimulating intellectual experience for me, I did not have the academic preparation or the skills to take advantage of it. Professor Thornton did most of the talking. He was an eloquent speaker who held our attention with accounts of British imperialism in Africa. Occasionally, perhaps to make me feel more included, he'd talk about India, but I was tongue-tied and intimidated, and could not enter into a discussion with him. The other two students often asked him questions or commented on some topic, but I cannot recall saying a single word the entire year. Professor Thornton did not push me to express myself. Perhaps he realized that I was feeling disconnected and alienated, and he let me be; I suppose he thought I would participate in discussions when I felt ready.

My university education in Bombay had emphasized learning facts. Courses were taught by lecturers in large classrooms. Of course, I had rarely attended them, having spent almost all my time at the coffee shops talking with my friends. Any conversational skills I may have learned at the coffee shops were not easily transferable to seminars at the University of Toronto. I was painfully aware of my rather limited knowledge of the subjects, and I was unsure whether I understood the material we were assigned to read. As the only foreign, non-white student in the group, I felt self-conscious. I certainly did not feel confident enough to form opinions about what we were studying, let alone express them in seminars.

I listened to Professor Thornton attentively, but not critically. If I did disagree with anything, I did not voice my reservations. In retrospect, I think that part of what kept me quiet was my desire to adopt a perspective similar to his and that of the other professors—the *right* perspective, I thought, from which to see the world (or at least history). At that time I believed that they had knowledge of the truth. Besides, there were only two other students in the course, and I did not meet other students or hear what their world views were.

Professor Thornton represented authority to me. Who was I to question his knowledge of imperialism, or of any other subject, for that matter? I did not have the confidence to challenge him. I came from a hierarchical culture where an individual is expected not only to respect elders and authority figures, but to defer to them. The combination of the professor's status as a white male, my cultural inhibitions and being in an alien, unfamiliar environment silenced me. I quietly listened to what I was being told.

Professor Thornton, for instance, did not ignore what African leaders had to say about imperialism, but he suggested that their writing was emotional, subjective, and tainted with nationalist ideology. Western writers, he added, were dispassionate and objective, and therefore gave more reliable accounts of African colonial history. This was a common view in academia at the time. The assumption that the values of university-educated, Western males represented a norm that was universally accepted was only beginning to be condemned. This perspective was just one of many possible, but it dominated almost all fields of study at that time, and was accepted by Third World societies as well.

My experiences in the 1970s of Western attitudes towards India were similar to those of the Indian novelist Mulk Raj Anand during his student days in London in the 1920s. He describes a conversation he had in a London tavern with English "man of letters" Bonamy Dobree, Gwenda Zeidmann, a student, and Nikhil Sen, a Bengali poet.

"Tell me," Gwenda said, "is Gandhi really for people or just pretending?"

"He is trying to abolish untouchability," I answered.

"But how can he?" began Bonamy Dobree. "A man who says he is a Hindu can't abolish caste...I understand this superior-inferior business is inbuilt into your religion."

"He knows people are orthodox," said Nikhil, "so he uses the idiom of tradition, but nibbles at the roots."

"I have read Kipling's story 'The Village Which Voted the Earth Was Flat,'" said Bonamy Dobree. "You people have a long way to go."

"I suggest, Sir, you take a chair in an Indian university for a few years," suggested Nikhil. "You may be able to go beyond Kipling's *Kim* to Forester's *Passage to India*."

"A good fantasy novel, *Kim*—what vivid prose Kipling writes—including those telling Hindu words!"

"Punjabi words," I whispered, as a minor counterattack against his ignorance...

"Nikhil, you can't change a Tory," Gwenda said affectionately. "Bonamy believes in the Pax Britannica."

"I admit," said Bonamy Dobree, moving towards a chair, "I do believe in the regenerative role of some of our people out there...After all, we did help to abolish the burning of widows...And you all speak such good English."[1]

During my first week at the University of Toronto I met Milton Israel, a genial American professor. He was over six feet tall, and since I am only five feet, I literally, as well as figuratively, looked up to him. Professor Israel was enthusiastic about working with me as a graduate student and immediately agreed to supervise my dissertation. At that time, he had only one other graduate student, a Canadian woman who was studying Hinduism with him. I thus found myself in the very strange situation of studying India in Canada with an American. With him I took an independent studies course on modern India, from the arrival of the British in the seventeenth century to their departure in the twentieth. This was not a regular course, but one designed for me specifically and taught on a one-to-one basis, so once again I missed out on being part of a group of students interested in a common area of study.

Professor Israel recommended that I focus on a few themes running through this long period of British rule, and one of my choices was the history of revenue collection in India. In the late-eighteenth and early-nineteenth centuries, the British divided up the land and set about determining who was responsible for paying taxes on it. This was part of an act called the Permanent Settlement, designed by Lord Cornwallis in 1793. We analyzed how a territory was acquired by the British and consolidated with neighbouring territories into a state for administrative convenience. No attempt had been made to group together people sharing a common language or religion, and we did not study the social history of revenue collection, which might have given me some knowledge about the people, their cultures, and their social institutions. Indeed, at the time, social history was not considered a serious subject for history, like politics or economics, and the only political or economic history that was considered worthy of study concerned the British presence in India. Now I wonder whether we were studying part of the history of India, or part of the British history of government and administration.

I was comfortable reading material written in the English language. My education had been entirely in English, and although I could read Hindi, I had limited facility with it. (In the intervening years, having had little opportunity to read anything in Hindi in Toronto, I have all but forgotten how to read and write it, but I can still speak it fluently.) The historians that I read in English, even the Indian historians, had developed their understandings of history and of themselves through colonial education in India or study in the West. These middle-class, English-educated Indian historians did not interpret history in any way other than that of their rulers. Western scholars defined the framework of their research and study, and Western liberal and bourgeois values and norms directed their research and writing. My birth and colour of skin did not by themselves entitle me to any insight into Indian history, and I hadn't studied much Indian history at home, but I did have a claim on being an Indian and an "insider" when I first came to Canada, (a greater claim than I have now, some thirty years later), and I should have resisted the Western biases more strongly and earlier on than I did.

The books that I read made of the history of the British in India what Guha calls "a pedestal on which the triumphs and glories of the colonizers and their instrument, the colonial state, could be displayed to the best advantage."[2] One of the most fascinating examples was James Mill's *History of India*, published in 1817. Mill's characterization of Indian history played a major role in guiding British governors of India, and his book was considered a classic, a must-read. But what was I to make of India or its history from reading Mill? As Amartya Sen points out, Mill "knew no Sanskrit, no Persian, no Arabic; he had practically no knowledge of any of the modern Indian languages; and so his reading of Indian material was most limited." In addition, he distrusted accounts written by "native" scholars; they "appeared to him to be liars." Indeed, says Sen, "Mill disputed and dismissed practically every claim ever made on behalf of Indian culture. He concluded that it was totally imitative and rude. The diagnosis fit well with Mill's general position in favour of bringing a rather barbaric nation under the benign and reformist administration of the British Empire."[3]

An opportunity to learn about the perspective of Indian nationalists did present itself, but I made little use of it. I was Professor Israel's only graduate student in modern India, and he gave me writing assignments rather than having one-to-one discussions. One assignment was to write an annotated bibliography on the economic policies of the British in India during the late-nineteenth and early-twentieth centuries. British and American writers said that the economic policies of the British government in India had helped construct an elaborate railroad system throughout India, promoting greater trade and commerce between India and the rest of the world. However, I came across books written by Indian nationalists like Dadabhai Naoroji and Romesh Chandra Dutt that condemned the "drain of wealth" from India to Britain from the eighteenth to the twentieth century. Since I was searching for the "truth," and presumed that the books had it, I was very confused when I found that the books disagreed with each other.

Recall that most of my previous training in history had come from textbooks that compressed whole debates on historical issues into a paragraph or two. In the large classes at Bombay University, controversies were resolved by the authoritative voice of an instructor. When I approached Professor Israel for guidance, he merely said, "You must make up your own mind."

Since Naoroji and Dutt's interpretations of India's history had been adopted by Indian nationalists, I first jumped to the conclusion that they were simply biased. However, both sides were very persuasive. I blamed my difficulty in deciding between the Western and nationalist accounts partly on my own bias in favour of the Westerners—an outgrowth of my colonial education—being challenged by my growing sympathy for the nationalists, but mostly on what I supposed was an irremediable inability to sift through material and come to conclusions.

I did not even take offence at Westerners' claims that India was the "white man's burden," at their portrayals of Indian society as standing in need of the "civilizing influence" of the British, or even at their frequent use of terms like "heathens" to describe Indians. They didn't mean that Indians were irreligious, but that they were non-Christian—and uncivilized and unenlightened. I did not challenge their language, or ask what they counted as civilization or enlightenment. I remained inarticulate and inert.

Historians were by no means the only people who portrayed India as requiring British help to overcome its backwardness. Missionaries provided gruesome accounts of cruel and inhumane treatment of untouchables by Hindu caste society. They did not say anything about the British treatment of their Indian subjects. Shashi Tharoor has recently given an amazing example of British barbarity in *India: From Midnight to the Millennium*, wherein he recounts that on two occasions the British ordered the thumbs of Indian weavers chopped off so their textiles would not compete with those being manufactured in Lancashire.

People like me, educated in mission schools, whether in India, Africa, or even northern Canada, were often alienated from their own culture. Sometimes the affront they felt at the images and messages in Western representations, along with the loss of dignity and self-esteem they experienced, radicalized them. Sometimes it motivated them to try to institute change and reform in their own society—in India, for instance, in marriage for women, in the caste system, and particularly in the position of the untouchables. Sometimes they tried to reconstruct and redefine their past in terms that contradicted the myths propagated by the colonizers, to define and affirm their own identities, or at least to mark out their differences from the colonizers.

Some Indian students in Toronto in the 1970s reacted to the shame and pain inflicted upon them through the image of "backward" India by promoting the contrasting image of spiritual India. They portrayed India as the home of an ancient civilization which had much to teach the world. Some, indeed, argued for the superiority of Indian culture. I responded neither by condemning the British nor by praising India. Unlike a number of people in the post-colonial period following the independence of many Asian and African countries, I did not become a political activist.

One explanation for my passive response to the denigration of India in the books I was reading was my limited understanding and knowledge of the country. Since I had been alienated from my culture by my schooling, I had no strong attachment to India, and I could put some emotional distance between its history and myself. While reading about the past, I located myself only in the present. My sense of cultural identity did not include India as a whole, but just my family and regional community. And I had no reason to think that Professors Israel and Thornton, or the other professors in the history department, judged me in the terms that were being used to describe India. I had not yet encountered much prejudice against me on account of my race, and I was quite unaware of the significance that others might attach to my national identity.

When I applied for admission to the department, I also submitted, as my professor friend in Waterloo had suggested, a brief proposal to write a dissertation on women in India. Although I had not studied women in my courses, and Professors Israel and Thornton had little academic knowledge of the subject, they were enthusiastic about the idea; they thought it was particularly appropriate for a woman in the 70s, when my research would give me an entry to the new and emerging field of women's history. I did not, until many years later, realize how difficult the terrain I had ventured into was.

Israel and Thornton recommended that I take an independent studies course with Jill Conway. Professor Conway was one of the leading feminists at the University of Toronto in the early 1970s, and later went on to become the president of Smith College. A specialist in American history, she had written her dissertation on American social reformers such as Jane Addams. My professors thought that Conway's work on social reformers in America would provide a good guide for my work on women in India, and she accepted me for an independent studies course with her. However, the opportunity to study with a leading feminist turned out to be of little benefit to me. Professor Conway was a very busy activist at the university, and when she was promoted to become its vice-president, she had little time to spend with students like me.

In the early 1970s there were very few books on women in India (or in any other country), and none written from a feminist perspective. I know now that the absence of women revealed systemic biases of male historians. They focused on big, datable events in the lives of rich and powerful men—wars, changes in government, and so on—and neglected social history. Since women in India, as elsewhere, had been prevented from participating in politics, business, or society outside the family, they were missing from the history books.

I found less than a handful of autobiographies or biographies of Indian women in the university libraries. These recorded the struggles of women who had been "rescued" by missionaries from the oppressive customs of Indian society. There were some discussions of women in books on social reform and the independence movement, but these were all written by men.

I found only scattered references to women in most of the standard history books on India. Most times, there were at best one or two casual sentences and no discussion. Accounts of the impact of British rule in

India were usually just silent on its effect on women. Take, for instance, the Permanent Settlement. This was supposed to set the amount of tax due to the government on a particular piece of land forever—to "fix it in perpetuity." The responsibility for collecting this tax was given to special revenue collectors, and if they failed to obtain it from the peasants because of drought, famine or any other reason, the land was sold. In practice, this meant that when peasants defaulted, they lost their hereditary right to work on the land. Since in such circumstances the collectors themselves often bought the land, the effect of the law was to displace peasants and create a new class of landowners. Access to a small piece of land, which could help a peasant woman provide nutrition for her children by growing a few beans and chilies, was often the difference between life and death at a time when many of them lived on the verge of starvation. However, I did not see (and still have not seen) any history that discussed how these changes in land ownership, the primary source of subsistence in the agricultural economy, affected women.

The absence of women from the histories frustrated me. How could I write a dissertation on women if none of the authors I read discussed them? Sometimes I would console myself with the thought that perhaps their absence was a blessing: I would not have to read an enormous number of books or analyze their discussions. I could merely look in the index of a book, see whether women were discussed at all, and if so, just read those pages where they were mentioned.

Missionaries had written about women in India, but their writings, full of ethnocentric interpretations of customs and traditions of Indian families, were written in language that was often offensive. There were two or three autobiographical accounts of Hindu women who had converted to Christianity and travelled to the West under the sponsorship of missionary societies. My reaction to these accounts was utterly unlike my detached reaction to the political histories. Reading the missionary accounts of women's lives horrified me. They said that Indian culture—specifically, Hindu culture—subjugated women and stunted their mental and physical development; they received little or no education and were forced into early marriages. They portrayed the worst cases as the norm, gave exaggerated accounts, and sensationalized some of their problems.

The missionaries' descriptive and narrative accounts of women's oppression portrayed them as victims of their culture or gender (there was less discussion then of class or race.) Reading these accounts made me reflect on the lives of women in my family, and the maid who worked in my aunt's house. I hadn't thought of Bahenji or Mano-ki-ma's difficult lives—one as a socially constrained widow and the other as an abused and poverty-stricken spouse—as two among many others. But as I did more research, I realized that what I had thought of as personal, individual, and isolated tragedies were repeated in other women's lives.

I did not believe that my memories, embedded as they were in Hindu society and the norms of my community, would be of any interest to other students. In the university context, I thought of myself as an "exotic other" who came from a culture regarded as "traditional." Why give people added material that would only reinforce their perceptions of Hindu society? Consequently, I kept my stories to myself, ashamed of the hardships imposed by Hindu society on its women.

After I completed some research, I obtained a fellowship from the Department of International Studies and History to travel to New Delhi to collect primary material—which meant reading the papers and diaries of politicians and social reformers. It was my first trip back since coming to Canada, and I spent about a year in Delhi and Bombay. I worked at the All India National Archives, where progress was slow. I had to submit a request for material hours ahead of time, and yet getting to read it still depended on chance and luck. Delhi had frequent, unscheduled power cuts, so at any time the lights and fans could go off, forcing everyone to cool their heels outside the building, often for an hour or two.

I did most of my work at the Nehru Library, part of a museum complex that had been the official residence of Jawaharlal Nehru while he was prime minister. The library had bright, airy rooms inside and gardens with tables and benches outside. Once the librarians there got to know me, they allowed me free access to the private papers of many politicians in the nationalist struggle, and let me take the material out to the garden when the power failed. There were no photocopy machines at the libraries, so making notes was a long, laborious process. Afraid I would never make much headway in my research, I persuaded a student who was short of money to help me with my note-taking.

The material that I collected on women in India was loaded with race, class, and gender biases. I should have asked a basic question of it: Who was saying what, and why? This seems like common sense now, but it was not so obvious to an intellectually insecure and impressionable student like myself. If I had asked "who," I might have realized at least that "what"

was not a pure, factual account of events or situations that would give me
the knowledge of the truth. I still believed that, in the case of each of the
authors, "who" was a disembodied intellect writing an objective account
for the sake of researchers like me who came to get it. I didn't fully see that
"why" they wrote what they did had much to do with their values, norms,
emotions, and feelings. Furthermore, my idea of analyzing "what" was to
extract it and put it into my dissertation. I thought that the only problem
I faced was the small number of sources.

Of course, I saw that Westerners and Indians gave vastly different
accounts of the lives of women in India. I figured that some were right and
others wrong, though I saw no way of deciding which. On one side were
the colonial administrators, missionaries, Orientalists, Indologists and journalists, among many others. Although they didn't agree about everything,
they all tended to share a belief in the superiority of the "civilization" of
Western nations. They discussed at great length what they referred to as
the "problems" of women in Indian society, such as their lack of education,
their restricted lives in purdah, the custom of early marriage, and the sanc-
tion against widows remarrying. Some Westerners condemned in its
entirety the "Indian" culture of which such practices were an inherent part,
and implied that the people should all adopt Western norms and practices.
On the other side were Indian social reformers, academics, and politicians.
They represented various ideologies (some were scholars of Indian religion
and philosophy; others were Western-trained lawyers), but they all tended
to be defensive about India and the norms and practices of Hindu culture.
It was mostly upper-caste Hindus who argued that a misinterpretation of
their scriptures had led to practices injurious to women, such as the custom
of early marriage. Other Indians simply stood their ground and defended
the norms and customs as they were.

I was depressed by the descriptions of the lives of Indian women in
much of the literature. When Professor Thornton and I discussed one of
my first drafts, he nodded sagely and said that I obviously felt deeply about
the subject. I took that to mean that I was allowing my feelings about the
subject to taint my "objectivity." I supposed that strong emotional reactions should be suppressed, that history should not reflect the race, class,
gender, or nationality of the historian. Given the prevailing values in academia at that time, I realized that acknowledging my own biases would
have been stupid and self-destructive, anyway. So I decided to hide my
biases by adopting an aura of abstract intellectualism.

Putting more distance between the subject of my study and myself had its costs. Since I tried to stand aloof from it, I could not use insights gained from living in India to critique the literature, though the sometimes gory descriptions of Indian women's lives in the writings of missionaries and Western males seemed to me to be distorted and inaccurate. This was not the way things were in "real life." Many of the writings generalized the norms of Hindus over the entire country, treated extreme examples as typical, and ignored the social context that helped explain women's roles. But I was even reluctant to point out, for example, that the horrors the writers related about Indian women usually applied only to upper-caste, upper-class Hindu women, not Muslim or untouchable women. They did not discuss differences among women that stemmed from caste, class, religion, and region.

In the end I wrote about the participation of women in the nationalist movement, which aimed at ending colonial rule and establishing an independent nation. I focused particularly on women's involvement in Gandhian politics and the Indian National Congress. Gandhi, a prolific writer, had regularly written articles and letters in nationalist newspapers about the need to improve the situation of women in families, communities, and society. His support of women had been critical in integrating them into nationalist politics, which included social reform. He stated that his goal was to "regenerate" and "rejuvenate" Indian society, by which he meant abolishing untouchability, alleviating the hardships of the rural poor, and improving the conditions of women's lives. He gathered a coterie of women followers drawn from a variety of backgrounds (including some British women) who lived in his ashrams and in whose well-being he took a personal interest. He even called himself their "mother" in letters to them and offered advice on diet, health, education, family relations, and a myriad of other issues. To raise the status of "women's work," he did chores such as cutting and peeling vegetables and feeding the livestock at the ashram. To advance the cause of untouchables, he cleaned toilets and ate and visited with untouchable people. Some of his women followers took on leadership roles in politics and social reform.

The underlying values of Gandhi's philosophy of non-violent civil disobedience, or *satyagraha*, included love and self-sacrifice. These attracted large numbers of women to join the nationalist movement. A few upperclass women's organizations, originally non-political, began to focus on gaining the vote for women and became integrated in nationalist politics.

At first, I was happy to find so many positive examples of women politicians in India. On further analysis, however, I found that this was not as radical as it seemed, for all of the women leaders came from prominent families—like Vijaya Laxmi Pandit, who was the sister of Jawaharlal Nehru—or they required the support of male politicians such as Gandhi. This was the case with Sarojini Naidu, who became president of the Indian National Congress. Although male politicians were staunch supporters of women's participation in politics, none advocated a revision of gender roles or questioned or challenged patriarchy.

I wrote my dissertation in Toronto. Now, as I sit poised over the keyboard of my computer, I remember with amusement my writing background at that point. I had written less than a handful of essays by the time I began to write the dissertation. I had never written any essays as an undergraduate or while attending law school in Bombay. The master's degree that I completed at the University of Waterloo required me to take three courses, but not to write a thesis. What's more, I did not write any essays in the courses there, but only final examinations. (I remember this particularly because I applied to some universities with PhD programs. One asked me for a sample essay, but I had none to send.) Professor Thornton did not ask his graduate students to write any essays either, choosing instead to give us a take-home examination. Jill Conway's course had required two essays, but Milton Israel's assignments, although followed by a written examination, had been annotated bibliographies. My writing skills, to say the least, were very limited.

I received little guidance from my male professors on how to analyze the data I had collected for my dissertation. Perhaps Professor Conway could have provided some insight, but the only connection between her work and mine was that we were both studying women's history. At that time, women were still thought of in a generic way. No one felt much need to take into account the effects of class or race on the experiences of gender in different cultures. We should have been asking how the experiences of one group of women in a specific cultural and historical context could help in studying other groups. We were still studying women through the prism of male experience.

When I gave the first draft of a chapter to Professor Israel, he took his time reading it and then returned it with no substantive comments, no suggestions for additional resources I should consult, and nothing on the strength or weakness of the argument I was trying to develop. However, he did note that his own dissertation had needed seven drafts; I took that as a polite hint that my writing needed a great deal of improvement. I did not get discouraged, and kept writing and rewriting over the next year and a half. But the routine did not change: I would hand in a chapter to Israel and wait months for him to read it. He would give it back with a maybe a comment or two, but mostly he left me to my own devices.

I wrote and rewrote the chapters and learned through trial and error. Eventually, Professor Israel pronounced that the dissertation was ready and could be sent to the internal and external examiners. One examiner, a Hindu professor, offered suggestions for improving the chapter on the "problems" of Hindu women. Other than that, there were few changes, and the dissertation was accepted. Three years later it was published in India as *Elite Women in Indian Politics*. In spite of its success, I think I learned much less from this experience about how to write history or conduct research on women's lives than from my later work in teaching social science courses and writing about the experiences of immigrant women in Canada.

I did acquire one practical skill in writing the dissertation; I bought myself a typewriter and learned to type as I went along. I wrote the first drafts in longhand, then typed the successive drafts, slowly and painfully. Since I had to do several drafts of each chapter, I became adept at "cutting and pasting." Eventually, each page would be laminated with handwritten and typed revisions on slips of paper that I had pasted over earlier versions. When a page got too messy to read, I would retype it. This process helped me improve my typing speed. Sometimes when friends asked me about my job prospects after graduate school, I would reply, "After I finish writing this dissertation, I will certainly be able to find a job as a typist."

My graduate studies had made me reflect on my position as a non-white woman in the academic world. My family had protected me in India, where I had led a very circumscribed life. Consequently, I was somewhat innocent and naïve compared to many other students from Asia, Africa, and the Caribbean. I worked at the university as a teaching assistant in a course on the Third World with a professor whose specialty was Latin America. The course attracted a few students from Third World countries. One day a black student approached me and said, "Vijay, how can we get rid of this white professor?" I was absolutely stunned to hear this blunt and straightforward denunciation of him. She argued that she did not want to learn about the Third World from a white professor but from somebody from the Third World, like me. "Me?" I responded in total disbelief. What also shocked me was her labelling the instructor by his race. Although it was usual for students to identify one of their professors as "my Indian professor," it was not until the 1980s that many referred to white people by their race. I mentioned this student to the instructor, but it did not seem to make him uncomfortable. He just laughed and said that she was already known in her program as a bright but militant student.

Reflecting on this incident now, I see that this student was light-years ahead of me. She had shown the courage to challenge the right of white males to speak on behalf of Third World populations. She had "come to voice" and was no longer silent. But the incident also raises some complex questions that remain unresolved even at the present time. On the one hand is the question of the right of academics to "appropriate" the experience of others in their research, which promotes their careers. That's exploitative. On the other hand is the danger of thinking that only those from a particular group—"insiders"—can speak for them, that only women can speak for women, or only men for men. But these questions about identity and perspective were not asked then, when it was still rare to hear even challenges to the norms of "objectivity" and "neutrality" that dominated university environments.

Over the five years that I spent as a graduate student at the university, I did slowly become more self-confident in articulating disagreements with some professors. I remember a discussion I had with two political science professors whose specialty was Latin America. I was a teaching assistant for one of them, and had been invited to her house for a course meeting. She mentioned an American anthropologist who had advised an impoverished Mexican woman with six children to take the birth control pill. She was critical of the woman for resisting the suggestion, blaming the strong pull of culture and its negative impact on women's lives. I gathered up the courage to side with the Mexican woman and asserted that the anthropologist had no business giving the woman such personal advice. "But, Vijay," she said, "don't you see it is for the woman's good? She already has six children. She is very poor." I held to my position and refused to budge. Once I got home, I thought I had been imprudent to risk offending my professor, but later I heard from others that she appreciated my intervention and had reconsidered her stance. That incident made me feel better about myself.

One of the first times I had a conscious realization of the effects of different perspectives was when I was reading a PhD dissertation written by a white student named Ruth Brouwer. It was a history of some Canadian women doctors who had lived and worked in India amongst the poor. I was happy to read about a Canadian-Indian connection, but I found that I disagreed with Brouwer's assessment of the doctors' accomplishments in India.

Women first graduated from medical school in Canada only in the late-nineteenth century, she wrote. Gender biases in Canadian hospitals made it difficult for them to obtain internships, and without them they could not practise medicine in Canada. Of these six doctors, two went to India as members of the Presbyterian Mission Society. There, they had professional and personal opportunities that were denied to them by Canadian society. In the course of their work they exercised power over males and females in some sections of Indian society. They dispensed medicine and provided some teaching for the poor, many of them untouchables. As missionaries and white women, they had prestige in colonial Indian society, and gained entry into the homes of local princes. They successfully lobbied the princes for land and funds for their work.

When the women came back to Canada on furloughs, they were sought out as speakers who could report on "exotic" India. The goal was to raise funds for their work amongst the "heathens" in India, so they emphasized the poverty there and the lack of medical services and education. I could understand why they talked about poverty, but it seems to me that they also reinforced the most negative stereotypes.

My disagreement with Brouwer, however, was over another issue. She had concluded that the missionary women were role models for Indian women. That was so much at a variance with my personal experience and knowledge of Indian society that I had no hesitancy in pointing out what I thought was a mistake. I asked her how women from a different culture and country, who dressed, looked, and behaved completely differently, could be role models for Hindu women. Upper-caste Hindus respect missionaries for their work amongst the poor, but a widespread assumption among them was that most Indian Christians were poor people from the untouchable caste who had converted to Christianity to gain material advantages (food, education, and jobs) offered by the missionaries. This was a rare moment of insight for me, but it left me feeling disgruntled rather than elated. Why, I thought, don't we have any accounts by the poor and untouchable of *their* perceptions and experiences of these Canadian women missionaries? The previously silent women from Canada may have come to voice in India, but the poor and untouchable Indians remained silent.

I also gained valuable insight into my "racial" identity and its significance in informing my perspective through attending some feminist events. One of the first times I met with Professor Conway, she invited me to participate in a march she was organizing in support of female faculty. I dutifully went to the rally and tagged along behind a small but very excited group of women who met at Sydney Smith Hall, where the history department was located, and then made their way through some other buildings on campus. They seemed to be absorbed in their own discussions and oblivious of me. Watching them chat and laugh in small groups while I stood outside these circles of friends, peering in, made me feel lonely. I did not have the courage to make small talk with anyone, and as the march went on, I became more and more depressed, alienated and homesick. Eventually, I drifted quietly back to the residence.

A much bigger feminist event occurred on campus shortly after this. Germaine Greer had recently published *The Female Eunuch,* and she came to give a talk in the university's large Convocation Hall. The publication of this book had caused quite a stir in North America; caught up in the enthusiasm, I determined to go and hear her. As I walked down St. George Street to the hall, I saw many women walking in the same direction. I looked around, hoping to locate a friend or see a South Asian face, but there were no other non-white women in the crowd, and again I felt alone. I got to the hall several minutes before the appointed time for the talk, but the room was already completely filled and there was barely standing room. I cannot recall what Greer talked about, but I do remember the palpable sense of excitement that filled the room that day.

I also remember noticing that many women in the audience, like Greer, were not wearing bras. I was surprised to see middle-class Western women without bras, but the sight of braless women is commonplace in India, so I did not interpret it as a particularly revolutionary or brave act. In India, poor rural women do not wear bras. Women in cities who work at a variety of menial jobs, such as providing unskilled labour on construction sites, do not wear bras. Beggar women do not wear bras; maids do not wear bras; old middle-class women do not wear bras. Middle-class North-American women who discarded their bras were taking part in a highly charged rejection of conventional and restrictive norms within their own class and culture, symbolically affirming their commitment to sexual liberation. But what was a daring and unconventional act in their culture didn't have that significance elsewhere. Going without a bra would have made me feel like a poor peasant woman, and I was too much of a "bourgeoise" to want that.

Something that seems mundane and trivial in retrospect but which was avidly debated at the time was the practice of men holding doors open for women. All kinds of sinister implications were attributed to this courtesy. Women such as my friends Alison and Barbara asked whether it implied that a woman was less able than a man to open a door. Did it symbolize her dependence on a man? The questions that loomed in my mind were somewhat different. When a man held open a door for me, I wondered whether it was an act of courtesy towards me as a woman, or if he was just being polite to an obvious foreigner. Would a man interpret my rejection of his "gallantry" as the uncultured behaviour of an Indian woman who did not know better? Or would he recognize a militant feminist demurely dressed in a sari?

Alison took me with her to some consciousness-raising sessions, but I felt out of place, and the discussions dumbfounded me. One of the dominant themes of many of these discussions was sexual liberation, and women at the meetings were often debating, avidly, sexual norms in male-female relationships. Women, they asserted, had a right to express and enjoy their sexuality. Coming from a culture that seldom discusses sexuality openly and is extremely prudish about male and female sexuality, the talk in this group scandalized me and left me speechless. Sometimes during the discussions my friends would glance at me furtively and smile mischievously. My face obviously revealed my shock at the talk.

Although at most times I tended, like other young people, to be self-centred and oblivious to the pain of other people, I knew about sexual exploitation of poor women, mainly through stories I heard from the maids who worked for our family. One magazine in India had exposed the plight of poor prostitutes in Bombay who conducted their business—literally—in cages similar to those for animals. (The neighbourhood where they work is known as The Cages.) So while the talk about having the right to enjoy one's sexuality was shocking, it revealed more about the self-centredness of privileged women. It made me feel awkward and an outsider.

However, we were all young and enthusiastic, caught up in the new ideas and intent on defying the traditional norms of our own cultures. We did not have the vision to perceive gender roles from the perspective of poor women, disadvantaged women or women in the Third World. I did not raise questions about the relevance of the discussions to the lives of poor women or immigrant women like myself. That had to wait for a future date.

My graduate studies in Toronto succeeded in making me aware of who I was and how I differed from others. Although I believed that I was free to define myself in the new social context of Canadian universities, my freedom proved to be more of an illusion than a reality. Theoretically, it opened up a range of choices and possibilities, but my everyday experiences (as opposed to conscious, thought-out decisions) steered me in specific directions. Besides, in my academic and personal interactions there were tensions between who I wanted to be and who the white population of professors and students around me thought I was or ought to be. Negotiating those tensions played a critical role in molding my intellectual and emotional being and in defining who I am today.

6

In Search of a Community

After three years of living in Canada, I stopped feeling like a bumbling fool. I had slowly learned to act appropriately...in an acceptable, "Canadian" way. I liked being on my own and feeling free. I could sleep in all day and miss my classes, or go to the library and do some research. Whatever choice I made, I did not have to explain myself to anyone or seek their approval. But though I revelled in my free and easy life and the seemingly limitless choices I had, at times I missed not having a family and a community to which I belonged. I had made friends with some Canadians at the university residence; I watched television with them, played pool and table tennis in the common room, or attended parties in the building. But I had also developed a separate network of friends among people from India and Pakistan, mostly women, some of whom lived at the residence. With them I sometimes cooked meals, went to see Indian movies, and discussed contemporary Indian politics.

Loneliness and nostalgia often troubled me. My room at the residence was nearly bare: a bed with a gray bedspread and a desk with an ugly metal lamp. I had few books and no pictures. I had a radio, but although I played it most of the time, it did little to dissipate my loneliness. The music, whether classical or "popular," was unfamiliar and I could not relate to it. Often, while sitting quietly in my room and reading, I would long for the familiar sounds of the streets of Bombay, which invariably make their way into most apartments. Here, there was no loud singing of beggar women

---

Notes to chapter 6 are on p. 282.

and children hoping to attract a handout of a few coins, no blaring honks from car horns, no noisy disputes, no hawking of goods from carts or passersby and no Hindi music blasting from the neighbour's radio. The still and quiet of my room in Toronto made me feel deserted, isolated, and lonely. Sometimes, afraid of another bout of nostalgic crying, I would rush outside and look for company to distract me and keep me from feeling sorry for myself. In times like these, it was comforting to speak to an Indian or Pakistani friend.

There were very few single Indian women at the university, and the ones I became friendly with were all from very different regional, linguistic, and socio-economic backgrounds. Since we could not be choosy, however, we all worked hard to overcome the differences in our backgrounds—and temperaments. We were all foreign students, feeling isolated and lost in the alien Canadian university environment. We all wanted a connection with our past and needed companionship and support in Toronto. We tried hard to be amicable and found common interests that sustained our friendships.

One day in the laundry room of the residence, I saw a woman dressed in a sari. Although her appearance indicated a background different from mine, I unhesitatingly went up to her and introduced myself. We found lots to talk about, and after a while we went up to her room and continued our conversation there. This experience of immediate familiarity and bonding occurred because of our common predicaments and shared sentiments about India and Canada. We were both Indian foreign students, trying to cope in our separate and different ways with Canadian norms. We were also both nostalgic and homesick for the friends, family and society we had left behind. In every other way, though, we could not have been more unalike.

The daughter of a Protestant minister, Nadira was studying for a PhD in education and supporting herself on a fellowship. She always wore brightly coloured saris and used lots of vivid makeup, which made her look flamboyant and theatrical. She had brought her sitar along with her from India and liked to entertain us by playing and singing classical Indian songs. At times, with her dramatic clothing and demeanour, she seemed more like an aspiring film star than an educator. She was strongly committed to retaining her Indianness in dress, appearance, and behaviour, and resisted any change that was not absolutely necessary. She was given to comparing Indian values and norms favourably to those of "Canadians" and, quite oblivious to my confused state of mind, advised me not to let my present surroundings influence my behaviour or change me. I found her commitment to rigid traditional Indian values and culture somewhat frustrating, and did not really support her attitudes towards other Canadians. I did not want to be like her, yet I would often find myself phoning her or seeking her out in her room for a chat.

I met two other Indian women at the university, and we would frequently see each other as a group. Sveta was from Bengal and had been raised in a middle-class, Hindu family. She had leucoderma, a problem of pigmentation that leaves the skin discoloured, and was very self-conscious about her appearance. Sveta, too, always dressed in saris, but hers, unlike Nadira's, were in subdued colours, and she never used any makeup. She had shoulder-length hair, but sometimes tied it up in a ponytail. In India, Bengalis are caricatured as arrogant highbrows, but Sveta was not much interested in art, literature, or classical music. Her manner was unaffectedly straightforward and warm, and she was generous and kind.

Sveta had impressed an Indian professor from Toronto while he was in Calcutta doing field work, and he had arranged to get her a job as a research officer in statistics at the Ontario Institute for Studies in Education. "OISE," now part of the University of Toronto, was just down the street from the residence. Although she lived in a walk-up apartment in a house nearby, Sveta felt isolated. She had been in Canada the longest amongst us and had sometimes visited with the families of the Indian professors who worked at her department. Being single, however, she felt out of place at their social gatherings, dominated as they were by couples and their children. Sveta was comfortable working with white Canadians, but she had not become friendly enough with any of them to meet them socially outside work; she was consequently lonely, and particularly on weekends. When I happened to see her one day at the cafeteria of the Institute, I did not wait to be formally introduced, but went up to her directly and began a conversation. I discovered that she was as eager to get to know me as I was to get to know her.

Another Indian woman, Asha, had been with me at the University of Waterloo. Although she too came from Bombay, her background was different from mine linguistically and socially. She had obtained a master's degree in French from Waterloo, but was supporting herself by selling encyclopedias door to door in small towns outside Toronto. She kept trying, unsuccessfully, to find a full-time job. We hung out together, despite having little in common.

Getting together with other women from India served emotional and psychological needs. When we met with each other or talked on the phone, we could take for granted some well-established reference points, which made it easy to communicate our thoughts and feelings and establish a rapport. Sometimes, when talking with Canadians, we felt self-conscious about our responses to things. We worried about being incomprehensible or, worse, being thought of as weird. Amongst ourselves we could let down our guards and relax. Generally we spoke in English, because that was the only common language between us, but our conversation was peppered with Hindi words and colloquialisms. Using a mixture of Hindi and English helped convey our thoughts more precisely and created a sense of familiarity and intimacy between us.

A common diversion for us was to cook an Indian meal and eat it together. I say "Indian," because we weren't particular about regional variations in cooking and were satisfied just as long as the food was spicy and vaguely reminiscent of "home" cooking. Sometimes Nadira would play the sitar for us after the meal. Although the rest of us did not really have much interest in or knowledge of Indian classical music, we didn't want to upset her, because it was she who most often did the cooking for us. I considered this entertainment the price to pay for a nice Indian meal. Both Nadira and Sveta preferred to retain their cultural norms; they felt no drive to know other Canadians or to learn their ways. Asha and I, on the other hand, were interested in learning about some Canadian practices, but were ambivalent about others, such as dating.

In some ways change was a necessary condition of survival. Although Hindu and Muslim cultural norms restrict social interaction between young, unmarried men and women, as foreign students in Toronto we were drawn by our social isolation to become friendly with some of the Indian and Pakistani male students who also lived at the residence or were studying at the university. Nevertheless, friendship with men from our own cultural backgrounds was fraught with tension, as we were unsure which rules of conduct—Western or Indian—applied to us in Canada. Sveta said she couldn't date the Indian and Pakistani men at the residence or on campus because she would lose their respect. "What will they think if I go out for dinner with them?" was her common refrain. Nadira was convinced that even though the men we were meeting espoused free social mingling of the sexes, in their hearts they were traditional and would look down upon us as not being "nice" women if we went out with them on a date. Mostly we were just naïve, but protective of each other. Once when I was planning to meet Tom—a Canadian and my future husband, as it turned out—Nadira cautioned me not to accept a cigarette from him. She said she had been told that accepting a cigarette was a code for assenting to sex!

I thought dating a man from my own culture would mean retreating into corners of the cultural framework I had come to Canada to escape. Besides, stories about who was dating whom circulated fast within the small community of single South Asians on campus, and I did not want anyone to know too much about me. This left me free to do as I wanted without fearing comments from others (although it also required some circumspection in making and dropping friends). In contrast, dating a Canadian gave me greater opportunity to present myself anyway I chose. I could express my ideas without fear that they'd be criticized as "too Canadian." Faced with the choice between the norms of dating prevalent among students on campus and the Indian cultural compunctions and inhibitions about it, I took the easy way out and adopted a double standard. I was casual about going out with white Canadian men, but adopted a more aloof attitude with the men from my own background. This caused some hard feelings and resentment.

Over the course of my many evenings in the common room of the residence, I got to know several of the white students who also spent time there. I became particularly friendly with Tom Agnew, who was always hanging around there in the evening and was teaching me to play pool and table tennis. Tom had just completed a master's degree in mathematics and physics, and had a job with Environment Canada. Although he was no longer a graduate student, he was reluctant to give up the camaraderie among the students at the residence and so continued to live there. Academically, our interests were completely different. I was studying history and feminism, and Tom was researching the physics of cloud formation. We also had completely different family and social backgrounds.

My Indian friends and I were keenly interested in keeping up to date on current happenings in India, but in the first few years that I was in Toronto, I only recall media coverage of very significant events, such as India's testing of nuclear devices. Today, news items and articles about India are regularly published in *The Globe and Mail*, and its Asia correspondent spends some time there. This change may reflect the newspaper's awareness of the growing numbers of immigrants from the region. At that time, however, news about India mostly came from American or British newspapers and magazines. Sometimes overseas editions of major Indian newspapers and magazines were available at the university libraries, but they were often very out of date.

Frequently three or four Indian and Pakistani male students joined us for chit-chat. I am surprised at how little our differences, especially in religion, mattered to us at that time. We did not know much about each other's countries, but their linked history, geographical location, and status as poor and "underdeveloped" nations created many points of commonality and solidarity. We felt a common need to defend India or Pakistan to our Canadian friends, even though our politics and perspectives differed in details. In India, I had felt no strong sense of nationality, but in Canada I had become conscious of it. To the Canadian professors and students on campus, I was not just "Vijay" but "Vijay, the Indian woman."

My friends and I were sensitive to descriptions of India and Pakistan as poor countries, and in our talk we highlighted signs of "development," such as emerging industries and technology, and the prosperity of the upper classes. We attributed a somewhat exaggerated strategic importance to India and Pakistan in the regional politics of Asia. Although none of us had very strong feelings about British and American imperialism, words like "underdeveloped," "traditional" and "backward," when used by Canadian students and professors as defining epithets for South Asia, evoked an emotional response from us.

There were differences between us as Indians and Pakistanis. The Pakistani students felt that their country was strategically more significant to American foreign policy. Since I was studying India, I knew that they were right, yet I did not support their arguments. Instead, I pushed the international prestige and stature of Indian nationalist leaders like Jawaharlal Nehru and Mahatma Gandhi, much to the annoyance of the Pakistani men. If the discussion got too contentious, we calmed things down by comparing the subcontinent with Third World countries in Africa. Then we could all congratulate ourselves on the strides our countries had made in becoming "developed."

For most of the 1970s (and again in the early 1980s), Indira Gandhi was the prime minister of India. Her strong leadership initially won international respect, but soon that turned to condemnation and criticism for her anti-democratic and authoritarian policies. Her leadership, however, was a source of pride to us as Indian women. She was also a handy device by which to blunt the aspersions cast on us as women from a "backward" and "traditional culture." We did not develop sophisticated, cross-cultural analyses of gender relations in India and Canada; that would have been beside the point. Our need was not intellectual, but emotional and psychological. We required a few choice phrases to soothe our wounded self-esteem as Indian women.

Typically, Nadira would rush in with the Indira Gandhi point for the latest victim of a negative remark about India or Pakistan. She would say with great indignation and self-righteousness: "Canadians could never accept a woman prime minister. But look at us! We are very liberal and progressive. We have a woman leader and she is ruling the country with a firm hand."

India became a hot topic of conversation in May 1974 when it tested its first nuclear device. My friends and I had mixed feelings as we followed reports in Canadian newspapers and discussions on television. We were glad to see India reported in the regular media, but we resented the criticisms that were being heaped upon it for its actions. The nuclear test, in our minds, proved with certainty the technological and scientific advancement of India. Could a "backward" country test a nuclear device, we rhetorically asked one another. We felt vindicated for our assertion that we were a more "developed" country than Canadians imagined. The nuclear test enhanced our self-esteem as Indians.

The media, however, worried about the "danger" posed to the planet by a Third World country, such as India, having "nuclear capability." I remember a political cartoon in a magazine that showed an emaciated, naked *fakir* (a poor man) with a begging bowl sitting next to a nuclear bomb. The racism and arrogance revealed by such images concerned me, but in the discussions with Canadian students in my seminars, I just repeated the arguments being put forward by Indian politicians that the nuclear explosion was for "peaceful" purposes, namely, to help in the exploration for oil. Indira Gandhi's shrewd negotiations of aid from Russia and United States enhanced our admiration for her leadership, but we gave little thought as to how the increased military budgets under her governance were affecting the availability of food for the poor.

My friends and I had little contact with Indians outside the university community. Each of us knew one or two Indian or Pakistani families in Toronto, but we had no contact with immigrants from our home countries on a day-to-day basis. Occasionally an Indian professor at the university invited us to his home, but the only time we saw groups of Indians and Pakistanis was when we went to Indian movies. We didn't see ourselves as part of a larger community of people from South Asia.

Since the introduction of the 1967 immigration policy, the number of Indians had grown steadily throughout Canada, and a large proportion of them had settled in Ontario. The new policy introduced a procedure for immigration that was popularly referred to as the "point system" because it assigned points to immigrants for attributes like education, age, language, and work-related skills. This policy, in contrast to previous ones, was supposed to treat people of all nationalities equally, but it did favour professionals, and therefore Indian immigrants. In addition, between 1967 and 1973, a large number of people of South Asian origin came from South Asia, the Caribbean, or Africa to Ontario as "visitors." (In an effort to stop people from jumping the queue or coming in through the back door, the government introduced legislation in 1973 that disallowed applying for immigration from within Canada.) Thus, in these few years, a population with diverse cultures from various parts of the world, but collectively referred to as "East Indians," and later as "South Asians" by academics and government agencies, came to live and settle in Toronto. All that united them was a geographical or historical link to South Asia and, in the eyes of white Canadians, the colour of their skin.

There were as yet no South Asian movie theatres or grocery stores. In the late 1970s an Indian bazaar and an entertainment district containing movie theatres and restaurants would emerge in the east end of Toronto. Such enclaves also sprang up later in other parts of Toronto, such as Scarborough, and in the nearby cities of Mississauga and Brampton. In the early 70s, though, a few entrepreneurial Indian men had set about meeting the social and recreational needs of the new immigrants by showing current Indian movies in high school auditoriums in the west end of the city on Sunday afternoons. The wives of the entrepreneurs cooked *samosas* and *pakoras* (Indian savouries) and made *masala-chai* (tea leaves boiled in a mixture of water and milk with spices and lots of sugar) and sold them during intermission at the shows. They were a big success, drawing in large crowds. My Indian and Pakistani friends and I sometimes went to these movies as well.

Most of the audience took the opportunity to dress in Indian clothes, and since different regions in India have somewhat distinctive styles of clothing, we could easily see that the group was a mixed one. We could also make a guess as to which people came from large urban centres such as Bombay, New Delhi, or Calcutta, supposing that they were the ones with short or shoulder-length hair who wore stylish saris in subdued colours and prints and very little gold jewellery. In contrast, we guessed that women who wore brightly coloured saris with a lot of gold embroidery and long, gold earrings and thick, gold necklaces came from smaller towns in Punjab or Gujarat. They often braided their hair or had it tied up in a knot; they used vivid red lipstick and nail polish, and put red powder in their hair parting, a traditional sign of being married. Other dress variations suggested that women might be Muslims from Pakistan. We thought that those wearing a dupatta and *churidars*, or leggings, with long, loose-fitting shirts were from Pakistan, although this Muslim style of dress was also popular in large cities in India. Almost all the men wore Western-style pants, sweaters, and jackets.

Some members of the audience did not seem to be from South Asia. They dressed in somewhat outdated Indian clothes, like those of women from smaller towns in India. We later learned that these were Indian immigrants from the Caribbean or parts of Africa—now sometimes referred to as Indo-Caribbeans—and their clothing resembled that of the regions and towns from which their foremothers had originally emigrated. What most distinguished these women were their different accents and behaviours—a mixture of Western, Caribbean, Hindu and Muslim. Some of the people seemed to us to be professionals, but dress and speech indicated a preponderance of working-class people at these movies.

In Bombay I had been raised on Western novels, music, and movies. My Westernized friends and I looked down on Hindi movies, with their escapist adventures, family tragedies, and lewd song-and-dance routines set to loud music. That kind of entertainment, we said in a high-minded way, was not for us. In Bombay I failed to notice the irony in my attitude. My father owned a movie theatre that showed only Hindi movies, and it was precisely the ones that my friends and I deplored that were the biggest box office hits, and so most profitable to his business. I had very seldom gone to see a movie in my father's theatre, however, or in others like his. I remember as a young teenager asking permission to go there with a crowd of friends and my father steering us off to a different theatre. The family theatre was in a working-class neighbourhood near a Muslim shopping district, and was therefore out of bounds for me, although no such prohibition applied to my brothers; they were expected to work at the theatre on a regular basis to earn their allowances. In Toronto, however, these movies provided a touch of home and transported me, at least in imagination, to the world I had left behind.

The audience, though, presented a dilemma for my Indian and Pakistani friends and me. Our sense of identity—who we were—had been defined by the small communities in which we had grown up, and we strongly identified with the families and friends we had left behind. In many ways our reference points and moral guides continued to be the values of our friends and families in India. In Toronto I had come to know some students from the subcontinent, but we recognized that it was our new location, more than anything else, that generated friendship between us. We had different goals and aspirations. Some of us wanted to go back home, while others, such as I, had ambivalent feelings. We were reluctant, however, to identify with what seemed to us a ragtag group of people at the movies, and we held ourselves aloof from them.

We were critical of the samosas and pakoras that were sold at these gatherings because they had a strong, spicy aroma. We were sure that Canadians unfamiliar with Indian food would disapprove of them. Besides, they were difficult to eat with forks and knives, and were consequently eaten by most of the people present in the traditional Indian way—using one's fingers. This did not stop us from devouring them, although we ate them with some guilt. We were embarrassed at having to eat with our fingers and constantly looked over our shoulders, apprehensive about being seen by the very few white Canadians in attendance. After eating, the audience would dump the paper plates in the garbage bins, spilling some of the leftover sauce and creating a mess, or they would simply leave the plates on the tables and chairs for others to pick up.

We were also embarrassed by the loud voices of some of the people, along with their unsophisticated use of the English language, their dress and their behaviour. We cringed at the confusion that occurred during intermission when the audience rushed to greet friends and acquaintances with noisy exclamations of happiness. Since entire families came to the movies, many small children ran around chasing and shouting at each other during intermission. Babies cried in discomfort and protest.

My friends and I considered ourselves to be superior to the audience at the movies. We were educated, middle-class, and aspiring to professional jobs. We had Canadian friends and knew how to interact with them. We

had manners. Compared to us, we thought, most of the others in the audience were ill-mannered and uncouth. It was an unpleasant shock for us as
we came to realize that the internal distinctions between us mattered little
to most white Canadians. To them we were all South Asians, an undiffer-
entiated category that was changing the face of the city.

Although Toronto was quintessentially an immigrant city, having
attracted European immigrants throughout the twentieth century, people
from the subcontinent formed the first wave of immigrants to the city
from Third World countries after 1967. Additional non-white immigrants
were coming from the Caribbean, other Asian countries and, to a lesser
extent, Africa. The media reported on a shortage of rental housing and
social services resulting from the rapid increase in population; the new
immigrants perceived themselves as victims of racism. However, the difficulty was not merely that of a WASP society feeling overwhelmed by all
the new languages, foods, and cultures of the immigrants, although some
argued to that effect. The problem was not the strain on social services
and housing, despite what some media stories claimed. Rather, a more-or-
less white Toronto was changing to a Toronto dotted with Indian, Pakistani, Asian, Chinese, and black faces. It was the fear of this change that
created tension and resentments among the white residents of Toronto
and led to racial conflict.

The racism that we Indian and Pakistanis consciously noted and discussed openly for the first time was of the name-calling variety. The chosen epithet was "Paki," which was commonly used to taunt us in malls,
subways and on the streets. Response to it varied, but it created a sense
of crisis within the community. Name-calling simply offended and
insulted some Indians and Pakistanis; they considered it an affront to
their dignity and honour. Others were apprehensive for their (and their
children's) physical safety. Professionals, who didn't think they would
encounter the same kind of verbal abuse as working-class manual labour-
ers, asked, "Why us?"

Matters came to a head in a subway incident when a male immigrant
of Indian origin from Tanzania was pushed onto the subway's tracks by a
youth and was rescued by a white man. Various groups of South Asians
organized dinners to honour the white man, taking the opportunity to
decry publicly the racism that was by then threatening their lives. The
incident generated a great deal of publicity, and the government
appointed a task force, chaired by Walter Pitman, then head of Ryerson

Polytechnical Institute (now Ryerson University), to investigate the prevalence of racism in Toronto.

The racism prevalent at the time gave Indian and Pakistani immigrants, along with newcomers of Indian descent from Africa or the Caribbean, a feeling of being under siege. Our common situation created the feeling of belonging to a community. I did not feel outrage at the name-calling. When an epithet was flung at me on the street, I would look the individual in the face and stare at him or her until we passed each other by. I never got into a verbal brawl, although I heard of many Indians and Pakistanis who did. These incidents did not mar my self-esteem or erode my sense of dignity, perhaps because I still anticipated going home to Bombay. The racism, to me, was just a phenomenon that I had to temporarily endure.

Actually, this was not the first time in my life that the issue of skin colour had come up. In Bombay, when I was a teenager, some of my aunts visiting the family would sometimes nod sagely in my direction and say to my father, "She is dark..." or more politely, "She is not as fair as her sisters." The implication was that they would have to use some extra guile to net a "suitable boy" for me to marry. My father, confident about his deep pockets, would shrug nonchalantly and laugh, and if I was anywhere near he would put his arm around me. Although his confidence was reassuring, I nevertheless had a sense that I was not as pretty as my fairer-skinned sisters.

Meena Alexander, whose family comes from South India, describes the way her grandmother, who was "fair-skinned," worried about Meena, who was "so dark," getting too much sun. The grandmother used to say: "Look, child, you are dark enough as it is. How will you ever find a husband if you race around in the sun? Now it's time to stop and do a little embroidery and let one of the maids plait your hair properly..."

Meena goes on to say she felt inferior to her grandmother. "Already by virtue of what I was, dark like my mother, I was a cut below her, and beauty was impossible. And I knew it was only because of the fine ancestral lines and the land holdings that she had permitted her son to marry such a woman. Then, appa [father] had gone to work in Africa. There was always the danger that I would become a jungli [wild] of sorts, ill-kempt, barbarous, impossible to tame..." She felt she had to "...overcome these faults: decorous behaviour, embroidery, and some musical skills...I had to learn my feminine skills, labour hard to grab hold of what beauty I could."[1]

The consciousness of skin colouring is akin to racism. People associated differences in skin colour with differences in social status, intelligence, and overall value. In India, light-skinned people are generally
assumed to be superior to dark-skinned people, regardless of the fact that
there are dark-skinned people of high caste, for example, and fair-skinned
people living in poverty. Where did this attitude come from? Some people
suggest that it has a long history in India. Colour-consciousness may go
back as far as the sixth century. The original settlers in southern India
were Dravidians, who were dark-skinned. They were conquered by
Aryans, light-skinned invaders who came through the Hindu Kush in
northern India and from Persia.

Other people argue that colour-consciousness is mainly a legacy of
colonial rule in India, dating from the arrival of the British in India. The
white-skinned British had colonized the dark-skinned "natives." My
aunts, like most Indians, also applied the conventional measures of physical attractiveness: a tall, slender girl was more beautiful than a short,
stocky one; a girl with finely chiseled features more beautiful than a snub-
nosed girl with a pudgy face. The standard of beauty in India is fair skin,
as innumerable advertisements in matrimonial sections of major Indian
newspapers attest.

Although I had felt the effects of prejudices like these in India and
had begun to encounter white racism in Toronto, it took some time
before I got involved in the political activities organized by groups of
South Asians in Toronto in the mind to late 70s. At the university in
Bombay, where I had spent my time dallying and drinking coffee, I had
participated in plenty of social activity, but never in politics. Perhaps
what propelled me into meetings, workshops and discussions in Toronto
was the excitement of being part of a community in an otherwise alien
Canadian environment.

Two Indian professors, one a Parsi teaching anthropology at the University of Toronto and the other a Punjabi professor at OISE, were organizing workshops meant to educate Canadians about South Asians, and
they invited me to be a panellist. These meetings presented some South
Asian history, explained our many religions and cultures, discussed
women in India, and, most significantly, threw a spotlight on the new
immigrants. We thought that if we could communicate that we were professional people (engineers, scientists, physicians, and teachers), the
racism against us would dissipate. We disregarded the presence of a sub-

stantial proportion of working-class Indians and Pakistanis in Ontario, preferring instead to focus on ourselves. However, through these meetings, I became part of a network of Indian and Pakistani men and women who were middle-class, professional and politically active.

I remember attending one meeting that was organized by a group of Indian women to discuss initiatives they could undertake to combat racism. Their emphasis was on finding a strategy that would draw attention to the positive attributes of the Indian population in Canada. The aim was to project an image that would show us as contributing members of Canadian society and indicate our desire to assimilate. Some of the women suggested going into schools and holding workshops for students and teachers on the different cultures of Indians. They described the distress their children felt in school lunchrooms when other kids said, "Your food stinks!" or "Your lunch smells awful!" or even just, "What is that?" They wanted to do cooking demonstrations in these schools so that the other children could learn about the different flavours and aromas of Indian foods. They suggested doing voluntary work at hospitals so that white Canadians could get to know Indians and Pakistanis and overcome their misapprehensions.

I worked mainly with organizations such as the Indian Immigrant Aid Service and the Association of Women of Indian Origin in Canada. The Immigrant Aid Service had been started by some Indians to help new immigrants from the subcontinent who were having difficulty gaining access to social services. However, the rise at that time in the name-calling variety of racism shifted the focus of its work and politicized it. Since this was the only organization besides the volunteer recreational and social organizations that had an office and a paid staff, it became the centre of activity for politically active students and professors. The Indian Immigrant Aid Service obtained funds from government agencies, and in turn contracted students and professors to produce research studies. The hope was to use the data they gathered to lobby politicians and educate Canadian society through print and electronic media.

My identity was being changed by being excluded from parts of white Canadian society and included in these South Asian groups. The process was a matter of circumstance, the changes imposed upon me rather than ones I chose to make. The racism that existed at the time made me conscious of myself as "different" from white Canadians. Many things about me were different: nationality, language, religion, and culture. But the name-calling variety of racism made me aware that white Canadians considered my skin colour the most important difference.

Brown-skinned people were considered different from the white-skinned population. And we were different again from "Orientals" and blacks. But my skin colour grouped me willy-nilly with many people I had difficulty relating to or accepting as members of my community. I knew the diverse origins and wide range of differences within the "South Asian community," but these distinctions, which partly defined who I was, were irrelevant to most white Canadians (and remain so even at the present time). They made only very broad distinctions. They may have been conscious of different religions, languages, and cultures within the white population, but they lumped together all blacks, all Orientals, and all South Asians.

At the university I had become conscious of myself as an Indian national. This was no longer a mere detail to be entered into an official government document, but had significance and import in my daily life. I perceived myself to be an Indian woman. Many of my friends also identified themselves by their nationality and referred to themselves as Pakistani, Sri Lankan, or Bangladeshi. People of Indian origin from Africa, however, were wary of defining themselves as Africans or even as nationals of the particular country from which they had emigrated. They often defined themselves by their religion or language: Ismaili (or Shiahs or Sunni), or Gujaratis. People of Indian origin from the Caribbean seldom defined themselves by nationality, for example, as Trinidadians, but instead referred to themselves as Indo-Caribbean. Sikhs who were emigrating from Britain defined themselves as Sikh, never as British.

The name that emerged for this diverse population of new immigrants was "South Asian." This replaced the former moniker "East Indian," which had been used to describe Sikhs immigrating to British Columbia in the early part of this century. I am not certain how the "South Asian" label emerged, and I have been unable to trace its origins. I think it was a convenient label devised by academics who needed a term to cover all the countries and cultures in the "subcontinent." Perhaps it was coined by government agencies. It still seems to leave out people from Tibet, Nepal, and Bhutan, covering just old British India, including Pakistan, and Ceylon (now Sri Lanka), but it is easy to see why community groups preferred it to narrower categories like "Indian" or "Hindu," and to derisive epithets like "Paki."

Salman Rushdie, in *The Ground Beneath Her Feet*, addresses the dilemma of immigrants who are always looking over their shoulders at what they have left behind, wary of the new norms and values to which they are exposed in the adopted land, and always negotiating, deliberately or otherwise, the behaviours and attitudes that they will retain or give up. His breezy advice is to be more carefree, to take the plunge into a new way of being. He writes: "What if the whole deal—orientation, knowing where you are, and so on—what if it's all a scam? What if all of it—home, kinship, the whole enchilada—is just the biggest, most truly global, and centuries-oldest piece of brainwashing? Suppose that it's only when you dare to let go that your life begins? When you are whirling free of the mother ship, when you cut your ropes, slip your chain, step off the map, go absent without leave, scram, vamoose, whatever: suppose that it is then, and only then, that you're actually free to act! To lead the life that nobody tells you how to live, or when, or why."[2]

Although at the time I was unable to commit myself to being Indian or Canadian, our lives in Canada were changing all of us. I had dated Tom Agnew for more than two years, and through him I was pulled into a "Canadian" family environment. Tom was from a working-class background and had always lived in Toronto. With his long, blonde hair and beard, he looked like a hippie. Now that he was working, he had taken to smoking a pipe in an attempt to appear sophisticated. He liked to travel and had spent two summers backpacking in Europe. Tom and I went out together to campus pubs or neighbourhood cafés. On weekends we went out to movies and dinner afterwards. We spent most of our time with other students on campus, and if they thought our relationship was out of the ordinary, they took care not to reveal their feelings. Perhaps if we had been part of small, close-knit, white community in Toronto, or lived in a small town with few non-white residents, I might have felt more self-conscious, but in the pubs and cafeterias that were our usual haunts, we felt "normal."

One day, Tom suggested that I go with him to his parent's home so he could show me the photographs he had taken in Europe. Visiting a Canadian family in their home was still an unusual experience for me, so I readily agreed. Also, I was curious to know where Tom came from.

I thought of Tom as a "typical Canadian," and when I met his parents and sister, I assumed they were an example of an average Canadian family. I took what I saw in their home to be the norm for all Canadians. Tom's mother was a plump, cheerful woman; his sister, Debbie, nine years younger than he, was tall, thin and blonde. He also had a brother five years younger. In India, when meeting older adults, an English-speaking Indian would call them "auntie" or "uncle." I was not then familiar with the Canadian norm of referring to a friend's mother formally as Mrs. so-and-so. I coped by avoiding the use of any name. (Two years later and just before we were to be married, Tom's mother broached the topic jokingly and asked, "So what are you going to call me—the old bag?" and then laughed uproariously. I started to call her Mom at that time.)

On that first night, Tom, Debbie, and I sat at the kitchen table while Mrs. Agnew continued with the preparations for the meal. Although Debbie and her mother tried to engage me in conversation, I felt somewhat shy and tongue-tied, and could say little. I already knew some details about the Agnews from Tom. The only one in his family to have gone to university, he was upset when his brother and sister had quit school at sixteen, and it had alienated him from them for a while. Their lifestyle, according to Tom, revolved around watching sports on television, listening to music and going to the neighbourhood pubs. He aspired to be different. But on that day, in that kitchen, Tom's mother and sister told me happy stories of their past.

Tom was reticent by nature, and he had shared very few stories of the university with his family and their friends. I found out that he had never taken any of his university friends home and so for them, some mystery surrounded the university and Tom's life there. His parents and siblings had attended his graduation; an enlarged picture of Tom on that day was displayed on the fireplace mantel. Tom had never introduced any of his female friends to his family, so they were more than a bit curious about me. They had all seen his slides of Europe, and Debbie had heard Tom's stories about them before, but she still expressed an interest and suggested we watch them in the living room. The slide show gave us time to become a bit more comfortable with one another.

I can vividly recall many details of the supper that day because it was so different from my previous experience of family meals. We ate at the kitchen table and had pork chops, mashed potatoes, and peas. Sometimes in India I had visited families who ate in the kitchen, but that was in the traditional style, sitting on a mat and served either by the elder women of the family or by the paid cook. Tom's mother, likewise, served the meal to us. Indian families almost never have a table and chairs in the kitchen. Perhaps what was most different from my own experience was the Canadian idea of the kitchen being the focal point for the family, with the mother and her cooking bringing the family together.

After the meal, Tom's mother began to clear the table and wash the dishes, while his father quietly departed for the television set. Tom jokingly urged his sister to get up and help, but she refused and the three of us continued to sit at the table. I thought it was normal that he would not jump up and start doing chores around the kitchen. I was probably expected to offer some help, but not knowing the routine or the customs of the family, I too continued to sit and observe, listening all the while to the banter between sister and brother. It seemed that quibbling about helping with the dishes was par for the course, for at one point Tom's mother turned around and, when our eyes met, smiled broadly and winked conspiratorially at me.

I imagine that my race must have been the most striking aspect of my identity for Tom's family. Interracial relations and marriages are recurring themes in many novels that discuss aspects of the immigrant experience. Although I read such books avidly, they usually discuss such relationships from the immigrant's perspective. I have only read one account by a member of the dominant group who discussed his interracial marriage—white novelist Clark Blaise, who is married to Bharati Mukherjee, an Indian. Even he sidestepped the difficult issues, however, merely saying that he was in love with an individual, and not a culture or a continent. By and large, members of the dominant society who do not care for the interracial or interethnic choices of their family members do not discuss their feelings in print.

I first met Tom's parents in 1974. I have tried hard to think of some incident or remark that would reveal their attitude to my ethnicity and race, but I can come up with none. Part of the explanation may be that everything about me—race, education, family, and experience—was diametrically opposite to everything that was known and familiar to them. I represented a bewildering array of differences that they did their best to accommodate. Another part of the explanation may be their own very circumscribed life experiences: they had only lived in Toronto and had seldom met people of different cultures or race. Besides, they were apolitical and knew nothing about India. I can imagine some other people reacting negatively when confronted by a potential daughter-in-law so different from themselves, or developing an attitude towards her, but in their case they were open-minded and hospitable towards me. I think perhaps the truth lay in their desire to keep Tom within the orbit of the family. Tom's education and life experiences had opened a chasm between him and his parents and siblings; he had become part of a world that was alien to them and about which they knew little. Since they wanted to maintain a close and happy relationship with him, they were anxious to accept whoever his friends were.

Neither Tom nor I had grown up in the middle-class, WASP environment that dominated the residence in which we lived. Our attitudes towards the past and hopes for the future had drawn us together in spite of our cultural differences. Tom did not want to emulate the students at the residence, but he did want a life for himself that was different from the one he had grown up in. Becoming friends with me was as different as it was possible for him to be in that environment. For me, dating Tom allowed me to set aside the values and norms of my own socialization. I was free in this relationship to be whatever I chose to be.

One evening I took Tom to meet my Indian friends at one of our get-togethers. It was hard, however, to integrate him in our conversations about India, and we had to grope around for topics to discuss. Our usual litany of complaints and grievances could not be recited for him, nor could we express our doubts about "Canadian" values and norms. Over the next few months I occasionally took Tom with me when I met my Indian friends, but mostly I kept these two aspects of my life separate from one another.

Alpna, a Hindu Gujarati woman from Bombay, also lived at the university residence and was dating a white Canadian named Michael. Alpna's background was steeped in Indian classical dance and music. In Bombay she had aspired to be a classical dance performer of the Bharat Natyam style (there are also the Kathak and Odippi styles), but in Toronto she was a graduate student studying for a doctorate in Sanskrit literature. Michael was a PhD student in mathematics. Alpna's two sisters lived in Toronto as well; one of them was a Bharat Natyam dancer who performed regularly at several university campuses in Canada. The other sister and her husband were professional photographers who had shown their collection of Indian photographs in several multimedia exhibitions around the campus. The entire family ardently championed classical Indian arts in Toronto throughout the 1970s and beyond.

Alpna and Michael decided to marry, and they invited Tom and me to their wedding, which was to take place in a room in Hart House, a Neo-

Gothic cultural centre built on the campus grounds in the early 1900s. Alpna's family tried to recreate Indian wedding décor in the room, and it was decorated in Gujarati fashion to mark the celebratory event; garlands of flowers trimmed the door frames, and on the floor were several small earthenware oil lamps, around which were drawings of typically Indian motifs, such as paisleys, executed in white flour. They had also scattered some pieces of Indian brass around the room, and posters of India were hung on the wall. Near the centre of one wall stood two low stools decorated with gold and red tinsel on which the bride and groom were to sit during the wedding ceremony. Alpna wore a sari in the traditional red colour decorated with gold embroidery and Michael was in a black suit.

About fifty Indian and white Canadian guests were assembled in the room. We sat on chairs facing the bride and groom. In Hindu weddings there is usually music—along with hustle, bustle, excitement and lots of loud talk. Entire families attend weddings, and children are everywhere. The atmosphere in that room, however, was solemn and serene. A priest sat on a floor mat facing the couple and chanted Vedic *mantras* to begin the wedding ceremony. Usually, wedding prayers are said in front of a small open fire, but since Canadian fire regulations do not permit a fire indoors, the family had placed some kindling in a metal container and prayers were said over that. At the end of each prayer the bride and groom poured spoonfuls of a potpourri of spices and herbs and clarified butter into the fire as an offering to the gods. Then they walked around the fire seven times to the accompaniment of prayers to complete the ceremony. Alpna and Michael walked to the older members of the gathering and, as a traditional sign of respect, touched their feet. The two white professors present at the ceremony were taken aback, and seemed somewhat bewildered by what was taking place in the area of their feet.

I was familiar with the ceremony, having watched it many times in India, but sitting with Tom in the presence of other white people, it all felt quite strange. Although the religious rituals were the same, transplanting them to Hart House had subtly changed them. There was a self-consciousness to the effort that had gone into creating the wedding scene that made it seem different and exotic to everyone in attendance. The ambiance of an Indian wedding, with music, women dressed in brightly coloured saris, and chattering crowds, was missing here. Instead, there was a group of white people looking interested but feeling out of place and lost. I suddenly felt conscious of myself as an Indian (and not just as a

Hindu) who belonged to a culture with its own well-established rituals and ceremonies.

Novels and, more recently, movies have looked at the attitudes of South Asian families to interracial marriages. *The Hero's Walk*, by Anita Rau Badami, is about marriage between an Indian woman studying in Canada and a white Canadian. When the young woman tells her father over the telephone that she wishes to marry the Canadian and break off her engagement in India, he says, "You will never come home! Never!" Caught up in anger over his loss of face in the community and loss of authority within his family, he cannot find it in himself to forgive her, even though he misses her. It is only when the couple dies in a car crash and their daughter is left without a family that the father overcomes his anger and comes to Canada to claim his granddaughter. The novel concludes with the father and granddaughter reconciling and accepting one another.[3]

Tom and I were caught up in the idea that we were free to pick and choose the values and norms that suited our own needs and temperaments. However, the way we conveyed news of our engagement to our respective families revealed how rooted we were in the practices of our disparate cultural mores. Tom felt that a decision to marry was a personal one that, once made, could simply be presented to his family as a *fait accompli*. They, in turn, accepted me into their family without much ado.

However, I felt that I had to seek my father's approval and consent, and since I was in my mid-twenties and more than anything else he wanted to see me marry, he readily consented, having more or less guessed that I intended to live in Toronto and would not return to Bombay except for holidays. My brother Subash had also married a white Canadian. He and Linda had decided to have a civil ceremony, followed by a small dinner for about a dozen people; no one from the family was present. After a brief holiday in Europe they went to Bombay and my father had a very small wedding reception for them. There was no Indian wedding ceremony.

In my case, my father merely asked that I keep him informed of my plans so that he could arrange to be in Toronto when we married. A few months later, he and Rita came from Bombay to attend the wedding, which was held in Tom's apartment and followed by a small reception for our friends and family. Debbie and Tom's female cousins had tried to give me hints about the ceremony but, wanting it to be casual, Tom and I had not fretted about any details. When Debbie asked who would be the bridesmaid, I replied "Rita," although there are no bridesmaids in an

Indian wedding. When she asked, "What about the flowers?" I merely suggested that she go ahead and get whatever was necessary. In India, flowers
are worn as a garland and pinned to the bride's hair, but neither Debbie
nor I knew the custom in each other's culture; a bridal bouquet was
brought along for me.

On the wedding day I wore a red chiffon sari embroidered with gold
motifs that my father had brought from Bombay, along with a heavy gold
necklace and dangling earrings. Rita wore a purple silk sari. At the appropriate moment I emerged from the apartment's hallway into the living
room carrying a bouquet of flowers, and in the presence of about thirty
friends and family we proceeded with two ceremonies—first Hindu, and
then Christian.

Tom and I were attempting to do our own thing; we had not
exchanged engagement rings and did not plan on exchanging wedding
rings, either. However, when the minister, a cousin of Tom's, enquired
about them at the last moment, my father pulled a diamond ring out of his
pocket, along with an eternity band for me and a gold band for Tom.

And so, observing some conventions, we were married.

Being and Becoming

I woke up this morning thinking about Bombay. I felt nostalgic for the girl I once was, and lonesome for my sisters and brothers. I put on a sari my father sent me as a gift some ten years ago, and memories came flooding back. I was reading Salman Rushdie late into the night, and his prose evoked familiar images of India. One thing he wrote has strengthened my resolve to examine how my experiences in Canada have shaped and molded my identity: "...the awareness of oneself as a homogenous entity in time, a blend of past and present, is the glue of personality, holding together our then and our now."[1]

First, my past. In my mind's eye I am the fifteen year old standing in front of the mirror scrutinizing the beginning of a pimple on my nose. Suddenly my aunt's face appears next to mine in the mirror. She looks grim. "Again," she says sternly, "you are wasting time." She begins one of her lectures about vain girls, with dire predictions about my fate if I neglect my school work. She ends, as always, by presenting me with a choice: either study or help with household chores. As I bend down to pick up a book, she says: "No one much cares what you look like. It is unimportant. You must study, become an intelligent woman. Then you will be welcome in other people's homes."

My widowed father is more indulgent. However, when I set my heart on a new pair of gold earrings, he resists buying them for me. "I *need* them," I tell him. At the end of his patience, he sits me down in his room and gives me a lecture on the values of Hinduism. The world and all material things, he says, are just *maya*, an illusion; they count for nothing. Significance lies in an individual's *atman,* and it is that—the soul—which must be nurtured. The atman survives the physical body on death and is reincarnated in another body, in a continuous chain of births and rebirths. The goal of the individual should be to free the atman from this chain and become one with the "truth" that is God. "These silly baubles do not matter," he tells me. "Focus on improving your mind." I look at him morosely and hand him the cheque I have prepared for his signature. Finally, he laughs at this well-practised routine, signs the cheque, and I am out of there!

The distinction between mind and body was a dominant theme in a course on Hinduism I took as an undergraduate in India. At first it was hard for me to grasp the concepts of being and becoming as they were presented in class. "Being" is the material body—flesh, bone, and blood. The body, however, is insignificant in the individual's quest for truth and purity in life. The process of "becoming" defines the individual, and in religious terms, enables a person to attain *moksha,* that is, liberation from earthly human desires. Devout Hindus spend their lives attempting to overcome human passions and subordinate their desires to the ideal of dissociating from material, earthly needs.

Though my aunt and father warned me against attaching much importance to the body, they did not ignore my gender, and tried to inculcate values in me which they considered appropriate for girls. My aunt was a traditional woman who thought in conventional ways. Her only departure from the norms of her community and society was a strong commitment to the value of female education. In all other ways, she wanted me to conform to the gender roles of a middle-class Hindu woman by learning household tasks and practising female modesty and decorum. My aunt valued obedience and forbearance in girls. She constantly reminded me that "good" girls should be seen and not heard, a refrain taken up teasingly by my older brothers when I argued with them or gave vent to my feelings. Frustrated by my constant talking back to them, they would pronounce me incorrigible and joke that I should train to be a lawyer.

At the age of fifteen, when I left my aunt's home and returned to live with my father, I found that his lessons sometimes contradicted those of my aunt. My sisters and I experienced greater freedom than might have been possible if there had been a female role model in our daily lives, since my father compensated for that absence by being overindulgent. In our new circumstances we were no longer cautioned by older women about the "truth" or "facts" of women's lives, and we could dream up possibilities that might otherwise have been nipped in the bud. Besides, my father did not care about tradition and convention. He wanted my sisters and me to be "modern and progressive," by which he meant that we should emulate the norms and values of well-off, educated, Westernized Indians. He often warned us against what he termed female weaknesses—emotion and sentimentality—and wanted us to assess situations in our lives dispassionately and intellectually, "not like a woman."

When I immigrated to Canada in 1970, I heard white female students at the University of Waterloo and later in Toronto avidly debating feminist ideas. Caught up in their enthusiasm, I started to read feminist books. Over the next few years I discovered that feminists were challenging the distinction, also made in Western metaphysics, between emotion and intellect. Feminists said that what had come down through history as objective and neutral knowledge was permeated by the values of its male proponents. Patriarchal societies had questioned women's ability to reason and had cast aspersions on their intellectual abilities. Women's "ways of knowing," based on their own experiences, were often different from those of males, and they reached different conclusions or emphasized different factors in arriving at conclusions.

The suggestion that women's reasoning did not have to conform to male standards in order to be valuable made a strong impression on me. Such ideas were still abstract, however, and I did not immediately start reassessing my values or my upbringing in light of them. I did not realize their concrete significance for my past or present life. Lonely and homesick in my first few years in Toronto, I was not about to indulge in a feminist analysis of my past. The present was unknown and intimidating, and I had first to know myself—discover who *I* was—before I could benefit in any way from feminist insights such as these.

In Bombay I had paid scant attention to "who I was," and rarely thought about the ethnicity or religion of my family. Then, there had been few personal or social crises that could have made me aware of myself or of my values. We discussed politics around the dinner table, but I was not involved in any political group and had no desire to be a social activist. The ongoing political tension, along with a war or two between India and Pakistan, did make me distinguish myself from the Muslims. Newspaper reports about the war evoked for my father and other relatives and com-patriots memories of their lives in Quetta, which was now part of Pakistan. Through these accounts I learned more about the history of the two coun-tries and consequently developed a heightened self-awareness of myself as a Hindu.

India's growing tension with China introduced talk about communism into everyday conversations. And during a food shortage, Prime Minister Shastri exhorted people to observe a "wheatless day" once a week, which meant giving up bread, a staple in the diet of most Indians. However, in our family what was meant to be an act of solidarity with the masses turned out to be serendipitous, because a variety of other dishes were pre-pared for the weekly no-bread meals and they became our favourites.

I remained detached—not unusual for a teenager—from any discus-sions about the problems of poverty and unequal social relations that I read about in the newspapers and magazines. The one magazine I read reg-ularly, at my father's insistence, was *Imprint*, which serialized classic American works of fiction. (I later learned that *Imprint* was part of a covert, CIA-funded operation meant to counteract Russian communist influence on the Indian middle-classes.) In my everyday routine, however, I had no reason to think about social or political issues, or to reflect upon their relevance to my identity. I was also oblivious as to how they informed my everyday experience.

In Waterloo, and later in Toronto, my name, dress, accent, manner-isms, and skin colour made me different from the white students and fac-ulty. I was not at first aware of these characteristics or of their power to define and identify me, but my interactions with white Canadians were slowly making me aware of their implications for my career aspirations. In Bombay I had enjoyed many privileges, but in Toronto I was an "immi-grant," with little money, no family and no real home. I wanted to assim-ilate, but the questions that were invariably asked by new friends and acquaintances only made me aware of myself as a middle-class, Hindu, mission-school-educated woman. These attributes set me apart.

The first time I became conscious of having a perspective different from that of my white professors was in a course on nineteenth-century British history, in which I was a graduate teaching assistant. Ann Robson, who taught the course, was a Canadian of British background. She was always friendly, perhaps overly considerate of me as a "foreign" student. The course focused on the condition of the working class in the Industrial

Revolution. Although we read liberal philosophers such as John Stuart Mill, there was nothing about the British Empire overseas, or how Asia and Africa contributed to the industrialization and prosperity of Britain.

I noticed this omission because as an Indian I found it hard to conceptualize British history without including the Empire. However, I did not have the confidence to discuss this with Professor Robson. To me, as an insecure "foreigner," she represented intellectual and personal authority. In tutorial discussions, I did my best to reproduce her perspective, subordinating my own understanding of the subject matter. Although in theory I had some power in tutorial discussions because I graded the assignments, I felt vulnerable. I was embarrassed when I mispronounced the names of the students, all of whom were white. I prepared diligently for my classes in order to prove myself to the students and win their respect for my teaching.

My anxiety was focused on my own intellectual abilities and on my desire to bridge the chasm between my students and myself. A book, or even an article, on India's role in British history would have enhanced the course materials, as well as making me feel more secure and boosting my self-confidence as a tutorial leader. While the course enabled me to broaden my knowledge of British history, its perspective was just one more challenge in my quest to adapt and assimilate to Canadian society. It did, however, sow in me a tiny seed of political consciousness.

Some of my friends saw me as a woman from a mysterious and exotic country about which they knew little beyond some stereotypical ideas regarding spirituality and poverty. Sometimes they described my reactions to everyday situations as "cute"—I guess meaning a little naïve and comical. The word "cute" suggested to me "sweet" or "charming" or "endearing," but I think it was for them a polite way of expressing mild exasperation.

The word is often applied to children or small animals. Calling my ways of looking at things "cute" was a way of diminishing their importance, either to spare me the pain of being criticized or to save my friends the task of scrutinizing their own ways of thinking. By dissembling, they didn't have to decide whether my reactions to things were right or wrong—they were just different! By being "polite" and avoiding conflict, they didn't have to take them seriously or try to understand them.

There seemed to be no malice behind the word, and being called "cute" did not erode my self-esteem, but the thinking behind it did make it hard for me to feel at home at the university. It was a "nice" way of saying I was different, and because I was "different," students and faculty members often didn't know how to make small talk with me. They were afraid of saying the wrong thing, of giving offence. Carlos Fuentes, the Mexican writer, saw an even deeper fear in boys encountering "foreign" students at an American school he attended: "What was different made others afraid, less of what was different than of themselves, of their own incapacity to recognize themselves in the alien."[2]

To an open-minded person, meeting someone "different" can be an opportunity to see themselves through different eyes. Taking that opportunity requires faith in oneself and the confidence to risk finding out how limited one's knowledge is, or how narrow one's own perspective. Perhaps some of the white students and faculty felt it was an imposition to have to stretch their boundaries to accommodate themselves to the presence of others. Perhaps their own reactions and responses to "different" people were a source of disappointment because they revealed the gap between their liberal ideals and their everyday emotions. The defences and pretences they adopted, such as calling someone "cute," made communication and interaction difficult between "Canadians" and people who were "different."

Increases in the number of Third World immigrants, particularly in Ontario, came at a time when French Canadians were questioning their lack of power and privilege vis-à-vis English Canadians. The federal government's attempts to appease them by appointing a royal commission to examine French-English relations gave further impetus to European immigrant groups, who also wanted a public acknowledgement of their right to maintain elements of their own cultures and identities. The Liberal government of Prime Minister Trudeau introduced a policy of multiculturalism that recognized the aspirations of these ethnic groups. Of course, it also served to "contain" their political demands.

The policy of multiculturalism attempted to change the expectation of most of the white Canadian population that new immigrants would assimilate and conform to Anglo norms. It sought to give immigrant groups some social and psychological space by granting them public funds for group activities that had as their goal the maintenance and preservation of their ethnic culture. In the 1980s, public discourse around multiculturalism emphasized the diversity of the Canadian population, described ethnic cultures as enriching Canada and Canadians, and envisioned a Canada that belonged to all ethnic groups equally (although the English and the French would have some special privileges).

The discourse on multiculturalism heightened my sense of self as an immigrant, but it also gave me some awareness of having rights, and opened up the possibility of criticizing white Canadians who persisted in treating me as "different" and a "foreigner." However, the suggestion that all ethnic groups and races were "different but equal" created additional tension for immigrants who wanted to preserve some aspects of their culture but also desired social mobility. Thus, for example, a woman was free to be "different" and wear the traditional Islamic *hijab*, or head scarf, if she so chose, to her place of work, but the problem lay in finding a job in the first place. Not finding a job in a multicultural society could seem, at a superficial level, to have little to do with the biases of the larger society, but rather to be an indication of the lack of initiative or ability of some groups and individuals. The policy of multiculturalism gave ethnic groups the right to maintain their culture, but it did little to promote their job prospects. The discourse of multiculturalism had the effect of making individuals' feelings of inadequacy in not gaining jobs and social mobility seem to be personal, individual failings.

I am reminded of a man named Vyoteck Sandiomerski, whom I knew at the university residence in the mid-1970s. Vyoteck legally adopted the name of Sandy, but retained his last name. Tom and I were close friends to Sandy and his wife, Moya, until his untimely death in the early 1980s. He was a friendly, vivacious man with dark, sparkling eyes and curly, black hair. Born in Poland at a time when there were restrictions on who could leave the country, he managed nevertheless to escape and migrate to Canada. When he came to Canada, he knew only the little bit of English he had picked up working odd jobs in Europe, but by the time I met him, he spoke the language fluently. Sandy disliked any talk that identified him as an immigrant, although it had been a substantial accomplishment to survive by doing odd jobs while he learned English and then to gain admission to the graduate science program at the University of Toronto. He was keen to assimilate and lose his "foreignness." Although I had only a vague knowledge of Poland, I had heard about the sufferings of Polish Jews in the Holocaust, and one day I asked him if he was Jewish. He staunchly denied it.

Moya was an American whose working-class parents had emigrated from Britain. Moya frequently talked to me about her grandfather, who originally came from Sri Lanka. Family legend had it that he owned vast tea estates there. Her grandmother was white and British, and her mother had married a white Briton, so Moya's ties to Sri Lanka were pretty tenuous, but the topic would come up from time to time. Perhaps she was trying to establish some common ground between us, or maybe she thought that somehow one day she might inherit those vast tea estates. Some time after she and Sandy had been married, Moya started shopping at a Jewish butcher shop. Noticing this change, I asked her why, but she merely said that she preferred it.

At Sandy's funeral, an elderly white Protestant professor read the eulogy and revealed Sandy's Jewish ancestry to the gathering in a parlour at the funeral home. It was obvious that no one but the professor and Moya had known about it. Even their son had no idea that he was half-Jewish. The revelation was a shock to all of us, and it was clear during the tea after the service that it embarrassed Moya.

Sandy's choice to hide his ethnic identity is not unique, but immigrants who feel compelled to do so live in fear of being discovered and humiliated. It is racism in the larger society that makes people want to "pass" as "just Canadian." Even today, sons and daughters of immigrants sometimes change their original names. They may say that they are too difficult for others to pronounce, or to spell, or to remember. Some of my students are embarrassed by their ethnic names, and ask that I refer to them in class by Anglicized names or nicknames. They may feel that having a "foreign-sounding" name will impede their careers. In the 1970s, feminists argued that the practice by women of adopting their spouse's name implied a willingness to subsume their identities under that of the male. In spite of that, some feminists who kept their own names (really their fathers') changed them when they married to things that sounded more "American" or "Canadian."

I changed my last name when I married Tom in 1974: Vijay Nangia became Vijay Agnew. I too liked the idea of adopting a name that people could remember and pronounce easily. In changing my name I was not hoping to "pass," for my skin-colouring gave away my ethnicity. I did not relate in a personal way to the belief of white feminists that changing one's name subsumed a woman's identity under that of her spouse. The change in name undoubtedly symbolized society's views of a woman's place in life, but the significant issue for me was the space I could create for myself within the new relationship, and the choices I would make as we went along. I thought that what I *did* would define who I was, rather than the label I attached to myself. Besides, I did not for a moment believe that an independent, productive woman—which is what I thought I was—could be transformed into a snivelling, cowering woman by changing her name, and so I did what suited me best rather than be constrained by fears of what some white feminists may think of me. I did not realize then, however, that the change would also advertise my association with a white man.

In the school year of 1974-75, I finished writing my PhD dissertation and continued my involvement around campus in anti-racist activities organized by Indians. The history department had routinely awarded me teaching assistantships and a research grant, and I had enjoyed living like a student. I was feeling a bit sad, though, because the defence of my dissertation would also bring to an end my student life. I was looking somewhat half-heartedly for a teaching position at a university in Canada, but had few hopes of finding one.

The omens were all bad. The rapid expansion of Ontario universities was coming to a somewhat abrupt end at the time; there was a freeze in hiring new faculty, and very few positions were available. When I discussed my job prospects with some of my professors, they told me that for the first time students of *Canadian* history were having difficulty getting placed. The implication was that I, having specialized in such esoteric subjects as imperialism and women's history in India, couldn't expect to find a job in that market. Now that I was married and committed to staying in Canada, the thought of not finding a job was becoming a major concern for me.

One day I was at home reading when the phone rang. The woman at the other end of the line identified herself as Suzanne Kline, the undergraduate coordinator of the Division of Social Science at York University. She also mentioned that she was the wife of Martin Kline, professor of African history at the University of Toronto, for whom I had worked as a teaching assistant. Suzanne was looking for someone to lead tutorial groups in a course on the Third World, and had heard about me from her husband and other friends at the history department. "Are you interested?" she asked. Since the job made it possible for me to continue to live in Toronto, where I had set down some roots, I grasped at the opportunity enthusiastically. Of course, I did not then know that this decision, made in a few seconds, would be an important one in my life: I have spent my entire teaching career at York.

I had made no application for employment, and I underwent no formal interview. The informal recommendations of professors who knew me at the University of Toronto's history department were enough. Ironically, I—an outsider and an immigrant—had tapped into the "old boys' network" and found a job. Immigrants are often kept out of jobs because they are not part of the network. Women have also been excluded this way, although they have had some success in forming their own networks. However, the old network got me a job.

I began teaching at York in 1976. Over the years I had slowly became conscious that changes in my name, dress, or mannerisms made no significant difference in other Canadians' perceptions of me. To them, my immigrant status and the colour of my skin were my most important characteristics. My experiences of exclusion at the university and my desire to understand white Canadians' perception of me were to determine the subject of much of my research and writing.

In the 1970s women were becoming a subject of research. Some women on the faculty at York shared the enthusiasm generated by feminism and wanted to teach about it. Few, if any, had formal academic qualifications in the field or had done much research on it, but they got together and designed a course called "On Women," offering it jointly through the divisions of Social Science and Humanities. I, too, wanted to teach a course on women. I thought I was well placed to do so, since I had written my dissertation on women in the nationalist movement in India. I also knew that the undergraduate director who had hired me was looking for faculty to teach in Women's Studies. However, when I asked her to consider me, she said peremptorily, "Vijay, your expertise is on women in the Third World. You cannot teach these courses." Her response reflected the fact that feminism was a white women's movement at the time. She assigned me instead to teach a course on immigration, even though my only real qualification for it was having worked part-time for a few months collecting archival material on South Asians in Toronto for the Multicultural History Society of Ontario. I was an immigrant, though, and that seemed to suffice. In the summer of 1978, before teaching the course, I read articles and books on South Asian and other immigrants in Canada.

My readings on immigration policy and on the varied immigrant groups that had come to Canada provided me with new insight into my social location in Canada, and helped to show me "who I was" in the full Canadian context. I was illustrating the adage that to know history is to know oneself.

I read about the first wave of South Asians who had settled in Vancouver in the early 1900s. There, isolated from white Canadian society, they had experienced extreme racism. I was shocked to discover that only a handful of women from India had been allowed to immigrate to Canada. Even greater difficulties were experienced by Chinese immigrants during the same period. Yet, the pain and suffering of the Indian and Chinese immigrants paled when compared to the tragedy of the internment of the Japanese during World War II. I read Joy Kogawa's *Obasan*, and it made a deep and lasting impression on me. The struggles of the Nisei (second-generation Japanese Canadians) to define their identity during the war between Canada and Japan resonated in my mind.

Before I read this literature, some of my own experiences had made me uncomfortable, but I had shrugged them off since I did not have the language or analytical tools to label them. Many of the incidents that had disturbed me were insignificant in themselves, but over time, as they accumulated, they reinforced my feelings of being an outsider. I began to see some incidents at the university as racist.

In the mid-1970s—as at the present time—there was only a handful of South Asian women on the faculty at York. Indhu is a South Asian who, like me, has taught courses there for several years. Some members of the white faculty call me Indhu by mistake. They confuse me with her, but of course never with Mary or with Jane. Yet Indhu's physical appearance is very different from mine. She is tall, and I am short. She has long, jet-black hair, and I have very short hair. She does not wear spectacles. When I meet people in the hallway and they say, "Hi, Indhu!" to me, I want to ask them what similarities they see in us. But I know the answer. They have only noticed skin colour.

This kind of tunnel vision was most boldly evidenced when I was working on contract, with no permanent office at York. Every year my office mate was always non-white. This struck me as odd, since there were so few non-white faculty members and teaching assistants. I had no objection to my office mates and enjoyed being with them, but the assignment did seem deliberate, not a mere coincidence. I often chatted with the woman who was in charge of space at the division, so one day I asked her why I was always assigned an office with another non-white person. "Oh!" she said. "I thought you would be more comfortable with your own kind of people." It's nearly incredible to me now that she said this, but it is clear what "kind" she had in mind. Not people who shared an area of research or study, or who were part of a teaching team in a course. She didn't sort people by religion. Her criterion was race.

Some people at least have the decency to be embarrassed. Just a couple of years ago I went to hear a renowned Indian feminist, Bina Aggarwal, give a talk in the Political Science department, one floor below Social Science. As I walked in that direction, I was approached by a middle-aged, white political science professor who asked me, without thinking, "Where are you from?" Nonplussed, I replied, "From the seventh floor." He abashedly tried to make amends by engaging me further in conversation.

My life of privilege in Bombay probably gave me the confidence to withstand what some would consider attacks on their self-esteem. I was simply annoyed by the perceptions of white faculty members and students in Canada. I was protected in many ways by the "ivory tower," with its enlightened values. How much more difficult must life be for my compatriots on the factory floor and the assembly line. Nevertheless, it was galling to have my skin colour be the only aspect of my identity that mattered. I had come to Canada to be free, and to grow intellectually. In Bombay I had felt hampered by the protectiveness of my family, constrained by their desire that I conform to custom and tradition. Now my skin colour became an impediment to interaction with most white Canadians in the university. Yet, I felt that I was ready to face the world as an Indian woman. Indeed, I began thinking like James Joyce's Stephen Daedalus: "I go to encounter for the millionth time the reality of experience and to forge in the smithy of my soul the uncreated conscience of my race."[3]

Many of the students who take my courses are children of European or Third World immigrants. But in terms of political consciousness of themselves as immigrants—for this is how they are perceived—they are not much different from me in the early 1970s. Many seem to be searching, if only subconsciously, for answers to their personal dilemmas by taking my courses.

At the beginning my courses on women or on immigrants, I ask the students "who they are." Most answer simply, "I'm just a Canadian," or "I am Jewish," or "My parents are Italian but I am Canadian," or "I am Chinese," or "I am an Indo-Canadian." When I ask them what made them decide to take my course, they are reticent, giving only polite replies. They do not say they wanted to learn more about themselves, but that they thought they should know more about immigrants. Or that hearing their immigrant parents talk about the "old country" had piqued their curiosity. As the course progresses, though, I find that these initial responses do not necessarily capture the students' sense of themselves. When they feel more comfortable with me, they discuss their ethnic and immigrant backgrounds, tell me stories about their immigrant parents, and share some of the experiences they have had with the larger, mainstream society. But they are seldom assertive about their ethnic identities.

Most of my students are quite apolitical. Their perspective has been shaped by the public discourse on multiculturalism, which is about including different cultures in mainstream society rather than about struggling against the power relations underlying Eurocentrism. In 1992 I saw a television documentary produced in the United States called *School Colors*. It described the experiences of high school students in Berkeley, California who demanded a change from their Eurocentric curricula. In particular, the students wanted to learn about black American history from a young black male teacher with long dreadlocks. The success of black-studies programs led Hispanic and Chinese students to demand their own area studies, too. I showed this documentary to one of my classes, but my students did not relate to the activism in the documentary. In fact, they were quite uncomprehending of the students in California and were not interested in becoming social activists. They wanted to find jobs after they graduated. They wanted a degree that employers would view favourably, and they didn't think studies in a non-Eurocentric curriculum would count for much with white Canadian employers.

I have found more commonality of interest with the few non-white faculty women that I have met at academic conferences at various universities in Canada. We gravitate towards one another either from being on the same discussion panels or from noting each other in the sea of white faces. After a day's formal events are over and we are looking for dinner companions, we often get together. Sometimes we are familiar with each other's written work, and it is fun to attach a face to a name. We quickly forge friendships based on common experiences at Canadian universities.

Now, as the time approaches every year to attend the national Congress of Learned Societies, I am comforted by the thought that I won't be sitting lonely and forlorn, drinking coffee or having lunch amidst chattering groups of white faculty members. I can meet one of these women or the black and South Asian men in attendance. Sometimes I feel self-conscious about doing this, and fear that I am ghettoizing myself! It's not that

I don't want to share a meal with the white attendees, or they with me, I assume. However, these conferences are occasions for people to network, and there is no perceived benefit in the academic world to schmoozing with a marginalized Indian woman.

My South Asian and black academic friends and I have invariably encountered some unpleasant experience of racism in our teaching in the year leading up to the conference. On one level I experience relief when I hear their stories, because they reassure me that I am not the only one to have encountered racism. I pick up tips on how to deal with unpleasant situations in the classroom or at departmental meetings. We share our success stories with each other—a paper or a book accepted for publication, a research grant—and we scrutinize these successes for clues as to what worked, and why. We swap stories of who has been newly hired, and to what position, and the hidden agenda behind the appointments. When I was going up for tenure, I turned to them for advice, and when asked by the university, they wrote letters attesting to my scholarship. I celebrated with them on being granted tenure.

My experiences at the university have made me realize that I have to struggle to protect my atman, rather than allow the perceptions of others to define me or be caged by the assumptions of colleagues and students. This reminds me of the lesson I learned from my father: the world is illusory, and only the soul is real.

Returning to Bombay

As a young adult I had been anxious to leave home, and it was only after I left that I realized I might sometime want to go back. Still later I discovered the truth of the saying that you can't go home again. Home in Bombay was a secure place with daily routines with which I was comfortable. I felt that I had a right to be there and that I was an integral part of the lives of my siblings and father. I had responsibilities and obligations towards members of my family, and they towards me, and we tried to live up to them. At home I could reveal doubts or anxieties about myself and find first criticism for having them at all, and then help in alleviating them. The atmosphere was imbued with love even though, being an undemonstrative family, we seldom expressed it in hugs and kisses. Caught up in the excitement of leaving, I imagined that home would always be there, constant and unchanging, and that I could come back when I chose. I have gone back to India periodically, but my life and studies in Canada have changed my perspective, and I am never quite "at home" there now.

By 1980 I had become much more comfortable in Toronto. I could navigate the streets with easy familiarity, guide lost tourists to all the major attractions, and zip up and down the aisles of the local supermarket to precisely the right location for needed groceries. Sometimes, if I was in a more pensive and vulnerable mindset, the cold air, sanitized floors and looming racks of the grocery store, with their twenty different types of

Notes to chapter 8 are on p. 282.

peanut butter, made me long for the chaos and confusion of the bazaars of Bombay and Delhi. Yet, when I visited India, I felt overwhelmed and defeated by the unceasing noise. Rushdie describes the "tumultuous sensations of the city, the scents of chana and bhel [lentils and puffed rice], of tamarind and jasmine, the shouting voices, because nobody ever says anything in these parts without first raising their voices; and the quarrel of traffic, the hooves, the sputtering exhausts, the bicycle bells, the brilliant lights of the sun on the harbour, the hooting of warships and the electricity of a society at the point of transformation."[1]

I vividly recall a trip to Bombay in 1980 when Nicole was two years old. I remember it more than some other visits because taking her with me gave rise to intense anxieties. I worried about whether she would adjust to the completely different food and if the visit would pose risks to her health. I made several visits to doctors for inoculations and prescriptions for diarrhea and other ailments, trying to provide for every contingency. These preparations made me think—like any Canadian going on vacation to Asia—about how different Bombay was from Toronto.

By 1980 I was also more or less settled into teaching at York University. One of the courses I taught was on the Third World. The readings in the course and the ideas and opinions of my colleagues made me question things I had previously disregarded, such as the wide gap between the rich and the poor. The course was taught, as many such courses are, from a Marxist perspective, and I found that one of the harshest critics of Western capitalist culture also had considerable contempt for India. As Oscar and Mary Handlin say in the introduction to their book *From the Outer World*, Marx regarded India as the "ultimate in human degradation— where man, the sovereign of nature, fell down on his knees in adoration of Hanuman, the monkey, and Sabbala, the cow."[2]

The Marxist literature on the Third World and the discussions with students in my classroom politicized me. I became critical of the colonial education I had received in India, and sensitive to comments about India's poverty. White Canadian students sometimes said that the "backward" cultures and societies of Third World countries had left them "underdeveloped" and poor. Students with immigrant Third World backgrounds would respond with remarks about the plunder and looting of colonial societies by European nations. One female Indian student told the class about the Kohinoor diamond. The largest and most conspicuous of the gems that were stolen from India, it now forms the centrepiece of the crown of the

Queen of England. The Indian students visualized an India awash with diamonds and emeralds, and directed the discussion away from poverty and underdevelopment to the history of oppression and exploitation.

Students from countries such as India chafed at the label "Third World," which ranked them down in third place below the superpowers and Europe. They resented this exercise of Western power and privilege in labelling countries and people. We avoided offending them with this negative term by calling our course "Problems of Developing Countries," but that title was still derogatory, for another reason. One of my Indian colleagues, when asked to teach this course, discreetly changed the title to "Problems and Prospects of Developing Countries."

On my trip to India with two-year-old Nicole I tried to observe the interactions of the poor and the rich. It is, after all, one thing to understand on an intellectual level the causes of India's poverty and its lack of technological development, and quite another to be struck in the face with the poverty—to bear witness to it. Many South Asian immigrants, prior to visiting India, take their children to poor and rundown neighbourhoods in the cities where they live in Canada to prepare them for the extremes of poverty seen everywhere in India. Such preparation is not usually very helpful, however, for poverty is experienced in vastly different ways in Canada and India. People living on welfare in a public-housing complex may be considered poor in Canada, but in India the same kind of housing and financial resources would be available only to middle-class individuals; "poor housing" is living in pup tents, discarded water pipes, or on little mats on the pavement. The numbers of people afflicted with poverty, and the striking and ever-present contrast between rich and poor, are also much more evident in India. Such disparity can raise issues of personal ethics and make one feel guilty about going to a restaurant or buying consumer goods while others are starving. In Canada, we can take comfort in the thought that the government provides for the poor, even if we are critical of the extent of help given.

I was very conscious in India of my position in what Marxists would call the exploitative and oppressive capitalist class. Neither the villains that the Marxists portrayed, nor perfectly upright moral human beings, the privileged Indians that made up my community seemed as full of contradictions and frailties as my friends and colleagues in Toronto. At the end of the trip, I returned to Canada in a state of confusion over the problematic relationship of rich and poor in India.

Airplanes from the west usually arrive in Bombay in the middle of the night to accommodate convenient departure times in European and North American locations. Nicole and I arrived in August, the tail end of the monsoon season. The heat and humidity completely enveloped us as we got off the plane and walked over the tarmac to the terminal. The line at immigration was composed almost entirely of Indians, and I, for a change, was just one of the crowd. There was no baggage carousel, and so suitcases were carried in manually by porters and placed in a cordoned-off area. There, chaos reigned, with passengers and porters pushing and shoving, people talking loudly in several different dialects and gesticulating to spouses and children, and everyone in a mad hurry to identify his or her baggage and be the first one out of the airport.

I cheerfully joined this confusion, weaving through the crowd of sleepy children and brightly coloured, floating dupattas to locate my bags and some porters to carry them for me. As I approached the glass wall separating the airport building from the outdoors, I swallowed a lump in my throat and tried to settle my nerves. Outside there was a mob of people straining to see the passengers they had come to meet while cars tried to make their way through the crowd with an endless honking of horns. The minute I became part of that horde of people, I began to panic and clutched Nicole, but luckily, just as fear was beginning to overwhelm me, my brother Devinder spotted me and elbowed his way through the crowd to rescue us. He immediately took charge, dealt with the baggage, paid the porters, and piled us into the car. It only took a couple of minutes to slip into my accustomed role in Bombay: letting the males in my family do things for me.

The drive from the airport to my father's home in the middle of the night presented the landscape starkly, without the usual masses of people obscuring the view. There were huge pipes near the airport that were being used as sleeping quarters by homeless beggars. Rags were flying in the wind from atop tin huts. People were lying huddled on the streets, apparently sleeping soundly, and garbage was liberally strewn on the streets. The worst thing was the smell of urine, which permeated the air. Memories of visits to an aunt's house flashed through my mind. She had an apartment in Bombay with a gorgeous, unimpeded view of the Indian Ocean. When I spent the night at her house I loved to wake up in the morning and go outside on the veranda to drink my tea and enjoy the scenery. Soon, though, I would see people in ragged clothes walking towards the rocks and defecating on them. I would feel frustrated and unhappy at having my idyllic view thus ruined, but when I complained, my aunt would retort sharply, "Where do you think they should go? Are they not human beings like us with similar needs?" I remembered her strictures, but nevertheless felt nauseated. I wondered how I would ever be able to bear such a stench for three weeks. However, once I got to my father's apartment and found him sitting up waiting for me, the happiness of being with him chased all other thoughts from my mind. The next morning, when I woke up and went out, I could not smell anything in the air. I guess my senses had automatically adjusted themselves to the environment.

Throughout this visit I was constantly nagged by a misgiving that perhaps I perceived my surroundings through "Canadian" eyes. I wondered how I could have previously failed to notice the infinity of crowds on the streets and the constant buzz of activity. Had there always been so much noise and confusion? Obviously it had been such a normal part of my environment that I had paid no attention to it. In Toronto, I had missed the feeling of belonging to a family and community. It was the desire for that which had brought me to Bombay, but the way I was now scrutinizing my surroundings marked me as an outsider, and it was galling to be treated by family and friends as a temporary visitor.

Coming "home" to Bombay as a mature woman and mother meant that I was now invited to women's get-togethers. Most of the women I spent time with socially were part of the leisured classes, and their primary responsibility was to manage their households and supervise the help. Some Marxists would describe them as women who did no productive work; after all, paid help did the cooking, washing, and cleaning. However, this does not capture the way these women thought of themselves. They considered the care that they lavished on homes and families and in building social networks critical to the well-being of their families.

Whenever I visited Bombay, I fell into the old habit of deferring to my father's wishes about whom I should spend my time with. He had ambiguous feelings about my joining the women for their morning coffee parties after the children had left for school and husbands had gone to work. On the one hand, he wanted me to renew my ties by spending time with them, but on the other he felt that they gossiped and wasted their time, and he did not want to seem to be encouraging me to do the same. The conversations that preceded such get-togethers constituted an ongoing dialogue between us.

The women, dressed in freshly starched and ironed cotton saris, would gather together in the one of their homes or sometimes more formally in a restaurant; the atmosphere in either case was relaxed and friendly. If we were in someone's home, we would often sit on the balcony, on cane chairs laid out on a carpeted floor. The maid would serve tea and coffee to us in fine china cups and saucers on a tray covered with starched linen with a matching tea cosy. Some of the women liked masala-chai, which, unlike the hastily prepared chai served at the Indian movies in Toronto, had been carefully and slowly brewed to draw out the rich flavours of cardamoms and cinnamon.

As the women talked, there was no sense of being rushed for time or being burdened with chores needing to be done. They shared with each other the happenings of the day or the week before. For example, if there was a rice or sugar shortage, they passed on the news as to which grocer had just received a stock of the desired item. Difficulties experienced by the children were thoroughly analyzed and solutions and strategies proposed. Similarly, news about the household help was shared, such as a cook's threatening to quit or attend to personal matters in her village just when house guests were expected. The discussion was frank, with little compunction about intervening in other people's lives or invading their privacy. Advice was freely dispensed. The women relied on each other for emotional and psychological support.

Although it is common for males to characterize such talk as idle gossip, it also builds and maintains useful networks. Through the constant routine of meeting and talking, information about particular families (and extended families) becomes known to the others. For example, the group knew that one of my brothers was, at the time, a physician in the United States. Thus, if someone needed medical treatment and could travel to the U.S. to obtain it, we could call him on their behalf for advice and information. They knew who among them was related to a politician, a senior bureaucrat, a lawyer, or other professionals. This information is invaluable to businesses in India, where much work is facilitated through influential contacts.

On a subsequent trip, when Nicole was six years old, she was puzzled that my sister-in-law did no housework and did not have a job. One day she asked, "Auntie, what do you do?" My sister-in-law responded cheerfully, "Nothing. I'm a lady of leisure." Devaluing the work that she did for the family as "nothing" echoed the way a male society values and characterizes women's work.

The women did not consider me one of them, an insider who could share their day-to-day joys and tribulations. They just wanted to impress me by showing me the new Bombay they were proud of—the new stores, hotels and restaurants, skyscrapers and overpasses, modern factories and research institutes. They told me of their frequent travels outside India. They emphasized the new availability of mass-produced consumer goods, such as televisions sets ("...much like Western societies," they said), which were not only available but were being widely bought. They narrated the details of their purchases of paintings and mosaics by prominent Indian artists, such as Hussain and I. K. Gujral, and of reproductions of antique Indian sculptures. Increasing numbers of Indians were affluent, they stated assuredly.

It would have been easy for me to contradict them by giving the statistics on poverty. I could have told them about the increasing gap between the rich and the poor in India since independence. However, they would have been affronted by a discussion of India's poverty. They wanted to talk about the signs of progress and achievement in India. To harp on about the numbers of poor in India or the ever-present signs of dehumanizing poverty all around us would have constituted bad manners on my part. It would have been like being invited to dinner at a friend's house and then finding fault with the furniture, dishes, and cooking. Besides, they now regarded me as a "Canadian," and an outsider. No doubt they thought I had forfeited my birthright of criticizing India or Indians.

The Marxist books that I had read in Toronto referred to people like my friends and relatives as the parasitical class. Critical of their consumption of consumer goods, these texts described them as oppressive and greedy: capitalists who had gained their wealth by exploiting the poor. Insensitivity to the needs of the poor and the working class had enabled such people to accumulate wealth and invest it in an ever-expanding range of ventures that made them more profit and therefore more wealth. But up close, at an individual level, they seemed generous and compassionate.

Anu, a neighbour who was also a relative, embodied this unconscious charity. Anu had a cook named Angela, whom I had known for several years. Angela had fallen in love with a driver and "run away with him." However, the man had abandoned her soon after the birth of a baby girl, and since Angela had not married the man, her relatives refused to have anything to do with her. Angela had nowhere to go. She came back to ask Anu for a loan to tide her over the hard times. She was adamant about keeping the baby, whom she had named Nita. Anu, who was without a cook at the time, offered to employ Angela and to let her keep the baby with her in the house, contrary to usual practice. Most of Anu's friends considered her offer an act of great generosity because of the limited physical space available to most families in Bombay, though others regarded it as foolish.

Anu and her family then insisted that Nita be fed and clothed at their expense. Nita went to a nursery school and then to grade school. Anu paid for the school fees. The family physician took care of Nita along with everyone else. Angela, though, wanted Nita to be aware of the difference between her situation in life and that of the family with whom she lived and worked. By the time Nita was eight or nine years old, Angela insisted that she refer to everyone formally by title—as sahib or memsahib[†]— rather than by name. She also started to teach her some simple tasks, such as serving water to people or waiting on the table at dinnertime.

Nita came by to see me when I was visiting Bombay. As usual, she was dressed well—in a Benetton sweatshirt and jeans—much like any middle-class teenager. (Anu's family owned garment factories and manufactured clothes for multinational corporations, so clothing was always plentiful.) She had completed Grade 10 and Anu had found a job for her in the clothing factory; she earned a good wage by Indian standards and continued to live with the family. But Nita's conversation with me revealed that issues of identity troubled her. Who was she? Who comprised her family and community? Her good fortune in finding a home and becoming educated had also left her without a community of her own. In the class-conscious Indian society, she belonged neither to the world of middle-class people nor to the world of cooks and maids. Anu's generosity had solved some problems for Angela, but it had created new ones for Nita. It made me realize that the everyday relations between the rich and the poor were more complicated than Marxists envisaged, and could not be reduced to straightforward and simple formulations of exploiter and exploited.

Within a day or so of our arrival in Bombay on our visit, I had slipped back into the routine of my father's household. By six o'clock in the morning the street was slowly coming to life and the noise of the milkman,

---

† The terms sahib and memsahib were most commonly used by Indian servants for their British masters and mistresses. However, they have since become part of the Hindi vocabulary and are often used to refer to rich people. Sometimes the word sahib is used derogatorily to refer to someone who is presumptuous or arrogant.

newspaperman, and street cleaners floated up to the apartment. Soon
after, various people began arriving to perform daily chores: wash the car,
do the laundry, cook or clean. Since many of them had been coming to
the apartment for years, they chatted for a few minutes with me. I enjoyed
being with people who knew me and to whom I did not have to explain
myself, as I felt I needed to do in Canada.

Although I have referred to people who worked in the house as
"household help," they are usually referred to in Bombay—and in other
parts of India—as *bai* (maid), *ayah* (nanny), or more generally as *nokar*
(a servant responsible for a myriad of tasks in the household). In some
very affluent households there are *khansamas*, or cooks. Referring to
them as household help may accord them a greater dignity than they
actually experience, but referring to them as servants might create the
impression that they are treated in an inhumane or cruel manner, which
is not the case, either. Having been made acutely aware of my class privilege in Indian society through my studies in Canada, I felt uneasy about
my own situation, and anxious about the feelings of people who worked
for our family. I worried about how my father's cook, Sushila, a woman in
her early forties, regarded me. I sat around all day visiting with other
women, drinking endless cups of tea, which she prepared for me, and eating meals she adapted to suit my taste and preference. Whenever I
attempted to go to the kitchen, I was politely ushered out of the cook's
domain. "What do you want?" Sushila would ask me firmly, urging me to
go and sit down. "I will bring it to you." I cringed when she brought me
a cup of tea or a glass of water.

I didn't have to worry about Nicole, either, because she too was being
cared for by others. She loved the hustle and bustle of the household, and
enjoyed talking to different people who came to the house. However, she
did not quite take to the food, which was not only spicy, but had a different taste and aroma from what she was accustomed to. Although she ate
her meals, it was without enthusiasm. Our doctor had recommended that
she drink no milk, so Sushila made fresh orange juice for her, but it also
tasted different. Mostly Nicole ate boiled eggs and freshly made *roti*, a flat,
unleavened bread, and remained healthy.

I saw only friendliness and goodwill when I interacted with the people who worked for our family. The skeptic in me was well aware that they
all expected to get a handsome tip, either from my father or me, during my
visit there. In a slight variation of the religious practice of making an

offering of thanks to the gods, middle-class Indians often give charity to the poor to mark significant events—such as a married daughter's visit to her parents. It may be a way to assuage guilty consciences, but nevertheless, the household help were all dropping hints to me while I was there. One person suggested that by the time we left, all of Nicole's clothes would be worn out and could be left behind for her granddaughter. Another announced the forthcoming wedding of a daughter. Yet another complained vociferously about the rising cost of living and the difficulties of feeding a family.

One day, to appease my conscience, I mentioned to Sushila that I did all my housework in Toronto, as well as work at the university. Sushila was horrified, exclaiming that it was impossible for any one person to work at so many things. She also declared that she would have to accompany me back to Toronto to help out. Or, she said, I could take her daughter, a sixteen-year-old who was keen to accompany me as a maid. For the rest of the visit she constantly harped on this topic. I had difficulty explaining that I could not possibly take either of them with me to Toronto. I mentioned the harsh winters, the social isolation she would encounter, and the difficulty she would have in adjusting to life there. Sushila, however, brushed these aside. She knew little about the West except that it was very affluent. Her logic was simple and straightforward: a maid in "America" could earn better wages than a maid in India. I presented an opportunity to her and she was loathe to give it up. My concerns were different. I had no need for her and did not want to have this financial obligation. There would be legal and immigration difficulties. Besides, I did not want to be dubbed a middle-class woman who was liberating herself by exploiting a poor woman. I firmly resisted her importuning.

When I came back from shopping, Sushila would eagerly ask to see my purchases. I would be torn by guilt and would fret about her feelings. What did she feel, I wondered, when she saw my shopping? From her perspective, I had a great deal of money to spend, and although she was well dressed and comfortable, in comparison to me she had very little. I detected little evidence of envy or resentment, though. Did she have a way of rationalizing her situation that enabled her to cope psychologically and emotionally with the evident difference between us? Did she accept her situation in life as part of her "karma"?

My readings on the Third World were of little help in understanding Sushila and the other household help. I wondered whether they were simply passive and ignorant, but that did not seem to be the case. In daily interaction they seemed quite intelligent and keenly aware of their own interests. Perhaps they had internalized their oppression to such an extent that they were no longer conscious of their continuing exploitation. Perhaps they saw themselves in comparison with many other poor people on the streets and in their villages and were proud that they had done so well. They had plenty to eat and drink and good clothes to wear. Perhaps it was simply the normality of the status quo and the acceptance by all concerned of the roles assigned to them by their culture. Acceptance kept the household routine moving smoothly and calmly.

When I mentioned my misgivings to my middle-class relatives, they thought life in Toronto had made me soft in the head. Nevertheless, there were social changes, and my relatives were adapting to them from necessity, although they didn't seem to understand what was occurring. One day, while I was visiting my sister-in-law, she exclaimed, "Oh! I must tell you what happened at your father's house last month." Velu, the untouchable who came to work in our house, had announced that his son was to be married shortly. A few days later the doorbell rang, and when my sister-in-law answered the door, she found a young man dressed in a business suit with an invitation in hand. He introduced himself as Velu's son, and said that he had come personally to invite my family to his wedding. My sister-in-law said she was flabbergasted: "What could I do," she wailed, "but invite him to come and sit down in the living room?" In the course of their conversation, the young man told her that he had graduated with a bachelor's degree from Bombay University and had found himself a job with the government.

My family disapproved of untouchability, by which they meant discriminating against other people on the basis of ascribed status or birth. They also did not believe in the traditional notions of purity and pollution fundamental to the maintenance of the caste system, or that sharing a meal with an untouchable would pollute them. But since class and caste oppression are interlinked, most untouchables also tend to be poor, and thus experience class barriers as well. Although my sister-in-law did not believe in untouchability, she was reluctant nevertheless to socialize with people from a stratum of society different from her own. (Such a bias is common in India, and almost all upper-middle-class Indians would never consider sitting down with their household help and sharing a meal with them.) But at that moment, she said, her mind was racing. She wondered whether he expected her to offer him tea and treat him like any other guest, and so she decided to share tea and savouries with the young man. I rejoiced at this change, but she had less consciousness of the significance of what she had done. She was more concerned that she had behaved in a "decent" and gracious manner.

Although there were these few beacons of change, I read several depressing accounts in newspapers of violence inflicted on untouchables in smaller towns and villages when they tried to breach caste rules. The anonymity that characterizes large cosmopolitan cities like Bombay provides more opportunities for untouchables to mix freely. They can travel on buses, eat and drink in restaurants, attend colleges and universities and, hopefully, find jobs.

I also remember an elderly aunt who phoned and invited me to go with her to the local temple on Tuesday, the sacred day of the week for Hindus. Although as a non-practising Hindu I usually don't go to temples, I agreed to make the visit with her. On the appointed day, my father reminded me as I was leaving the house to take some money so that I could buy some food to distribute to the poor, who were always gathered outside the temple. He handed me a small bag of coins to give to them.

Charity is an integral part of religion, but even when I lived in India I had heard people make critical remarks about the wealth hoarded in temples and the corruption of the priests. Some of the books that I had read in Toronto alleged that India's lack of industrial development was because of the penchant of middle-class Indians to turn their capital into jewellery to hang around the necks of women and gods. So I was not about to make any donations to the temples or to the priests, whom I considered to be greedy and grasping rather than religious and devout.

The walk to the temple through the bazaar took a few minutes, and then suddenly the scene transformed into one imbued with religious symbolism. A line of little carts was strung with the marigold garlands used by Hindus in their devotional rituals. Filling the beds of the carts were cups made of dried leaves that contained fresh rose petals; these would be sprinkled on the statues of the gods during prayers. Further along were vendors with decorated stalls selling sweetmeats and fruits to be given as offerings to the gods and later distributed to the poor. I bought a few dozen bananas and took them with me to the temple. It was crowded, and we had to wait in line to get to the statues. There, my aunt prayed for a couple of minutes and the priest blessed her by gently touching her head. He did the same to me, and to the bananas I was carrying. I do not know whether he was being polite or reminding me to make a donation, but I resisted the perceived hint and refused to put my hand in my purse.

Outside the temple door were two lines of children, some of whom looked to be about four years old, waiting along with some adolescents to get their share of the fruit and sweetmeats. A man with a stick was trying to maintain some order amongst them. I started to distribute the bananas and money, but pandemonium broke out immediately as the children mobbed me. Bewildered at the speed with which the orderly line had disintegrated, I stood immobile as money and fruit were quickly snatched away. Less than a minute later, my hands were empty. Seeing this, the older children ran away, but the younger ones hung on to my clothes and begged for food and money. I was upset, since clearly the older and stronger boys had grabbed more than their share and the younger children had been unable to get anything. I was still trying to comprehend what had happened when I was accosted by women with babies in their arms, also begging for food and money. One enterprising vendor came over and sold me his remaining few dozen bananas, but within seconds the pushy older children had grabbed these too. Disgruntled, I started walking away from the temple with my aunt, who enquired acidly, "Feeling better?" I kept quiet and continued walking.

At home I gave vent to my frustration by complaining to my father about the unfairness of what had happened at the temple. His cynical and sarcastic remark depressed me further: "Stop fretting!" he said. "Nobody eats the bananas, not the young or the older children. They are already back in the vendor's basket and are being sold to the next gullible fool who comes around." I was saddened by the futility of my gesture, and of similar gestures made by countless others in temples across India. I wondered what I could possibly do to help the little children or the women with babies in their arms. Could individual acts of generosity make a difference to a small child? Faced with the enormity of the problem of the poor in India, what could I do?

I had spent a great deal of my time with my relatives in their homes or going out shopping or to restaurants. I dubbed these places "the five-star India." After I had done enough of this, I had an urge to see some other aspects of Bombay. Although not inclined temperamentally to be very adventurous, I wanted to see the life of the common people (without thinking too much about what or who I meant by that). However, since my arrival in Bombay, the inhibitions and restraints of my youth had reasserted themselves and made me think that it would be unsafe for me— a middle-class woman—to go to a poor district. I worried that I might not have the courage to look poverty straight in the eye. When confronted with the horrifying reality, I knew I would feel devastated.

I decided to visit what I termed "the three-star India." This was as close as I could get to the "real" India. I took a walk around an area of downtown Bombay called the Flora Fountain, built in 1869 to honour a British governor of the city. The fountain is an ornate structure built in stone, with mythological figures topped by a representation of Flora, the Roman goddess of flowers. The fountain has long since gone dry, and is now used during the day by vendors to display their wares and at night by street people as sleeping quarters. The statues are liberally covered with pigeon droppings. The fountain stands at the junction of five main roads, and this is also the neighbourhood where the university, High Court, museum, and stock market are located.

Flora Fountain is full of stately buildings that at one time must have conveyed the grandeur of the British Raj. However, the stone of the buildings has faded in the sun and is now covered with layers of dirt and soot, giving it an unattractive, grey-brown colour. Balconies on the façades of the buildings are festooned with awnings and enclosures of all shapes and styles in glass and wood. The enormous cost of space in downtown Bombay makes considerations of beauty incidental. "Who cares?" I can hear developers and lucky residents saying of their reluctance to restore the buildings. "Why should I give up an opportunity to provide for the education or marriage of my child? For the sake of beauty...or history?"

Arcades that were originally designed to allow people to escape the heat of the sun link the buildings. They were chock-a-block with people as I walked through, jostled by the hordes of humanity: pushing and shoving, eating and drinking, hawking and begging. In this crush of people there was no choosing one's pace; one had to go along with the momentum of the crowd. At every step I was met by aggressive salesmen trying to push their wares while I tried desperately to bypass them. Goods were displayed on every inch of the walls and jealously guarded by their sellers. There were magazines, clothes, plastic tumblers, imported perfumes, radios, shoes, food, and any number of assorted items. Even though I walked fast and adopted a determined gait, that did not stop beggars from touching my arm and pleading with me.

The beggars that I saw here remind me of the scene described by Salman Rushdie in *Midnight's Children* when the protagonist's middle-class mother visits a neighbourhood in old Delhi near the Red Fort in 1947:

> Under the pressure of these streets which are growing narrower by the minute, more crowded by the inch, she has lost her "city eyes." When you have city eyes you cannot see the invisible people, the men with elephantiasis of the balls and the beggars in boxcars don't impinge on you, and the concrete sections of future drainpipes don't look like dormitories.
>
> My mother lost her city eyes...Look, my god, those beautiful children have black teeth! Would you believe...girl children baring their nipples! How terrible, truly! And, Allah-tobah, heaven forfend, sweeper women with—no!—how *dreadful!*—collapsed spines, and bunches of twigs, and no caste marks; untouchables, sweet Allah!...and cripples everywhere, mutilated by loving parents to ensure them of a lifelong income from begging...yes, beggars in boxcars, grown men with babies' legs, in crates on wheels, made out of discarded roller-skates and old mango boxes...[3]

The crowded arcade on one side and the noisy road on the other frightened and overwhelmed me. I became less concerned about seeing the "real" India and more intent on getting out of there. In the road traffic, swirling dust and clouds of smoke replaced the congestion of people. I had to constantly watch my step and keep off the little sections of pavement occupied by the shoeshine men, the palmists and astrologers, the *sadhus*, or holy men, and the trinket sellers. I had to take care not to put my foot into the piles of rotting banana peels or into the dirty, reeking puddles.

I passed a cart equipped with a sugar-cane press for squeezing juice. It was well decorated with marigold garlands and a row of glass tumblers attractively filled with limes to attract customers. But I was not enchanted. I worried instead about the unwashed glasses and flies buzzing above the sugar cane. Someone coming to India for the first time might find the cart with the sugar-cane press "quaint," just as they might find the manifestations of poverty and underdevelopment "exotic." To me, the cart meant dysentery and diarrhea, and I did not indulge myself by drinking the sugar-cane juice. That would have put me in touch with the "real" India! When I got home, my father asked if I had enjoyed seeing the "real" India. I could not answer.

The contrasts between the lives of the rich and poor in India have provided material for many filmmakers and journalists from Europe and North America. The middle-class and the rich are caricatured, their ambitions made to seem petty and selfish. I, too, was finding my middle-class friends and relatives self-centred and shamelessly acquisitive. Their lack of concern for the poor seemed heartless to me. Their fascination with Western consumer goods amidst so much poverty seemed morally and ethically wrong. However, if I voiced my qualms—even mildly—they turned the tables on me by retorting, "Don't you go to restaurants in Toronto? How much do you spend there?"

"Yes, but..."

Even though I felt conscience-stricken, I could not resist going to some of my favourite restaurants. One of them was the Sea Lounge in the Taj Mahal Hotel. The hotel is located on the coast of the Indian Ocean, right in front of Gateway of India, a high stone archway built in 1924 to commemorate the visit of George V and Queen Mary in 1912. The Taj, as it is commonly called, is a "flamboyant stylistic mélange"[4] of Gothic Revival and Indian decorative elements built in 1904 by a Parsi businessman. A British architect designed it, but somehow a mistake was made and it was placed backwards, and so the palm-covered garden entrance faces a side street. The façade of the building has arched windows with stone sills and is topped off with a dome. In the 1970s, a grand marble foyer and an additional wing were built, linking in a "weird mixture an old dignified world and a brash new one."[5] The area around the entrance of the building is cordoned off to keep beggars and vendors from harassing the guests, who get out of their cars in the protected enclosure and are greeted by a doorman dressed exotically in a long white coat and large red turban. When they leave, the doorman summons their drivers on a loudspeaker in the parking lot, and guests are able to step directly into their cars without having had any unpleasant encounter with the "real" India.

Inside the hotel there are wide, marble hallways lushly carpeted with rugs and decorated with beautifully carved and polished brass planters. Lavish fresh floral arrangements are visible throughout. Some Indian paintings and antique tapestries hang on the wall. The Sea Lounge is located on the second floor, and its walls are covered with more examples of Indian painting and tapestry. The waitresses, mostly young and pretty, are dressed impeccably in printed silk saris, with their hair neatly tied back. Their appearance is more elegant than that of most guests. Huge picture windows provide a view of the Indian Ocean. The road alongside the coast is full of beggar women with babes in their arms, children hoping to get tips by per-

forming tricks for the entertainment of passersby, and an assortment of
vendors and hawkers. If one sits at a table a little away from the windows,
one can enjoy an unimpeded view of the ocean without having, again, to
cope with the "real" India. A meal at the Taj costs more than a month's
wages of household help and factory employees. Eating there generated
uncomfortable ethical questions for me. My brief excursion into the "real"
India made me doubt myself and troubled my conscience. Nevertheless, I
had returned to my comfortable home and favourite haunts.

Most of the people I met in Bombay were religious. But rituals such as
going to temples, giving alms to the poor and celebrating religious holidays dominated their religion. The more devout attended early morning
prayer meetings to hear readings from Hindu scriptures and participated in
singing at religious gatherings. The household help also participated in
these rituals. They brought flowers and sweetmeats from the temple for
me. Many times they came to work wearing the red powder that had been
sprinkled on their foreheads by the temple priests.

On the roads, too, I found religious India. Sadhus were sitting on the
pavements in their saffron robes and ash-smeared foreheads, meditating
and selling religious beads. There were dozens of them outside temples or
simply walking with bowls in their hands. The sadhus made lavish prom-
ises of praying for the individual's eternal salvation and moksha in return
for a few coins. It seemed to me that the sadhus were more interested in
the pockets and purses of the people they encountered than with their
spiritual well-being. But everyone has to eat.

I didn't find much "other-worldliness" or "non-materialism" among
the people that I was encountering, although my father, who was now
semi-retired, did live an atypically ascetic and simple life. He always wore
a plain white shirt and pants. He ate only vegetarian food and consumed
no alcohol or tobacco. Sometimes he would go to his workplace for a couple of hours, but usually he checked up on his affairs by telephone. He
spent most of his time reading books on philosophy, meditating, and chatting with people who came to his house. There was very little television
programming in India during the 1970s, but he never watched it, anyway.
He never went to movies—not even in his own theatre—or to restaurants. His only entertainment was to go for walks. Yet I would not categorize him as "otherworldly" or "non-materialistic."

Hinduism is sometimes thought to be more a way of life than a religion.
It does not prescribe disengagement from the material, physical world

through all the stages of one's life. Rather, each stage has a specific set of duties and obligations. During the "householder" stage, men have to provide for their families, and women to nurture and care for them. However, once these duties have been fulfilled, the individual is expected to withdraw from worldly affairs and search for the Divine, seeking to become one with God. The people I met did not seem particularly conscious of this prescription, nor were they motivated by a desire to fulfill their religious obligations. They were not inspired by the Gandhian ideals of the virtues of simple and cooperative living. They were firmly entrenched in the physical and material world around them, much like people in Canada. Their goals were personal, individual, and material.

In trying to help individuals I encountered in Bombay, I was assuaging my conscience. Acts that were without much meaning in the larger context nevertheless relieved my anxiety. These small deeds did not provide equanimity; I continued my visit somewhat uncomfortable with the situation but resigned to accepting it as it was.

I gained some insight into myself as well. I learned that I was not inclined to be noble when my acts required me to sacrifice my own desires and goals for others. I came to the conclusion that I had no right to criticize upper-class people in India for being materialistic and acquisitive if I too was unwilling to put the needs of others ahead of my own.

9

A Third World Academic

On a cold, windy day in the fall of 1976 I arrived at York University to teach. The bus dropped me off outside the campus and I walked the rest of the way to the nine-storey Ross Building, the nucleus of the university. I was preoccupied, nervous about meeting the administrators and students, but still I noticed as I trudged along that the grounds on either side of the road were nearly barren. On one side, at some distance, there was a row of apartment buildings, and on the other was a parking lot. I decided to walk around a bit to familiarize myself with the campus before going to my class, but there was little I saw that was pleasant or reassuring. As I walked around I was further chilled by a cold wind that tunnelled between the unadorned buildings. I saw very few faces like mine, and this heightened my sense of foreboding, making me feel wary and insecure. Although I did not realize it at the time, the uninviting landscape was an ominous sign of what awaited me at York for the next few years.

My life at York has become tolerable; I have become more comfortable with being an outsider, accustomed to invisibility. Being "marginal" seems normal, an integral aspect of my working life. It is, however, a continuing manifestation of the destructiveness of race, class, and gender discrimination.

When I am in a classroom with young students, though, I feel invigorated by their energy and enthusiasm for life and learning. I enjoy planning and preparing for my classes and look forward to explaining complex

---

ideas to them. My students educate me by asking probing questions that force me to rethink some of my dearly held opinions. Such discussions keep me in touch with the changing norms of our times and I go on with my career despite some of its other disappointments.

Over the years, the physical and social landscape of York has changed. Pyramid oaks and chanticleer pear trees that were planted several years ago have matured, and in the fall, when the branches are full of colourful leaves, they provide some relief from the bleakness of the grounds. Along the pathways there are modern sculptures by some of York's students. On one side of the Ross Building, a new entrance to the university has been built, complete with an artificial pond, fountains, walkways with blossoming bushes, and archways with ivy.

When I walk around the campus today I see more faces like my own among the students. The university is, after all, located in a part of Toronto with a high proportion of immigrants. But the men and women working at York who belong to racial minorities are mostly secretarial staff. There are few faculty members from Third World countries; that situation has improved only very slightly from what it was some twenty years ago. In 2001, the faculty at York numbered approximately 1,100, of which about one third was female. In that year, I could count only ten full-time female faculty members from India, and less than a handful from other nations such as Egypt and Iran. There were two black female professors and a few more non-white male faculty members on campus.

The forbidding atmosphere on that first day at York did not distract me. I was determined to take on the tutorials that had been offered to me. I thought that even though the job was not all I had wanted, I seemed to have made as good a beginning as I could hope for, given the hiring freezes in most Canadian universities at the time. My aspirations were to lecture and, after some time had passed, get a full-time position either at York or the University of Toronto. Teaching tutorials gave me a toehold at the university, and the income from York was important to me, even though Tom had a secure job. I did not want to be a dependent spouse.

My experience of teaching at York over the last twenty-five years has been far from ideal. Sometimes, when I am feeling particularly disheartened, I grumble about white faculty colleagues and administrators. Since I teach courses on women and on India, at times the classroom is full of tension around race, class and gender, and that gets me down as well. Tom encourages me to give every incident the most positive interpretation possible rather than becoming mired in bitterness or frustration. He says I should disregard the race and gender discrimination and not grow a chip on my shoulder. His cheeriness doesn't inspire confidence in me; I suspect that since his experiences are so vastly different from mine, he doesn't understand the discrimination that I encounter at the university and cannot relate to my plight. A professional-looking, clean-shaven and well-dressed white man, Tom's physical presence lends him credibility and authority in most situations in Canada (and in most other countries as well.) He evokes confidence and trust among white Canadians. My experiences are radically different. I have to work hard to win the respect of my students and colleagues and to get them to accept me as a credible and knowledgeable woman. Respect is seldom given to me automatically.

Tom and I have quite different perspectives. They are not only a matter of race and gender, but also relate to our areas of expertise. Tom does research on climate in the Arctic. He benefits from the bias in contemporary society in favour of the physical sciences. My research, however, is in the social sciences; it deals with culture, values, and norms. Tom says his research is objective and value-free: where is the subjectivity in satellite data about ice formation?

If I am in a mood to argue, I can respond by saying that research on ice in the Arctic is an indulgence of Western industrial society, and shows an utter disregard of the millions of people dying of malaria and cholera in Africa and Asia. When we get to this stage, though, he shakes his head, mutters under his breath, and finds an excuse to go into his study until I have calmed down.

Some feminists, like Evelyn Fox Keller, have identified gender biases in scientific research similar to those found in the writings of the fraternity of "Dead White Males" central to Western culture. Feminists argue that all knowledge has hidden social and political dimensions. Debates about "the politics of knowledge" have focused recently on what is taught in schools and universities and who teaches it. I am reminded of an assignment Nicole received when she was sixteen years old. It was an essay on the shipping trade between Britain and Canada. Asked to read it after she had finished writing it, I found that it just repeated much of the information in her history book about the emergence of the lumber trade in the early Canadian economy. I suggested that she include something about the "human cargo"—immigrants, that is—that the ships taking lumber around the world brought back to Canada. I had to work hard to persuade her, because her book did not mention this, and the class had not discussed it. Eventually she added three or four paragraphs on the contribution of these immigrants to the Canadian economy. The teacher commended her on her originality.

In one of our parent-teacher interviews, the teacher told me that he was pleased with Nicole's very active participation in class discussions. Perhaps she had adopted some of my views on feminism; these had come through in the discussions in class. Some of her classmates started calling her a feminist, and she did not object to it very strenuously. Eventually she became, in the eyes of her friends, "the feminist" in her school. One boy in the class, a computer whiz, downloaded some articles on feminism from the Internet and gave them to her. Later, in secret, he told her about having what he called "two moms"—his mother and her lesbian partner.

Nicole liked the hint of notoriety that attached to being a feminist. She decided that since many of her friends knew little about feminism, she would start a feminist club at the school. She wrote a proposal for it, which was approved by the student council and the principal. The club met a few times, but with just a few girls, it fizzled out.

I think experiences like these in high school made Nicole more confident and self-assured, and she became less concerned about conforming to its white, middle-class norms. The environment of the university and curricular issues were very much in my mind when it came time for her to decide which university she would attend. I wanted her to have a liberal arts education that would show her that there are different ways of answering questions. My own experiences of getting a white, Eurocentric education at the University of Toronto added to my desire to help her find a university that would introduce her to non-Western cultures and histories but not limit her to only East-Asian or Latin American Studies, the usual alternatives. Tom, on the other hand, wanted her to study math and physics and become an engineer. He did not give much thought to the low female-to-male ratio in these faculties or attach much significance to the biases she might encounter looking for a job in this male-dominated field. These things were of primary concern to me, however. I was apprehensive of her feeling alienated and isolated or experiencing sexual harassment in that very male environment. Eventually, Nicole chose to pursue a liberal arts education and was accepted at Harvard University.

Proponents of change in university curricula believe that what we know about ourselves and how we come to know it have serious consequences for our sense of self. Self-knowledge is essential, furthermore, for self-esteem and self-respect. Identity, though, is to a great extent socially constructed, and the absence from the curriculum of some subjects, such as the role of Asian immigrants in Canadian history, may give students a message that their ancestors contributed little of value to society, so their experiences are not worthy of study.

Conservatives resist change and argue in support of the status quo— particularly if they have been well served by it personally. At York we have historian Jack Granatstein, who seems to be a leading proponent of the status quo. Although, naturally enough, he argues strongly in favour of teaching history to students, his ideal curriculum would exclude the history of race and gender discrimination in Canada. Such accounts, he argues, are mere complaints about public policy and therefore not worthy of inclusion in the history of the "Canadian nation and people."[1]

When Nicole was planning to attend university, I read about some encouraging developments on campuses in the United States. Some academics there argued against the Eurocentric curriculum that prevailed almost everywhere in North America. They pointed out that the absence of women, people of colour, and homosexuals from curricula reflected their marginalization and oppression in American society. Some of the controversy centred on "the canon"—the classical texts of Western literature and philosophy. Critics argued that it included only the writings of white males and was therefore exclusive, racist, and sexist. They said that far from being objective and unbiased, knowledge constructed by dead white males reflected the power relations of society. White European males had "imposed their ideas, their canon, and their self-serving readings of history on everybody else."[2] Although some wanted to add writings of non-Western people and women to the canon, others objected to the very idea of a canon, since it was both patriarchal and hierarchical. A student slogan at Stanford said, "Hey, hey, ho, ho…Western culture's got to go."[3]

A number of conservatives, such as Allan Bloom, Dinesh D'Souza, and William Henry III, challenged the arguments for a curriculum more sensitive to the needs of oppressed groups and a racially diverse student population and faculty. They decried the "tyranny" of the cultural left and their imposition of "political correctness" on campus. Critics of "radical" feminism such as Christina Sommers condemned what they called the politicization of the curriculum by feminists at universities and colleges. Sommers argued that feminists were revising women's role in history and attributing significance to women who hadn't really possessed it in the past. Others argued that courses on non-Western cultures and societies promoted cultural and moral relativism. They complained that qualified white males suffered from reverse discrimination. Students, they argued, were being admitted to prestigious universities and professional schools on the basis of their race, class, and gender identities rather than on their academic merit. Meantime, qualified and deserving white males were being left out. What would happen, they asked, to American leadership in research and scholarship?

In Canada, the debate about changes in curriculum has frequently focused on the need to make education multicultural in response to the changing ethnic and racial characteristics of the students. However, adding another course or two in one department or another does not alter the structural inequities of race, class, and gender, or the hierarchies that exist at the university. These courses are sometimes taught on a provisional basis, with no continuing commitment of faculty time. Their fringe status in the curriculum does not lead to incorporation into the discipline.

Yet even small improvements have provoked a backlash from academics who still support Anglo-conformity. Granatstein argues that all immigrants, whether they came one or twenty years ago, should quickly assimilate into the white Canadian (i.e., WASP) norm. He would not want even "one cent" of government money, municipal, provincial, or federal, spent on helping immigrants celebrate the culture—language, drama, music, and so on—of their countries of origin.[4] Neil Bissoondath, a Canadian author of Indo-Caribbean descent, also attacks multiculturalism, and urges people to assimilate and create one Canada with a unified homogenous culture rather than a Canada fragmented by national, regional, ethnic, and religious identities.

Change has come about, but it has been modest, low-key and slow. Its pace frustrates people like me. Perhaps university administrators would respond with greater alacrity if more students demanded change, but my students nowadays tend to be apolitical and skeptical of academic arguments about the power relations embedded in knowledge. A few students, however, do express their dissatisfaction with the regular curriculum and take two or three courses with me because they are committed to studying with non-white faculty members—the few of us who are there. My goal is to encourage them to relate their everyday life experiences to the more theoretical knowledge they are acquiring at the university.

My experiences at York have shown me that some of the resistance to change comes from faculty members who have a vested interest in the status quo. York is comparable in size to a state university in the United States. Unlike some of those, however, it has not given up liberal education in favour of business or information technology. The university requires students to take a variety of "general education" courses in humanities, social science, and natural science subjects. (These courses are the bane of computer science and math students, who would much rather focus their energies on their chosen field.) Still, one encounters race and gender biases there.

Members of the white faculty at York seem to find it hard to discuss race and racism. They would much rather it be kept shrouded. They react defensively to the mildest critical comment, and seem to fear hearing that they might be implicated in racism. They believe themselves to be liberal, progressive human beings who are scrupulously fair and consider all people equal. But I am often treated as an outsider. Sometimes I feel like a guest who needs to be well mannered and polite. I hesitate to mention the biases of my colleagues in faculty meetings or committee discussions.

When I do try to break the silence about race in curriculum or faculty appointments at York, I often meet blank stares or a rude brush-off. In the mid-1990s, I was the affirmative-action officer for the Division of Social Science. In the course of discussing the appointment of a new faculty member, I asked about the number of females and non-white applicants for the advertised job. A white male professor haughtily responded, "Vijay, we do not look at applicants by the colour of their skin or by their gender." He seemed to be saying that the committee is composed of liberal human beings who are blind to race and gender. His manner, however, suggested a subtext: "Who the hell do you think you are, to question me or the committee on such an issue?" My feeling was that he was responding to the physical me—an Indian woman—and was overcome by indignation that an Indian woman dared to question him. The chair of the division, also a white male, was embarrassed at the rude response and hastily jumped in to give me the figures and diffuse the tension. A white female was hired.

Sometimes I find that white faculty members may be sympathetic and say, "Oh yes, we know there is racism in Canada." I guess I am supposed to be grateful that racism has been acknowledged, but I feel hurt nevertheless. They seem to think that racism isn't much of a problem, or that it is so big a problem that it isn't resolvable by any practical action.

Even a general comment about structural and institutional racism may offend members of the white faculty. It breaks the unwritten rule of polite company against talking about race. In the early 1990s I was on a Faculty of Arts academic policy and planning committee. In one discussion I noted that there were not many courses dealing with non-Western subjects. The associate dean, a white male, asked me acidly, "Don't you teach a course on India?" The fact was, I had been at York for fourteen years before I could introduce and teach that course, and even then there was no commitment of full-time faculty to it. I suppose he was proud of this addition, but I was conscious of the length of time it took to make that small change.

The governance of York through committees makes the process of decision-making slow. All curriculum changes and faculty appointments are initiated at the departmental level and make their way up through various committees to the dean. Although this prevents administrators from imposing decisions by fiat, they have the power of persuasion and may sometimes encourage change in the departments by making additional resources available to them.

A new course must have the broad support of the predominantly white faculty or be initiated by faculty leaders who can generate such support. Every department has an academic plan, which identifies its long-term needs for faculty appointments and replacements. In any given year a department can identify some appointments that have to be made immediately if it is to continue to offer courses already listed in the calendar. Some courses are essential, while others can be skipped for a year or two. The courses and programs that already exist generate most faculty replacements and appointments. The chair of a department identifies a need for people with specific kinds of expertise after discussion with faculty members. The chair takes the list of needed appointments to the dean, and then the negotiations and horse-trading begin. The system perpetuates the inclusion of subjects that are already part of the curriculum, while excluding others.

White faculty members claim to be committed to a diverse curriculum and non-Western areas of study, but when resources are limited or scarce, as they usually are, liberal principles come into conflict with vested interests in existing areas of study, and marginalized areas of study lose out. A new area of study, they say, "wouldn't be pragmatic." They often view the allocation of resources to these new areas as a loss to their own, and steer discussions towards strengthening existing areas. If a non-Western course is suggested, they ask, "Wouldn't it be stretching us too thin?" "Wouldn't it be wiser to try to build on what we have by strengthening existing areas of study?" "Shouldn't we focus on doing better what we already do?" The process is quite civilized and polite. There is no need for individual faculty members to argue directly for exclusion. Everyone is off the hook.

Curricular change is further complicated by issues of what is taught, how it is taught, and who teaches it. In the mid-1970s, when I first started teaching at York, I led a double life. The gap between theories in the classroom and everyday practices in real life was large. Questions that concerned me as a woman and an immigrant were often excluded from classroom discussions, and since I did not have confidence to articulate them, they remained largely relegated to the margins of my consciousness. I hoarded feminist ideas in one compartment of my mind and spent a great deal of emotional energy managing the tension between what I thought privately and the way I presented myself to colleagues at York, docilely accepting their treatment of me.

Recently I read a 1999 memoir called *A Border Passage*, by Leila Ahmed, who was born and raised in Egypt, studied at Cambridge, and is now an academic at a university in the United States. Many of her experiences at Cambridge resonated with me. They also reflect the gender and racial discrimination that exist at universities in many countries. I am reassured and feel better about myself when I see that others have had similar experiences.

Like others, I accepted the disjunction between the classroom and my everyday reality because of my desire to survive. There were few faculty positions available to women in my area of expertise. Besides, the administrators at York knew that I was married and had little choice, if I wanted to teach at a university, but to continue with the contractual jobs they offered each year instead of making a permanent commitment to hiring me. Such contractual jobs were widely recognized at the university as being exploitative, and yet I accepted them year after year. That further accentuated the disconnection I felt between the theories of liberation we were grappling with in the classroom and my own private struggle.

Some of the courses in which I lectured at York were on the Third World. The teaching team for these courses was made up of faculty and teaching assistants, and included both black and white men and women. The course changed periodically as some faculty members and teaching assistants left and others joined the course, but gender and race shaped the hierarchy in these courses. The departmental administrators—white males and females—assigned the tasks that people would perform in the courses according to personal judgement and the social consensus existing at the university at the time.

When I first began teaching, the faculty at York was not unionized. Full-time faculty members formed a union in 1977 and the contract faculty formed one soon thereafter, but appointments to particular teaching positions were still often negotiated in person and with the help of "networks." The procedure gave the responsibility and power of matching individuals and course assignments to the administrators. Individuals like me, who were on contracts that were renewed annually, were dependent on their goodwill. Over the years, the union negotiated a variety of provisions for the protection of individuals from the exercise of arbitrary power, but at first these were ignored with impunity. A grievance that I launched with support of the union helped to entrench the principle of seniority, but that was not until the early 1980s. Although things slowly improved, there is still a great deal of discretionary authority resting in the hands of administrators.

I have taught several courses on the Third World with middle-aged white men. At first I was the teaching assistant and tutorial leader in these courses, only later becoming a lecturer. The allocation of positions within the courses was frequently determined by the administrator's perception of who would be the most appropriate lead member (called the course director) of the teaching team. I was seldom deemed that individual, in spite of my academic qualifications. Tenured white women, tenured black men, and other whites, blacks, and South Asians joined in the teaching of these courses, but white males almost always led them. This gender and racial hierarchy contradicted everything we lectured on in class. But the contradictions were seldom, if ever, acknowledged, and the status quo in many of these courses did not change until the early 1990s.

The presence of Third World people like me lent legitimacy to the courses. We could be compared to the dependent bourgeoisie through whom Marxists say colonial masters ruled and exploited their colonies. These "compradors" provided colonizers with contacts and networks through which they could exploit resources available in the colonies or sell their manufactured goods. We were like the English-educated civil servants who worked for the colonial governments in India, dressed in

Western clothing and contemptuously referred to by the British as "babus" for enthusiastically adopting the mores of the colonizers.

Wanting to be self-supporting, I colluded in my own oppression. Thus, while my mind was eagerly devouring the ideas of liberation and emancipation, I was a colonized subject teaching in these courses. Even though I knew I was being oppressed and exploited, I quietly acquiesced in it. How could I be critical of others' lack of political zeal, their choice to survive rather than join uprisings against oppressive landholders? Hadn't I also "sold out" to put bread on my table?

When I first started teaching these courses, the prevailing assumption was the objectivity and neutrality of knowledge—and of the professors who presented the knowledge to students. We did not disclose our ideological biases or those of the authors we assigned to the students to read. The bright students figured out our biases but mostly kept quiet about them, perhaps attributing them to failure on the part of their professors to transcend their own opinions. Other students just accepted what we presented to them as the one and only truth about the subject.

During one class in the mid-1980s, with about two hundred and fifty students, I was wrapping up my lecture on Marxist theories of underdevelopment when one particularly bright and assertive young man raised his hand and launched into an attack on the ideology of the course. Some other students, drawing courage from this young man, presented their understandings of underdevelopment in Third World countries, and I gave over the rest of the class to student discussion. The class enjoyed this lively exchange and was excited about the challenge they were presenting to faculty. I suppose, in a way, it had been easiest to challenge me as authority—I was an Indian woman. When it was the turn of white faculty members to lecture, however, they completely ignored students' responses and continued with their personal, Marxist analysis as if nothing had happened.

Feminist arguments have compelled scholars and professors to disclose their perspectives, be they liberal, Marxist, conservative, or feminist; such disclosures are thought to enhance the students' and the faculty member's understanding of themselves and whatever phenomena are under study. Understanding different perspectives increases tolerance of other people. What sounds so much like common sense now, however, was not part of conventional wisdom in the Third World courses with which I was associated in the 1970s and 80s.

The students were only assigned books, chosen by the faculty, written from a Marxist perspective. Understanding Marxist ideas required a complex intellectual negotiation for me; they resonated quite differently in my mind than in the minds of the white (and perhaps other non-white) professors. They could quite blithely spout phrases like "class oppressors" and "socialist revolution," but I came from a family of the sort that the white faculty was reviling as "class oppressors," and their derisive comments made me uncomfortable. The socialist revolution that they thought necessary in Third World countries would have destroyed most of my immediate and extended family in India.

When I first joined these courses, I would sometimes hesitantly suggest a book written from some other perspective. The team would listen to me politely and smile broadly when I finished as if I had made some kind of pleasant joke. Then they would go on talking about whatever they had been discussing previously. I learned to keep quiet. Over the years, I became more and more reluctant to speak, although I felt that my silence was construed as a sign of lack of intelligence or of ideas.

We did study India. In fact, the courses often began with a deplorable movie about it made by French film director Louis Malle. It focused, as one might guess, on poverty. We never saw Richard Attenborough's *Gandhi*, and I did not have the authority, nor the confidence, to suggest it. We studied the African National Congress, but no Indian nationalists. Discussing the Third World from different perspectives was not acceptable to the Marxists in these courses, and we never asked our students to read even one sentence by Gandhi in the many, many years that I was part of these courses. To do so would have provoked laughter from the other faculty members.

When I think of these courses as I imagine they appeared through the eyes of immigrant students, I am even more upset at what happened. Most of my students reacted defensively, while the more militant tried to assign blame to Western imperialism. Their reactions, and my own, were often emotional, as we perceived such discussions as reflecting on our self-identity. I wanted the students to take pride in their cultural heritage. In the early 1990s I started to teach a course on the history of India. The course currently attracts mostly students who are the children of Indian immigrants. I show the movie *Gandhi*. The students get to know that their parents come from a country that is not just full of beggars and mendicants.

We did read some books written by people from the Third World in those earlier days, but their views were all in synch with the ideology of the white Marxist faculty in the courses. Their voices, which just rehashed the arguments made by white scholars, became surrogates for those of my white faculty colleagues. Feminist and non-white scholars have explained that major publishers tend to support books that build on existing theories and hypotheses in the prevailing discourse of any subject area. New books in the subject give the existing theories greater credibility. Books that present different interpretations and analyses of data, or challenge prevailing wisdom, have a much harder time being accepted by major publishers, and thus become marginalized in the discourse in which they seek to make an intervention.

Since the 1980s, however, the "appropriation" of the voices of oppressed groups by privileged outsiders speaking on their behalf has been condemned as an exploitative exercise of power. I do not know how my colleagues coped privately with this. I only know that no one discussed it in my presence or in the lecture halls. I have seen only one article by a York professor on the subject: "White Teacher, Black Literature" by Leslie Sanders. She explains that people often choose areas of study that help them articulate questions that concern them most intimately; they hope to learn from the experience of others. However, she adds, they must take responsibility for their choices. The study of blacks by a white woman such as herself can be "problematic" and be negatively interpreted by them.[5]

The issue of who has the right to speak for a group is contentious, because it raises questions about authority and the exercise of power. Feminist thinking on the issue has changed over the last twenty years. It began with the assertion that only women have the right to speak for themselves, disputing the right of men to speak on their behalf, but lately there is a recognition that identities are not fixed in perpetuity, and values are not perfectly correlated to gender or colour. My physical appearance is that of an Indian, but I have spent most of my adult life in the West and I often speak from a Western perspective. Of course, I thereby risk being called an Oreo cookie—brown on the outside and white inside. To suppose, however, that anybody speaks from a single racial perspective, let alone for all members of any race, seems to me to be just another form of racism.

bell hooks is a distinguished black feminist, a professor of English in the United States. hooks argues that experience provides a standpoint from which to speak. She says that if she had been given the choice of taking a course on African-American critical thought from a progressive

black professor or from a progressive white professor, she would have preferred the black professor. She believes the black professor would have had
a "unique mixture of experiential and analytical ways of knowing—that is,
a privileged standpoint." This doesn't come from books or observation,
but from "the passion of experience, the passion of remembrance."[6] A progressive professor from a Third World country gives a positive symbolic
message to students who may feel insecure in their social identities. If we
aspire to give students more than mere information or analytical and writing skills—to convey values—then the experience of learning from a
member of an oppressed group is valuable.

At most universities in Canada in the 1980s it was almost unimagin-
able for men to speak directly on behalf of women or for a man to teach a
course on women. The same logic was not always applied to the courses
on the Third World with which I was associated. I sympathized with the
white people who had spent years studying and gaining expertise on the
Third World, but I was disappointed that they failed even to reflect on
their situation in writing or in the classroom. Another opportunity for
teaching and learning was lost.

White faculty members teaching courses on the Third World could
have examined their motivation for choosing to study Africa or Latin
America in the first place. Were they young idealistic students critical of
the imperialism of their own and other European nations? Did they see
themselves as making amends for the destructiveness of colonization and
helping to mobilize oppressed people through their research and writing?
Were their choices of areas for research influenced by the politics of their
times? Discussing these questions would have taught the students more
than the texts that we asked them to read.

White professors could have discussed the psychological and social
difficulties that white and black people faced when collaborating with one
another in Africa, Latin America, and Asia, where liberal and Marxist
white people contributed to liberation movements but eventually had to
stand aside as local people took on leadership positions.

I am reminded of a conversation between Charlie Andrew and
Mahatma Gandhi in the Attenborough movie. Andrew was an Anglican
minister and reporter who met Gandhi in South Africa, where he was
developing his political strategy of satyagraha (literally, "truth force").
Gandhi's work was at the time unknown outside a narrow circle. Andrew
helped to bring it to the attention of a Western audience by writing sev-

eral articles on Gandhi's political campaigns and the ashram he had set up in Natal, where residents lived simply, grew their own food, and eschewed all social-status distinctions.

When Gandhi returned to India in the 1920s, Andrew followed him there, and the movie shows a scene in which he visits Gandhi in jail. Andrew asks, "How can I help you?" To which Gandhi responds that he can help most by going away! Seeing Andrew's shocked expression, Gandhi softens the blow by explaining that Indians can take the movement forward: "We do not doubt ourselves. But others may doubt us, and believe that we are not so able as long as you are around."[7]

At first, I was simply grateful to have the opportunity to lecture and teach tutorials in courses on the Third World, but over the years I began to feel discouraged. The difficult questions that I had relegated to the edges of my consciousness became more insistent and troubling to me. The course directors sometimes quizzed me about my views, but then brushed them aside as "personal observations." My knowledge was "experiential," they said, and therefore not valuable. I resented this treatment, but to add to my travails, I was made to feel ashamed of myself. One day a new, white teaching assistant in the course told me rather arrogantly that I was not politically savvy and not assertive enough, so I was treated as invisible, a wimp. No one would presume to treat *her* that way, she said.

Feeling despondent, I twisted and turned in my bed all night, crying tears of frustration. Either I really lacked understanding and intelligence, or as an Indian woman, I was simply expected to bow to the authority of the white men. There were black men participating in these courses as faculty and as students, but the white teaching staff seemed more apprehensive of them, fearing complaints of racism. I had the double whammy: race, and on top of that, gender, which feminist academics say are integrated and interconnected. And unlike the new woman who held me in such contempt, I was not someone with influential friends and relatives among the administrators. I comforted myself by rationalizing the situation: it was the structure of race and lack of networks that disadvantaged me, not any personal qualities or failings. I was not completely inadequate, I told myself forgivingly. And with that thought, I finally fell asleep.

I think of the effect these courses must have had on students who came to our lectures week after week. All of us—the entire teaching team—let the students down. The word "race" was seldom mentioned in class. It came up in the discussion of apartheid, but never in any other context. We thus ignored a reality of the students' experience, particularly those who came from Third World countries, and we provided little incentive for our white students to question their own stock of received wisdom. The courses provided many "teachable moments" on race and gender oppression, but we ignored them all.

Donald Kennedy, president of Stanford University from 1980 to 1992, writes in *Academic Duty* that if universities are going to prepare students to take on leadership positions, they must not only impart facts and knowledge but also the ability to think critically. Professors, he says, should impress upon students how values inform interpretations and evaluations of all kinds of phenomena, interactions with others, and beliefs about what is important in life and how society should be governed. Kennedy distinguishes between teaching values and teaching *about* values. It is not for professors to promote particular values, he states. Rather, they should provide students with information drawn from different sources that enables them to reach conclusions for themselves. Let the students compare, analyze, think, and decide for themselves, he concludes, on the values they support.[8]

Occasionally, when the white male who taught the evening course on the Third World was unavailable, I had the opportunity to lead it. This course attracted several Third World immigrant students, people working at full-time jobs and older than the twenty-year-olds taking it during the day. The atmosphere in these classes was quite different from that of their daytime counterparts. These students felt freer to speak their minds and engage me in discussions. They could discuss their own experiences and share their observations with others in the class. They did not hesitate to contradict me and, if necessary, tell me I was wrong. I wondered if they would be so frank and ready to argue with a white male with gray hair. If a white student was rude or presumptuous, they would jump to my defence; I was in front of the class, and yet I was one of them. They thought of it as their class—a class in which they perceived themselves to have several advantages. For their part, the white students got a chance to look at life and experience from another perspective and examine and reflect upon what they already knew. They accepted me as a logical choice to teach the course. They sometimes thought I was biased in favour of Third World countries, or that I got carried away with feminist interpretations, but my bias itself became a lively question for debate and discussion in the class.

The department, without intending to, had provided the students and me with an experience that was educational and empowering.

In this seminar I connected the experiences that the students and I brought to it with the knowledge that we were gaining from the books we read. Students shared stories about "back home" and related them to theories of underdevelopment. After our discussions, students looked back on their previous experiences with new insight. At times, this new understanding would make them laugh, and at other times they would become angry and dismayed. Hooks would say we had become engaged participants in the class, rather than passive consumers of information.

The class also changed my perception of myself. I was not compartmentalizing information and knowledge, but was making connections between my mind and atman. My experiences of living in a Third World country and in Canada became more meaningful for me. The class gave me faith in myself, and the knowledge I was acquiring was healing my "uninformed and unknowing spirit."[9] I realize now that since I felt good about myself in that class, I was probably a better professor. What's more, some of my non-white students may have become more able to envision themselves in front of a class someday.

At the same time, feeling my own continuing lack of power in the Third World courses that I taught during the day, I gave up teaching them. Eventually, the administration made some new appointments in Third World studies. In the early 1990s an immigrant man from Chile with expertise in Latin America was appointed to teach one of the courses. A black immigrant man whose specialty was Africa was appointed to teach courses on Africa in the mid-1990s and an immigrant man from Uruguay with expertise in Nicaragua, Argentina, and Chile was appointed to teach in the Latin American Studies program in 1998. White women who had been teaching courses on Africa and Latin America lobbied the administration to make an appointment from a special fund set aside for affirmative-action hiring related to subject matter and supported the candidates through the hiring process. The situation slowly improved, but I had moved on to teach courses on India and Women's Studies.

———————

I woke up this morning and looked in the bathroom mirror. It was the same face I see every day...the daily routine makes me less aware of the telltale signs of aging. I don't know when my skin lost its smoothness and crow's feet appeared around my eyes. I know that these signs of aging mark me, but most times I do not consciously see them. Sometimes, absorbed in pleasant memories of the past, I see reflected back at me in the mirror the unconventional, daring young woman that I once was, rather than the professorial and sombre fifty-five-year-old I now am. When I see photographs of myself I realize how I appear to others, but I'm reluctant to identify with the middle-aged woman I see in them, and I complain about the photographers...they should airbrush these pictures, perpetuate the image of the young radical woman that I remember.

In my own mind I am sometimes still a vulnerable, marginal immigrant woman trying to make her way in the academic world, an outsider in her department and in the university community at large. At the beginning of each school year, I experience some anxiety over presenting myself to the students and gaining their cooperation and respect. When I first started teaching, students sometimes mistook me for one of them. Now age sets me apart, and there is no doubt in their minds that this woman, dressed in a suit or jacket, must be the professor. I still think of myself as a critic of race, class, and gender hierarchies at the university, but perhaps nowadays the students perceive me differently.

As a professor I represent some power and authority in the classroom, though my race and gender somewhat undermine them, but as a feminist I think I should abolish power and authority. Students and professors— young and old, black and white—should have solidarity with each other. The classroom, however, teaches me some lessons on applying feminist principles within a patriarchal Eurocentric framework.

My feminism becomes a barrier to accepting some of the motivations of students who take my Women's Studies courses. Most of my students are not driven by idealism or ideology, but have a variety of mundane reasons for being there: they need a course in social science to fulfill their requirements; their friends are in the course; they think it will be a nice change from their major; its timing suits their schedules. My interaction with the students leaves me little doubt that most of them are not interested in changing or transforming society, but anxious to find their own place in it. There is a generation gap between the students and myself. Some of the students are not yet aware of having been discriminated against or of being oppressed, or experiences of discrimination have as yet left little mark on them. Feminist views may be expressed in terms that they find hard to relate to, let alone be moved by. They study feminism dispassionately, and it only occasionally speaks directly to them.

Some students take my Women's Studies course as an elective. They may choose my course from a vague desire to know more about women's lives, but with no political motivation. Feminist ideas provoke self-reflection in some of them and they begin to analyze their previous experiences from a new perspective and thus gain better understanding of them. They become committed to feminist ideas. But others seem to have thoroughly absorbed the oppressive codes of society as adolescents and learned to submerge their own voices. They are sometimes alienated by the ideas that we discuss in class, and become critical of me and of other students.

Another group of students that comes to my classes consists of Women's Studies majors who have already taken a number of such courses to fulfill the requirements of their programs. Their familiarity with feminism makes them comfortable engaging me in discussions. They are often ardent supporters of equal pay for equal work and are critical of the politics of sexual relationships. However, although they often discuss the relationship between experience, activism and theories, this does not necessarily mean that they are committed to feminist political goals. They may not even have worked in a feminist organization or attended feminist meetings or rallies.

Many students take a course with me because of what I *am* rather than of what I know; they think that as a non-white person I may know things that white people don't. Some white students take my courses because I am non-white and they think of themselves as progressive women. Sometimes taking a course with me is a white student's way of making a political statement about herself as non-racist, progressive woman. The socialization of such students, however, is still sometimes a barrier to their accepting me. They know how different perspectives and what feminists call "locations" (such as who you are and from what perspective you are speaking: sexuality, ablebodiness, age, race, class and gender) skew interpretations, yet they often want me to say the same things as their white Women's Studies professors. When I don't, they sometimes find it hard to accept my views as being equally valid.

Some South Asian students take my Women's Studies courses because of my ethnicity. They sometimes have a vague, though usually unarticulated, desire to identify with me. A fine-arts student used to corner me during coffee breaks to talk about some event in the South Asian community or discuss her aspirations of becoming a feminist painter. She once brought her paintings of Hindu gods, set against an abstract background, for me to admire.

These students are proud of me as a South Asian, without actually saying so. Last year a student came up to me after class and said, "I thought you should know that Professor [so-and-so] at the University of Toronto is using your new book in her course." Other South Asian women take my presence in the classroom as evidence against the stereotypical assumptions of their white classmates. Sometimes, when I debunk some claim about the alleged oppressiveness of South Asian (that is, Hindu and Muslim) culture, they nod approvingly in a self-satisfied manner. They seem to be saying to the white students, "See how wrong you are!"

The South Asian and black students expect—correctly, as it happens—that regardless of what the course outline says, the class will discuss racism more thoroughly than Women's Studies courses taught by white professors. Some of these students claim to have experienced discrimination in other courses, and they use the opportunity provided by discussion in my class to let off steam about racism at the university. Some are aggressively assertive of their own social identities and are disgruntled if I advise them to tone down their rhetoric about racism being prevalent at the university and in society. By their demeanour they seem to ask, "Whose side are you on?" I sympathize with their sense of grievance because they are seeking support in understanding their everyday reality, but as a professor I also have the responsibility for ensuring that the class is comfortable for students of all ethnic and racial backgrounds. Thus I am torn, and sensitive to the accusation of having become "whitewashed."

Last year Genevieve, a student from the Caribbean and a single mom in her mid-forties, came to see me several times in my office. She had been in the workforce for several years but was now studying full-time, anxious to finish her remaining courses and get her bachelor's degree. She had established a friendly relationship with me right from the start of the course. She assumed that I shared her beliefs about racism at the university, and often gave me her impressions about different courses and professors. In class, Genevieve always sat with two other mature black students and took a protective stance towards the other young black women in the class. She was militant about what she described as the racism in some Women's Studies courses…"with these white professors." Genevieve was now committed to taking courses only from non-white faculty members.

Genevieve chided me in my office about my moderate stance. "Vijay," she said, "you should not tell us to tone down our criticisms." I responded meekly that I also had a responsibility towards the white students in the seminar, who would be uncomfortable with her anger. "They'll feel trashed," I said. She replied sanguinely, "So do I in many classes at this university. Now they know what it feels like." I am very sympathetic to women like Genevieve, but they make me feel that being part of the university compromises me. I have to be the voice of moderation, in part because the course must function for Chinese, South Asian, black, and white students of varying ethnicities, and not become an arena for "guilt-tripping" mired in personal accusations.

I rationalize that if I am too sympathetic to black, Asian, or South Asian students, I might further inflame their passion and they may drop out, convinced that the university is racist. My goal is to help students validate their understanding of racism as they encounter it and yet keep them in the system so they can complete their degrees. I think that getting a good education and a good job will be personally rewarding for the students and create a critical mass of non-white people at all levels of the work force.

My feminist values have also come under scrutiny by my students. Every year, like most other professors, I prepare a schedule of discussion topics and readings for each week's seminar. In one isolated case a white student asked, "Vijay, who made up this course outline?" I said, "I did," waiting to see if there was a point behind her question. There was. She said, "*You* get to choose what *we* read. The class has no say in it." I was exercising power over the class, she implied, imposing academic goals on them, subordinating them.

Like many others who think of themselves as feminist professors, I had presumed that I could combine feminism with my profession as a social scientist. However, white males and their values dominate this profession, like many others. As a professor I am part of the university, and universities too maintain and perpetuate these values. Including Women's Studies programs and offering courses in various faculties was a victory in the 1970s, but in becoming part of the institution, the field lost much of its radical oppositional voice.

Feminists who teach Women's Studies may replace substantive challenges to the system with "window dressing." We dress casually in jeans and sweaters, sans makeup, but forget that we are still exercising authority over students—and, for that matter, over university office staff, too. If we dislike the hierarchical structure suggested by the traditional arrangement of the classroom furniture, with rows of chairs facing a podium, we move the chairs into a circle. That encourages students to interact with each other, but it doesn't alter the fact that power and authority in the classroom belong to the professor. Even the pretense of dispensing with power and authority is something we do at our discretion, and they can be reinstated any time we choose. We take a "class vote" to determine when we should have a break in a two- or three-hour class, but that is not fooling anyone; we are only indulging ourselves in creating an aura of non-hierarchical relations. The students care about grades, and the professors hold the power of grades in their hands. Women's Studies courses do not differ substantially in their academic goals from other courses at the university.

This issue reminds me of a conversation I had with another professor at a Learned Societies Conference in Alberta in the mid-1990s. Abigail was an untenured professor at a western university. She was a single mom in her late forties. We had gone to a ranch on an organized group outing for dinner, and Abigail and I decided, while waiting for a table in the dining hall, to take a short walk to admire the scenery. In the course of our conversation, I asked Abigail what books she had assigned to her students in her Women's Studies course. She replied blithely, "We are not reading any books. We use our own life experiences as data and analyze them."

Did Abigail just ask the students to narrate their own life experiences without applying feminist theories? My Women's Studies course fits a much more traditional model. I expect the students to read some books and articles about feminism and to improve their critical skills. I assign essays and I expect them to do some library research and present arguments in those essays. And, of course, I make judgements about the quality of the students' research, their competency in discussing ideas, and the originality of their thought. My approach can be criticized for perpetuating the hegemonic culture that favours middle-class students who already have the skills I am rewarding. In making value judgements about them, I am exercising power. I have adopted the norms that dominate the university, and I impose them on my students, including those from other cultures.

Abigail believed in what feminists have dubbed the "authority of experience." Her goal was to reveal how the power relations of race, gender, and class that society accepts structure everyday life as normal and natural.

Asking the students to talk about their experiences gives primacy to their voices. It validates women's experiences and breaks their isolation. In talking with each other, women find common patterns, for many of the problems they encounter stem from systemic biases. They realize they are not individually to blame for limited education and training or lack of professional success. However, Abigail was denied tenure; many of the professors who evaluated her were critical of her teaching and research procedures. She fought that decision for several years, but was unsuccessful.

Although the course I teach is structured along conventional academic lines, some meaningful discussions do happen in my class. There is time in my class for students to tell their personal stories, but I try to connect the points made in their stories with the feminist theories we're studying. Students react to feminist books in terms of what they say about their lives, confirming or refuting their perceptions of their culture and society. Sometimes the readings enable a student to gain more insight into an incident that offended or angered her—for example, a boyfriend's expectation that she make coffee for him. Other students, more content with the tenor of their lives, are annoyed at the writers who document the oppression of women. "It's not so bad," they say to me. "I too want to stay home and raise children." And, "My mom is happy, and she has always stayed at home."

The students have personal responses to what they read, responses that reflect their locations and contexts. The experiences of white, urban, middle-class "Canadian" women seem to be the norm, and the experiences of working-class women, or Italian or Greek women, are discussed in relation to the norm. Any student in the class may find she is voicing an opinion that comes from a very different perspective from that of others.

I may feel sensitive about exercising the authority given to me by a patriarchal institution, but my students expect that of me. They often like me to assert my authority as the professor and "take charge" of the class. They demand that I follow conventional teaching methods and stick to the schedule, lecture to them in class, provide notes, and grade their papers and examinations. Few students want a free-flowing discussion whose subject matter may never be on the examination. Students complain if they think their classmates are talking too much about themselves. They liken that to mere chit-chat, unsuitable for a classroom. Yet, I sometimes feel that I'm being untrue to feminism and catering to system-induced student expectations. Sommers characterizes Women's Studies classes as "therapy sessions" devoid of any academic merit. My courses are not so touchy-feely, and my goal is pedagogical, not therapeutic.

The Women's Studies program is like a middle-aged woman unconscious of how she has aged and lost her youthful vigour and dynamism. Over the years it has been transformed from a radical oppositional voice to just one more academic field, sometimes invisible, like a middle-aged woman, and often unfathomable to all but the most select among its theoreticians. The idealism that drove women professors to start the program in the 1970s has waned, and the culture of the university now dominates Women's Studies classrooms. Perhaps this was inevitable. Becoming an established, respectable part of the university has meant that Women's Studies has had to abide by the rules and regulations that govern curricula, even if they conflict with feminist principles of non-hierarchical relations, consensus building, empowering the oppressed, and making space for all voices to be heard.

My experiences in the classroom sometimes compel me to reflect upon the contradictions of Women's Studies at a university. Social change and transformation can occur piecemeal, but they require engagement, challenge, and resistance to values and norms that oppress women. The physical space of the classroom enables us to articulate our oppressions and empowers us individually, but I am not sure how this cacophony of voices can take us forward collectively. Feminist theories provide no clear moral and political direction, and feminist practice seems to be immobilized by competing voices and identities. Feminists like me have not substantially transformed the institution by our presence. Rather we have imperceptibly been drawn into the system and used its values in the interest of our own self-preservation.

10

In the Company of Mothers

For a woman of my class, community, and regional origins in India, marriage and motherhood are the defining events of life. Marriage in many ways determines how a young woman explores and develops her potential, for it is dependent in large part on the cooperation and support she receives from her spouse and his family, to whom she becomes primarily attached. Motherhood integrates a woman even more closely with her husband's family and her interests and those of her children become inextricably entwined with theirs. In a biracial and bicultural marriage such as mine, however, few traditional rules of conduct applied, and that seemed at first to give me flexibility and choice. I felt free to observe or discard the values of my upbringing as I chose and to pick up the norms of white Canadian or WASP culture that best suited my needs and temperament. I did not realize that my values had been shaped by my past experiences and that in reality, they dictated the choices that I thought I was freely making.

White feminists argued that sexual relations within a marriage reinforced the social power of the male within the family and oppressed women. A marriage, these feminists argued, often subsumed a woman's identity under that of her male partner. I had no fears of being dominated and controlled by Tom, for he is a gentle and mild-natured human being, and I a fiercely independent one. Besides, when I was with him I did not feel like his appendage, and I did not think I was being treated as a "tro-

---

Note to chapter 10 is on p. 283.

phy" or a mark of his progressiveness. Nor did I think, if I thought about it at all, that getting married posed a threat to my self-identity. I felt no desire to sit down and write a prenuptial contract with Tom outlining my rights and responsibilities or the division of housework, although several books I read recommended doing so, particularly if a woman wanted to have an egalitarian relationship within marriage. My self-assurance was like that of many other young women who imagine themselves and their relationships to be somewhat exceptional and outside the norms that were applicable to others.

I did not analyze my relationship with Tom through a feminist intellectual prism because feminism did not speak to me or of me at the time. In the 1970s white feminists were focused on gender oppression, and gave scant regard to race and class as integral parts of a woman's identity. Their limited vision put a distance between me and "their" feminism. In the early 1980s feminists of colour in Britain and United States criticized white feminists for what they thought were their anti-family attitudes. They said that, given the racism of white society, women of colour needed the support of their men and the comfort of their families, although they did not deny the sexism inherent in family relations. My life in Toronto had made me conscious of my race; I was sensitive to racism but secure in my gender identity. The question that I had in mind was this: if patriarchal domination was common to almost all cultures, why were some cultural traditions, such as those of India, particularly reviled?

Looking back now, I can give an intellectual explanation of my behaviour, but that does not quite capture who I was in my late twenties. My choices were not based in theoretical ideals; I followed feelings and emotion rather than reason. I guess I relied on intuition, as V. S. Naipaul, in his Nobel lecture, said he has done: "I have trusted to intuition. I did it at the beginning. I do it even now. I have no idea how things might turn out, where in my [life] I might go next."[1]

Intuition, however, is partly a product of an individual's socialization in a particular family and culture. I came from a society that expected a woman to adjust to her spouse and his family. None of the women in my family's social circle, despite occasional heartbreaking difficulties, had questioned the family as an institution. I had no personal knowledge (as opposed to what I read in books) that marriage represented a problematic relationship that had to be carefully negotiated. My intuition about marriage, as informed by Indian culture, told me that it was a good thing.

I was happy to be with Tom, and gave no conscious thought to the dangers of losing my identity or sense of self within my marriage. I felt no urge to experiment with new feminist ways of being and behaving and was mostly content to let things take their course. In retrospect, I am awed by my self-confidence—or arrogance—although some may perceive my lack of thought to be unconscionably naïve and stupid. They may well wonder, is she really a feminist scholar? Fortunately, whether due to luck, chance, or the mix of temperaments involved, marriage and motherhood turned out to be happy life situations for me.

My first experience of living in an apartment in Toronto was in a condominium that Tom had bought before our engagement in a big complex just south of York University. Our building overlooked a flat expanse—plenty of weeds but not a tree in sight between the university parking lots and us. It was one of a row of seven or eight buildings with a string of town-houses on the end. The buildings themselves had a simple, functional look, with no interesting architectural features. I was reminded of my father's apartment in Bombay, but compared to all but the most exclusive apartment buildings in Bombay, these looked fine to me. Of course, there were no watchmen and no personal drivers hanging around the entrance, as is usual in Bombay. But each building had a lobby with an upholstered sofa and a table with a pot of plastic flowers. The lobby and halls were wallpapered and carpeted, and the elevator almost always worked.

Tom had bought the condominium after working for a few months at Environment Canada as a research meteorologist; I was still a graduate student and teaching assistant. We had little money, but Tom was able to persuade the bank to give him a loan to cover the down payment. We were proud of the apartment, which had three bedrooms, a sunken living room, and wall-to-wall carpeting. I enjoyed its spaciousness and was glad to have put the tiny bedrooms and shared kitchen and bathrooms of the graduate residence behind me. The few pieces of furniture we had were mostly shabby and old, given to us by friends and relatives. We had a bed and a dresser and a dilapidated chrome-and-arborite kitchen table given to us by Tom's mother. Like graduate students, however, we were pleased with the innovative ways we could furnish our apartment without spending any money. Our ingenuity at turning the assortment of tables and chairs given to us into something resembling a living room was what mattered to us at the time. We had little desire to assert our status and taste through home furnishings. Our friends were in much the same position, and we competed to see who could be most creative, with the least amount of money, fashioning bookcases from planks of wood and bricks and assembling dining tables from old, scrounged doors.

Many of the people living in our building seemed to be immigrants. I sometimes heard bits and pieces of conversation in languages other than English—most often Spanish. When I encountered people in the elevator, I tried to strike up a conversation with them, but they almost always gave only monosyllabic replies. At first, I thought they were reserved because they did not speak English, but over the next year I learned that the casual informality and friendliness that characterized apartment living in Bombay were not the norm in North York. Here you did not talk to strangers in elevators or drop in unannounced on your neighbours, or ask to borrow some missing ingredient for dinner. I wished I could spot a neighbour and say hello to them; I thought it would make me feel more at home in my new environment. However, I seldom saw anyone during the day, when the building had the feeling of being mostly deserted.

I had no complaints about loud music or cooking aromas. If there was a fragrance of spices wafting about, I did not attach any importance to it, since that is the norm in most apartment buildings in Bombay. I know some white Canadians complain about what they refer to as "the smell of spices" and "loud foreign music." Writers such as Neil Bissoondath have written short stories that describe the outrage of immigrants at having parties rudely interrupted by police who have been summoned by irate neighbours. I, however, was curious about my neighbours and wanted to get to know them, and any music—loud or soft—would have given me some clue about them. Instead, the building was lifeless and quiet, with only the occasional cry of a baby or the sound of small children playing.

This life behind closed doors threw me on my own resources and made me feel lonely and isolated. I missed my father and sisters in Bombay, and my friends at the graduate residence. With them I shared common interests, but there was no obvious commonality with my new neighbours, most of whom seemed to be working men and stay-at-home moms. I had no dog or baby to use as an icebreaker in a conversation. I moped and complained to some white Canadians friends about feeling isolated, but they just shrugged it off and said knowingly, "It's only when you live in a house that you have a sense of being part of a community." My Indian girlfriends tried to reassure me by suggesting that my feelings of being isolated were not unique to me. I was simply learning "the way Canadians are"—

formal, aloof, and protective of their privacy. The immigrant families in my building were conforming to the norms of white Canadian society. They kept to themselves, inside their apartments.

After living in the building for a year, Tom and I decided to move. By the mid-1970s the prices of homes had gone up dramatically (a trend widely believed to have been caused by property speculators), and our condominium had appreciated in value. This gave us some equity to use as down payment on a townhouse. Besides, I had completed my PhD and was teaching as part of the contract faculty at York, so we could afford to make larger house payments. The banks at the time used a formula that took into account the full income of the male and half that of the female in arriving at the amount that could be borrowed on any property. They asked questions about my education (but not about job security), and gave us a mortgage.

Our desire to move from the apartment did not arise from finding it small or inconvenient, but from a sensitivity to comments from our friends and relatives, who hinted that living in a condominium building was okay as a starting point, but that we should move once we were financially able or if we decided to have children. Since nearly everybody I knew in Bombay lived in an apartment building, it was difficult for me to understand this bias. One drawback of living in an apartment frequently mentioned was the lack of a backyard, considered a prime requirement of a healthy childhood in Canada.

Now, after several years of living in a house, I find that having a backyard is somewhat overrated. Backyards are no doubt aesthetically pleasing, but their use seems limited to small children for an hour or two on summer days or occasionally during winter when there is fresh, powdery snow. In my experience, children much prefer a basement or family room in which there is a television. Had I known how unhandy we were, or had I thought about all the chores attendant upon being a home owner—the mowing, the shovelling, the taking care of mechanical problems in the house—I would have stayed put in my apartment for many years.

Living in the townhouse reinforced my perception that people in Canada have little interest in engagement with their neighbours. Townhouses, moreover, seem to be designed to minimize contact with others. Ours was located in a picturesque environment bordering a ravine, a tennis club and a golf course. It was in a new development that had attracted some families with small children. The realtor, though, praised features that he said enhanced the owner's privacy. He pointed to the double garage with a remote-control lock that would enable us to drive straight in without getting out of the car, and a door in the garage that would take us straight into the house. The backyards of the townhouses were open and unfenced, and there was a small slope that made it an ideal snow slide for young children, but very few of them used it. The more affluent families had enclosed sections of their backyards to give them even greater privacy.

Townhouse living did not lessen my sense of disconnectedness. In the summer months, an Italian woman and I would sit facing each other across our backyards on the weekends. We waved and said hello when we saw each other, but only occasionally exchanged a few polite sentences. The interactions I had with my other neighbours while putting out the garbage or shovelling the snow were formal and polite. We were strangers to each other and seemed to have no reason to talk besides being courteous, and so acknowledged each other's presence in a distant way. I do not know how much of this had to do with my being an obvious foreigner, but I was self-conscious about being an immigrant and wary of doing anything that might be considered inappropriate, such as engaging people in anything but the briefest and most mundane conversation.

Over the first few months, some of the neighbours became familiar figures, but they seemed to have little incentive to convert the familiarity into even a casual friendship. Much later I would hear from other families in the neighbourhood that they had felt similarly isolated. Unfortunately, we had seen no way to convey our shared feelings, and remained enclosed in our private spaces behind closed doors. We didn't question what I think were WASP, middle-class norms. To me, townhouse living was just another Canadian experience that contrasted with my life in Bombay, and I felt I had to make the adjustment to this new way of life.

Our interactions with friends, neighbours, and relatives made me aware that Tom and I were on the margins of some social circles—liked and even loved perhaps, but still outsiders. Occasionally when I was in a sombre mood or feeling lonely, I imagined an idyllic situation for myself. I reflected that if I had married a man of my culture and background and stayed in Bombay, I would have had to make little effort to be part of an extended family and community. Here in Toronto, I was an immigrant and now part of a biracial couple, and I felt vulnerable and insecure. My lack of community and my feelings of being an outsider concerned me. Since the need to belong was mine, however, I took the initiative of adapting to the norms of my friends, neighbours, and relatives.

My biracial marriage and emotional needs dictated that I assimilate. However, I cannot claim that I made a conscious, well-considered choice; rather it was a response to the people I met and the experiences I had. I did not cling to ideals about how things ought to be for immigrants such as myself; instead, I responded pragmatically, believing that since I had freely made the choice of spouse and country, I had to make it work as best as I could. Thoughts of family and community particularly concerned me when I was pregnant with Nicole, but I gave little thought to the difficulties of becoming an employed mother, and I had no ideal vision of myself as a mother or any grand plan for us as a family. Although wary and cautious, I was nevertheless patient and hopeful about what the future might bring.

I wanted to be a mother, and while I was pregnant I was full of happy expectations; I did not at all think of questioning the origins of my desire. In the 1970s I had read feminist writings on motherhood, but these views did not resonate in a personal way with me. White feminists wrote that biology was not destiny, and argued that while reproduction was an integral aspect of the female body, the rearing and nurturing of children was a socially imposed norm. These writers argued against compulsory motherhood, and asserted the right of women to choose whether to have children or not. Men, too, were imprisoned in their roles, they conceded, and were, despite stereotypes to the contrary, capable of being loving, nurturing caregivers to their young children.

In the early 1980s I read that some black feminists in the United States were disputing the idea that gender provided a basis of commonality for feminist politics. They argued for recognizing the differences in women's experiences within the family and in the workplace. Mothering, they said, was experienced differently by them (and other non-white immigrants) than by their white, middle-class, and university-educated "sisters." Given the racial context in which they socialized their young, women of colour mothered their children in ways that were dissimilar to those of their white counterparts. (Nobody, at that time or even now, has said much about mothering in a biracial context.)

Despite much complex theorization about motherhood, feminists have found it difficult to explain why significant numbers of women around the world want to be mothers. Rationally speaking, it does not make sense for women to willingly choose what some might characterize as the drudgery of child care. But with full knowledge of the difficulties of combining paid work and mothering, I did make the conventional choice of becoming a mother. Since there is little satisfactory explanation of why I, like many other women, revel in being a mother, I wonder if there is something deeper and more elemental than socialization in such a choice. Although I do not embrace the concept in the classroom, my views on what motherhood entailed were primarily derived from experiential knowledge—the "authority of experience." My experiences of being a child in a family were similar in many ways to those of my friends and students. The stories I heard about childhood and growing up in other families described mothers as being the primary caregivers around whom the family routine revolved. Mothers were mostly assigned praise or blame by their children for whatever did or did not turn out right in their lives. Fathers were often seen as secondary figures. Perhaps there were dark, unsavoury secrets of family violence and incest, but the veil over these issues had not been lifted in the early 1980s, and such things were seldom discussed openly.

My memory of childhood was of being loved. My aunt had been a full-time mother and we had paid help, so my personal experience of the drudgery of housework and child care so often foisted on mothers was limited. I had no friends in Canada who were mothers and from whom I might have acquired an inkling of the constraints that a small child imposes on one's daily routine. Besides, since I viewed motherhood as a normal event in a woman's life cycle, I did not feel the need to read up on the subject extensively. Consequently, I gave little thought to the day-to-day difficulties of raising a child and maintaining a career. I imagined that a child would add happiness to my life. Over the years, I found that motherhood, although it entailed a lot of hard work, was a "labour of love." I also discovered that my ego slowly became wrapped up in my daughter's well-being, and I wanted others to see me as a responsible, caring mother who was doing her job satisfactorily.

Nicole was born, much to our delight, in 1978. With her birth, our needs changed, and along with them our perspective of family and community. While previously I had wanted to assert my independence and distinctive personality apart from my family, now I needed a family with whom I could share my anxieties over mundane issues of child care. I became alarmed when Nicole did not gain the two pounds in weight that, according to books, babies were supposed to gain every month in the first year of their lives. I reviewed my routine to identify what was I doing wrong, and wanted very much to remedy it. I was filled with self-doubt, and worried about being considered a negligent mother. Stricken by these fears, I telephoned Tom's mother to report the bad news. She laughed and tried to calm me down. Little coughs and colds became anxious times for me; I would feel compelled to rush Nicole to the hospital's emergency ward, but a telephone call to my mother-in-law would usually settle me for a couple of hours. Tom was more relaxed, but I had less faith in him than in his mother since, like me, he had no previous experience of child care. Sometimes, sensing my tension, "Mom" would simply come to our home and take over Nicole's care. She would casually suggest, in an attempt to distract me from obsessing over my new responsibilities, that I get some sleep, go out shopping, or go to the university.

I was an immigrant mother, but unlike many who lack family support in these small daily happenings in their lives, I had lucked out by having Tom's mother and family here in Toronto. Since Nicole was the first grandchild, she was greatly loved by his parents and siblings. We also had contact with Tom's cousins and their children, all of whom lived in Toronto, so over a time I felt reassured that we too were part of a larger family.

My childhood had been spent within a large network of grandparents, aunts, uncles, and cousins, and since I had no major complaints about my own upbringing, I naturally wanted to reproduce the same family environment for Nicole. In the next two years, fortuitously, both my sisters decided to immigrate with their families to Canada. Their husbands worked with multinational corporations in Bombay, and since Toronto offered a range of job opportunities, they chose to come here. My brother Subash and his wife Linda had children as well. So now we had a diverse set of relatives: Indian, Canadian, and a mixed family like ours.

Now I could call up my sisters and speak to them in Hindi, although more often than not we switched back and forth between English and Hindi any number of times, depending on the topic of our conversations. Emotional reactions were expressed in Hindi, as small pithy phrases communicated them precisely; opinions about school, work, and politics were expressed in English. However, it was the familiarity of the interaction more than its language that was comforting, and it took some of the edge off being an immigrant in an alien culture and society.

I became more slowly integrated with the local community and neighbours when Nicole was about two years old and needed playmates. She found William, another two-year-old, who lived right across from our townhouse. My routine was to pick up Nicole from the daycare centre at four o'clock, and invariably we would see William waiting by his window when we drove into our lane. Sometimes Nicole had had enough play at daycare already, but William, who had spent the day alone with his mother, looked forward to playing with her, so we frequently went over to their house for a visit.

William's mother, Jane, was in her late thirties and had a sad story. She and her husband had been married for several years with no children until, to their surprise, Jane became pregnant with William. Unfortunately, soon after William's birth, his father died instantly from a stroke. Jane, who had been a middle manager in a bank in Montreal, decided to move to Toronto and to stay at home for the foreseeable future. She was blissfully happy to be a mother and content to be a stay-at-home mom. She never complained about her day, which she spent entertaining William, doing her household chores, and reading. With her ready smile and knack for funny one-liners, people were happy to be with her.

Jane and I liked each other and became friends, but it was, in many ways, a surprising friendship. I was an Indian immigrant and Jane was a Canadian WASP. I was a working mom whose child went to daycare; Jane stayed at home. We never discussed these differences between us. I was interested in gender, race, imperialism, and underdevelopment, but since I was looking for social relations in which Nicole might find playmates and friends, I had no desire to stir up a potential hornet's nest by opening debates on controversial subjects like those.

Jane and I had enough to talk about concerning raising kids and the ordinary goings-on around the house, and these were safe grounds for social chit-chat. However, I can imagine a conversation between her, the stay-at-home mom, and me, the Indian feminist, going something like this:

Jane: Vijay, you look exhausted! Did you have a hard day at work? How about a cup of coffee? I suppose you don't drink beer?

Me: A cup of coffee would be nice, thanks. I had a long day, but it was interesting. I heard a feminist professor from the United States talk on motherhood at noon between my classes. She says almost all cultures expect women to take on the care and nurturing of chil-

dren, but that this responsibility—she said "burden"—has been
imposed on women by a male-dominated society. It prevents them
from following careers in science or art. There aren't any operas by
women!

Jane: I don't know what to make of all this feminist talk. I tend to resent
her calling child care a burden. I find staying at home with William
very satisfying. Maybe these feminists come up with these theories
about women being oppressed because they are basically frustrated
and unhappy women. I *want* to stay at home with William! I don't
care if feminists think I am oppressed or not.

Me: But, Jane, don't you see? Right from the time you were a child you
were encouraged to think that your ultimate destiny was to spend
your life doing housework and looking after children. This has
been drilled into us from the time we are babies. It just *seems* that
we voluntarily choose to stay at home or take careers like teaching
and nursing. Look at your floor! It's shiny and spotless, as usual.
Did you scrub it again today? The kids will dirty it in no time. I
don't know how you have the patience to do it again and again.
Such a waste of energy.

Jane: To each his own, I suppose...or her own! I would rather clean my
floors than have to read all that feminist junk. I find it depressing
and discouraging. Some of their theories are really outlandish. You
must have the patience of Job to get through them.

Me: Well, I'd better get off this feminist talk. What did you and
William do today?

Jane: We had a fun day. We built a house with Lego and then Edith came
over with her two-year-old to watch Sesame Street. Uh, oh! Look,
Nicole is hitting William again. Don't you think daycare makes
children aggressive? Poor kids, they have to fight for attention with
the daycare staff.

Me: Well, Jane, some women have to work. You would be really
shocked if you heard how many single moms are living in poverty
in Canada. They have to pay the rent and feed their children.
The feckless fathers of these kids refuse to honour their child-
payment orders. Women are struggling hard to live up to their
responsibilities towards their children.

Jane: I know that's the hard part. But take you, for example. You don't
have to work. You could get by without working. You want a career
and you're ambitious. Besides, you like going to university and
meeting your friends there. But I think that you are going to regret
it one day, because you'll have missed all the fun of staying at home

with Nicole. Children grow up so fast, and before you know it they're gone. Don't you miss Nicole when you're sitting in your office and reading these useless feminist books? I bet Nicole misses you and cries for you at the daycare. See how happy she is now, when she can see you watching her!

In reality we had no such conversation, comparing the difficulties of working a "double day" with the tediousness of staying at home with a small child. We did talk about our family backgrounds, and through those conversations it became apparent that our own experiences as children and young women in families shaped our choices and determined "who we were."

Jane had been raised in a small town outside Toronto and was strictly a meat-and-potatoes kind of person. She had lived mostly among other WASPs and was content with the cultural norms with which she had been socialized; she felt no need to question or change them. She saw the future in terms of her WASP upbringing, and she assumed life would continue in much the same way as it had in the past. Coming from different backgrounds dictated our choices of working or staying home. Our choices had been more a response to our families and cultural backgrounds than a conscious commitment to an ideology. Jane's middle-class family and friends believed that a woman should stay at home with her children. The only reason for a woman to work after the birth of her children was financial necessity. Jane had made a career for herself as a bank manger while she was childless, but now she wanted to do what was expected of women in her community. She was fortunate to have received a handsome settlement from the bank and from her husband's insurance company that allowed her to stay at home.

Jane had a bachelor's degree and was a voracious reader, but she was not curious about other cultures or societies. She did not know much about India, and had taken little interest in the immigrants that were coming in from Third World countries. I was not inclined to be censorious, since a few years earlier I too had not known much about Canada. I did not urge her to take an interest in new immigrants or learn about their cultures, or point out to her how her views were derived from her WASP upbringing (as mine were from my Hindu culture). Perhaps Jane might have risen to the challenge if I had posed it, and she might have taken the time to become knowledgeable about other cultures, but my usual inclination is not to hector people, and I did not want to put her on a spot. I was content to have my neighbours respect my "differences"—without assigning an inferior value to them—and accept me for what I was. I did not look past that into their views on race and class, and I was not offended by their absorption with their own cultural norms.

I was the only non-white individual in the townhouse development where we lived, but in the single-family houses in the neighbourhood there were plenty of Chinese, South Asian, and black families. At the neighbourhood mall we saw many of them shopping and eating in restaurants. Jane regarded me simply as a mother and a neighbour and not as representative of a culture or people. My different cultural and ethnic background did not seem to concern Jane, since our attitudes towards children were essentially similar. We were both indulgent parents, with "flexible" rules that got broken constantly. When that happened, we were inclined to gently admonish our children rather than impose punishment.

I was committed to continuing with my teaching career, and I never contemplated taking time off or quitting my job. However, other norms that were constraining in their own way replaced the traditional ones that had applied to other women in my community and family. Although I had not been personally raised by ayahs, the practice was common in many families of my acquaintance. My sister-in-law in Bombay had ayahs taking care of her children even though she did not do any paid work. All of my friends in Bombay had similar arrangements. The idea that the best care for children is provided by their birth mothers was not part of my family's experience or value system.

The expectation of those around me was that I should continue with my career, and no one was particularly sympathetic to my struggle with the demands of a double day. Tom took some pride in my education and would have thought that giving up my job was unnecessary and foolish, particularly since we had easy access to daycare. My father would have been disappointed if I had chosen to stay at home, as he did not have a high regard for housework—or housewives. Like many other men, he thought they were frivolous and idle. My sisters would probably have ridiculed my feelings of guilt and anxiety about leaving Nicole at the daycare. Since everyone around me supported my choice to continue with my job, at first I suffered little of the guilt common to many white Canadian middle-class working mothers, but over the years some of that began to rub off on me as well.

It was different for Edith, another neighbour with a child the same age as Nicole and William, who joined us on some evenings. Edith had always lived in Toronto and had taught at a high school for several years. She had married in her early thirties, and when her daughter Candy was born a few years later, she quit her job to stay at home. Edith considered being a stay-at-home mom a symbol of her economic and social status, and she was determined to be a "good" mother who would put selfish working women like me to shame. She viewed her responsibilities with utmost seriousness. Edith prided herself in keeping Candy "mentally stimulated" throughout the day by reading to her for long hours, never allowing her to watch *Sesame Street* or any other television programs for children. As Nicole, William, and Candy seemed to be developing at the same rate, it frustrated her that there was no visible sign of her good mothering. Still, Nicole did often have a runny nose from viruses she picked up at the daycare, and Edith would virtuously assail me with this fact while regaling us regularly with the minutiae of Candy's good health.

Edith wanted to inculcate the right food tastes in her daughter by making home-cooked, nutritious food—unlike, she said, the prepared, prepackaged and sugar-enriched baby food available in stores. Her condemnation of baby food in jars made me feel guilty when I fed Nicole. At first I tried to follow Edith's example, and I boiled and puréed vegetables and meat alike. However, the preparation exhausted me and by the time the food was ready, I was in a bad temper and did not care if she ate it or not. Once a visiting relative from Bombay watched me go through this elaborate procedure and asked me kindly, "Why are you doing this?" She thought perhaps I was short of money and could not afford to purchase prepared baby food from the store. When I repeated Edith's arguments about the evils of sugar-enriched baby food, she shook her head in complete bewilderment. She did not commend me on my attempts to be a good mother, and her remarks left me with little doubt that she thought I must have been a borderline lunatic to give up the convenience of prepared food. "A working woman like you has no time for this craziness," she pronounced. I went back to feeding Nicole baby food from jars.

One day Edith suggested that I join her in making a birthday cake, since Nicole and Candy's birthdays were within a couple of days of each other. I thought that it would be an interesting experience since I had never baked a cake and I could feel virtuous like Edith. This turned out, however, to be no simple cooking venture. The cake had to be made "from scratch." We would turn back the clock and do what I imagined stay-at-home women did fifty years before.

Preparation for the baking day required a special trip to the grocery store to buy all the ingredients and the paraphernalia for cutting and decorating the cake in the shape of Mickey Mouse. Back home, we got as much flour on the counters and the floor as in the mixing bowls. ("More cleaning!" I fumed under my breath.) Cutting the cake was supposed to have been the creative and fun part of the project, but trying to cut pieces in the right shape was a harrowing experience. The icing, when we tried to spread it on the cake, came out in discouraging gobs, producing awful, unanticipated lumps. This project took up the whole day, trying my patience and putting me in an abominable mood. The result was a pathetic-looking cake that only someone with a great deal of imagination could have perceived as resembling Mickey Mouse. That experience cured me of any further desire to emulate Canadian foremothers, and I vowed never again to bake another cake from scratch. From that time on I ordered birthday cakes from the bakery.

After living in the townhouse for five years, Tom and I decided to fulfill the middle-class Canadian dream and move to a detached home. The value of our property had appreciated a fair bit in the five years we had lived there, and our incomes had also gone up. We got a more expensive house and, of course, a larger mortgage. The new house was in Don Mills, then considered a suburb of Toronto, on a tree-lined street with single-detached bungalows on very wide lots. The area had been developed soon after World War II, and the bungalows that dominated the street were in fairly uniform design. What most attracted us was the lot, which was full of mature trees. There were two lilac trees and two crab apple trees directly outside a large "picture window." They looked stunningly beautiful when they flowered in the spring and early summer. There were also two large oaks in the backyard and several tall cedars that gave us almost complete privacy from our neighbours.

Many years later, I read a feminist article on the lives of middle-class mothers who lived in Don Mills during the 1950s and 1960s. The suburb had originally attracted families whose fathers left early in the morning for work and whose mothers stayed home with the children. The women were quite content with traditional roles and absorbed in the daily routine of their children. The author highlighted the dominance of traditional roles then prevalent by describing the elaborate ruses one woman used to disguise the fact that she had taken on a part-time job (not because she wanted to get away from the tediousness of her daily life but because the family had run into financial difficulties). The article analyzed the WASP values that dominated the community. Immigrants from Third World countries had not yet come in any significant numbers to live in Toronto.

By the time we went to live in Don Mills in the early 1980s, the families who lived there had changed considerably. Our street was predominately white, but had some Chinese and South Asian families, and an occasional black family as well. There was also a mix of lifestyles, with some stay-at-home moms and others who went outside the home to work. Happily for us, we found that our next-door neighbours, a Jewish family, had a daughter, Sara, who was exactly the same age as Nicole. Two doors over on the other side of the street lived a family from Sri Lanka whose daughter, Sudha, was about two years older than Nicole. I found the ethnic mix of my immediate neighbours interesting, and got acquainted with both families, although they did not have much interaction with each other.

Novels often portray Indian immigrant family life as having a dual nature. Home life is imbued with traditional Indian norms, while the school and workplace are dominated by WASP culture. All immigrants need to accommodate to this culture, although how much they choose to integrate and assimilate depends on many things. Cultural and class conflicts become interwoven with generation gaps, and the novels set in Canada or Britain have more often than not portrayed such problems through the eyes of the young members of immigrant families. I found Meera Syal's award-winning 1996 novel *Anita and Me*, set in a small British town, particularly enjoyable.

Written from the perspective of Meena, an only child living with her Punjabi parents in a working-class neighbourhood, it portrays this compartmentalization of private and public life. Meena moves easily between the family, school and home, and becomes close friends with Anita, the impoverished child of a white British mom on welfare. Meena's engineer father and school teacher mother are hurt and humiliated when they encounter racism, but they are unaware of their own class biases. They believe that if they buy a house in a middle-class neighbourhood and get their daughter into a private school, they can shield themselves from bigotry. Meena comes under intense pressure to study for examinations that will get her accepted into the private school while Anita, left more and more to her own devices, drifts into sexual experimentation. The novel ends with the girls coming together one last time, implicitly recognizing that they must go their separate ways.

The experiences of a biracial family like ours were different. There was no divide between the norms of the dominant culture and our family life or any feelings of "us versus them." Our neighbours were professional, middle-class, two-parent, heterosexual families much like ours, and broadly speaking, we had similar values and aspirations for our children. However, we met our Indian and Canadian relatives separately, in tacit recognition by all concerned that they were vastly different from each other and shared no common interests.

We hopped between the two cultures. When we visited Tom's family, we followed WASP cultural norms of behaviour and interaction: we were more reserved, careful in respecting the privacy of others, and had quiet, uncontroversial conversations. We often ate beef stew or pot roasts with mashed potatoes, peas, corn, and carrots. When we met with my side of the family, we were loud and boisterous, freely commenting on every conceivable topic, and arguing avidly over what we referred to as Indian and Canadian norms. We ate spicy food but spoke in English to accommodate the non-Hindi-speaking adults and the children, none of whom understood the language. Like all immigrants, we talked a lot about "home" and the "old country," whether it was politics, a newly published book, or merely bits and pieces of gossip about old friends and relatives there.

Sara and Nicole were close friends and often played together. Sara's mother, Rachel, was a pretty woman, always stylishly dressed, who had a bachelor's degree from McGill University. Raised in a prosperous family in Montreal, she was proud of being married to a successful lawyer who worked long hours to keep the family in comfort, and more than happy with the perks of being a well-to-do housewife. Their house was beautifully decorated with plush, upholstered furniture and colour-coordinated carpets and drapes. The kitchen was fully equipped with dishwasher, microwave, and garbage disposal—the latest kitchen gadgetry. Their walkout basement was divided into a family room with a television set and a large area where Nicole, Sara and the other children played. There was another small room, which was used as a bedroom by their live-in Filipina nanny. Rachel had her own car and she entertained herself by playing tennis and working out at a health club to which she belonged.

Rachel seemed content with her life. She did little housework herself and thus could hardly complain that her husband did not share in these tasks. He was more or less an absentee father, but that did not bother Rachel; it left her free to pursue her own interests at her leisure. Rachel was charming and discreet, and, although she tried not to let on, I got the distinct impression she felt sorry for slobs like me who had to work at a job.

The cultural mix in our neighbourhood and families meant that talk of ethnic and cultural differences was frequent, routine, and normal. Rachel kept a kosher kitchen, so at the age of five Nicole became aware of the different dietary codes. When Sara ate with us, which happened often, we talked about which food was kosher, and it often provided a good excuse for the children to have a soft drink instead of milk at mealtimes. Sara, however, seemed to have a particularly sensitive nose for the smell of bacon. When we had it for breakfast, she would often come over. At the table she would righteously inform us that she was not allowed to eat bacon because she was Jewish. Then, when she thought we were not watching, she would quickly pop a piece into her mouth. Invariably Nicole would see her do it, and there would be loud complaints that Sara had done a "forbidden" thing—or there would be conspiratorial giggles from both girls.

We also had what Rachel dubbed "Jewish ducks" in the neighbourhood. They lived in a garden a few minutes from our house that had a stream. When we took a walk there, we would take bread to feed the ducks. It had to be bagels, though, because both Sara and Nicole insisted that this was the preference of the ducks. Rachel declared that the ducks were obviously Jewish.

Sudha's parents were both immigrants. When we met them, her father, Raja, taught auto mechanics to high school students in Toronto. After establishing himself here, he had returned to Sri Lanka and had a marriage arranged for him with Shanta. Shanta had been trained as a psychiatrist in Sri Lanka, and on coming to Canada had quickly completed all her qualifying examinations and residency requirements and was now working as a psychiatrist at a major downtown hospital. They were both Protestants and attended church regularly on Sundays. Shanta did not quit working after Sudha was born, and the couple did not have a nanny. Rather, Sudha went to daycare until she began junior kindergarten, when Raja took over much of her daily care.

Raja was a devoted "Mr. Mom" for Sudha. He was cast in that role because as a teacher he had a short workday, whereas Sudha's mother worked long hours. Shanta did not drive, so Raja drove Sudha to her private school in the morning and went back in the evening to bring her home. He watched Sudha after school, arranged for her to play with friends, drove her to dance and swimming lessons, and did a variety of other tasks for her. Raja had assumed the care of Sudha as a pragmatic response to their family situation, and not because he had any particularly strong belief in sharing the responsibilities of child care with his wife. And although he was happy to be a "Mr. Mom" to Sudha, he drew the line at cooking and cleaning. Often he would go late in the evening to bring Shanta home from work or from the subway, and when she got home she had to prepare the meal for them. Sometimes Shanta would complain about having to cook when Raja had been home all evening, but she was not really discontent with her family arrangement.

Raja was acting out of character for a South Asian male, but his attitude was matter-of-fact, and he showed little self-consciousness in being a "Mr. Mom." To me, Raja was just another parent, albeit a special one, because he was South Asian like me. We babysat for each other, shared driving, walked both girls to the park together, or simply sat at the kitchen table while the girls played together. Raja's interaction with Sara's family, however, was distant and formal. They seldom communicated directly with each other, and consequently Sudha was limited to playing only with Nicole or with Nicole and Sara in our house. I had read feminist literature about domestic workers and thus went out of my way to befriend Sara's nanny, Nora, but she would have none of it and kept me at arm's length. I was her employer's neighbour and friend, and she wanted to keep our interaction at that strictly polite and formal level.

One evening there was a bad snowstorm, and we were all reading quietly at home. Rachel called to ask if she could bring Sara over to play with Nicole for a couple of hours. It was an unusual request, given the weather and the lateness of the hour, but Rachel explained that she had had an argument with Nora and it had resulted in her asking the nanny to pack up her bags and leave the house. She did not want Sara to witness Nora's departure. I agreed to have Sara come to our house, but was torn with indecisiveness and guilt. I was concerned for Nora and wondered where she would go in the severe snowstorm that was raging outside. Although I was quite willing to have Nora stay with me for the night or until she could make some arrangements, at the same time I had absorbed the WASP value of minding my own business, and thought it would be inappropriate for me to interfere in the household affairs of my neighbours. Fortunately, Nora, whom I happened to see a few days later at a shopping mall, had been resourceful. She had called a cab right away and was living with some friends while trying to find a job as a retail sales clerk.

Sometimes Raja and Shanta would invite us as a family to the dinner parties they hosted for their friends from Sri Lanka. At these parties I would meet other psychiatrists from Sri Lanka who had been classmates of Shanta or had met her in Toronto. A very traditional South Asian atmosphere pervaded these dinner parties, and even though many of the women were psychiatrists, they assumed very conventional female roles. Since everyone had come as a family, there were always children clinging to their mother's legs or running around the house. The women usually sat in small clusters talking to one another, and the men did the same in another part of the room. The women had the responsibility of minding the children and sorting out their quarrels, while the men continued talking, smoking, and drinking unconcernedly. The women helped Shanta get the dinner on the table, made sure the children ate, and helped with tidying up. When I first went to these dinners, I assumed that these professional women with well-paying jobs would act differently from the stay-at-home mothers, and when they didn't, I was amazed and a little disappointed as well.

My personal network of South Asian friends had contracted in the previous few years, primarily because family and work took up most of my time. Now I mostly met South Asians as university colleagues or through my volunteer work in immigrant women's organizations. However, I continued to meet many South Asians in my sisters' homes. Most of the men, given my brother-in-laws' professions, tended to be corporate executives, although some were in private business as well. Their wives were employed in offices or were stay-at-home moms. They visited each other's homes frequently, where they ate mostly Punjabi food, talked in Hindi, Punjabi, and English, listened to popular and classical Hindi and Western music and sometimes watched television. On these occasions men and women both drank alcohol, but women seldom smoked cigarettes.

There were many signs of Westernization at both formal and informal gatherings. Fathers and children, rather than being formal and distant from each other, had a somewhat egalitarian relation as they shared jokes and laughed together. There were none of the traditional Indian restraints on male-female interactions, and conversations between men and women occurred easily. There was many a discussion comparing "Indian" and "Canadian" values and norms. Most of the Indians were committed to assimilating WASP culture, but were not prepared to modify all their core values. They strongly avowed their commitment to the traditional Hindu ideal of taking care of the male's parents. Daughters are conventionally responsible for caring only for their parents-in-law, and I never heard either men or women challenging such a value. Similarly, both men and women had traditional expectations of each other's roles and responsibilities within marriage. Changes in traditional Hindu, Muslim and Sikh values did occur, but mostly in response to necessity and circumstance. For example, a male would share in the housework and child care, to greater or lesser degree, if his wife did paid work outside the home. My feminist values, as much as my interracial marriage, created a social distance between me and most of my sisters' friends. I integrated myself more with my academic friends and neighbours.

We lived in Don Mills for only three years before we decided to move again. We were greatly influenced by a book we read on investing by Morton Shulman, a former coroner in Toronto and a successful businessman. He predicted that property values in Toronto would rise within the decade, and his advice to readers was to buy the most expensive house they could afford. We had accumulated considerable home equity by then and had made some other good investments, so we decided to take Shulman's advice and buy ourselves a bigger home in Rosedale, near downtown Toronto. This house had two studies, a family room, and lots of space for Nicole to play with all her friends. It was old and required renovations, but we figured we could do those as we went along. We took a big gamble on buying such an expensive home, but over the years it proved to be a good investment, and one that we have enjoyed immensely.

As a graduate student, I had heard complaints from other women who felt that their identity was absorbed by that of their spouses on marriage. Later, as a professor, I chafed at the fact that my race was always considered the most important aspect of my identify. By the time we moved to Rosedale, however, I realized that in much of my life outside the university I had become simply "Nicole's mother." I first became aware of this when Nicole was five and started attending school. Perhaps it was the way school routines brought mothers into daily contact with each other that created this persona. I, too, did not know the names of many of the mothers with whom I regularly spoke. I merely identified them as the mothers of Nicole's classmates.

The Toronto Montessori School was located in a large, brick building surrounded on all sides with playing fields. Although it was not a grand building with pillars, elaborately carved wooden doors, or marble floors, it had large, bright, airy rooms with very high ceilings and many mullioned windows. The hallways were wide, with sparkling, tiled floors. The building had only one entrance, which was opened in the morning at quarter to nine, then locked for the day and not reopened until fifteen minutes before the end of school. Parents had to walk their child to the door of the classroom and fetch them there in the evening. Consequently, parents clustered at the entrance, in the hallways, or outside the classrooms before and after school. This provided me with a close-up view of some of their habits and norms.

Since there was no daycare before or after classes, the school attracted children from families that had a stay-at-home mom, nanny, or parent whose working hours coincided with the school hours. Most of the children came from traditional two-parent families, and I did not know of any single moms whose children were at the school. A few of the students fit the stereotypical image of rich kids who attended private schools, but most were just children of professionals, and some had interesting ethnic backgrounds. In addition to the WASP and Jewish students, there were many whose parents were from Eastern European countries or were immigrants from the Far East (primarily Hong Kong) or South Asia. But there were no black children at the school. Some of the students were from interracial and intercultural homes, with a British father and an Iranian mother, or a white Canadian mother and an Egyptian father, or a Filipina mother and a white American father. Although I went out of my way to say hello to the South Asian mothers of the students, I talked mostly to the mothers of Nicole's friends.

Ethnic and racial tolerance was the rule in the school, perhaps a tacit recognition that the fee-paying, middle-class parents of the students would have loudly and vociferously complained of anything less than that. The children all took their lunches to school, but I never heard any stories about children being teased about their food—even if they brought anything other than sandwiches. There was, on one occasion, considerable alarm over a candy thief who snuck into some lunch boxes to get the most desired chocolates. Sometimes when students from the school came to our house, I would quiz them about their knowledge and awareness of their ethnic background. A ten-year-old girl once got fed up with my questions and said, "Mrs. Agnew, my parents are from Hong Kong, but I am Canadian." That remark pretty much summed up the attitude of most of the children at the school.

Many of the mothers were professionals—doctors, dentists, lawyers or teachers, but whether career women or stay-at-home moms, they were self-assured and articulate. They exuded a sense of well-being that came with success, class, and status. Becoming a professional woman was in itself an achievement, and it gave the women confidence to express their views on the teaching methods of the school and on the values and norms that the school (and by implication we parents) ought to be inculcating in our children. But there was little political consciousness. The mothers did not measure themselves in feminist terms, and they did not envision the future for their daughters along those lines. These mothers had rarely taken time to reflect on the social factors that had brought them to their elevated positions. Rather, they perceived their professional achievements in individual terms, as the rewards of their own hard work.

Most of the women were comfortable with the status quo, which had served them well professionally and socially. Their attitude differed sharply from the one I was familiar with at the university. There, white women professors often felt that they had to express, at least towards me, some awareness of their racial and class privilege, usually through some form of self-deprecation. However, what they deemed to be politically correct made me feel that they were being condescending, and treating me not only as an outsider but also as an inferior.

At the school, among the apolitical mothers, I was simply one of the crowd. These mothers were devoid of guilt about their social and class privilege. Their sense of entitlement did not necessarily make them callous; they didn't lack a social conscience, and many willingly donated money (if not time) to worthwhile causes. They seemed to take the view, however, that social activism was not their calling, and so they were content to leave the work of bringing about social change to those with more inclination or motivation to engage in it. They focused instead on promoting their own and their children's welfare. My academic interests heightened my awareness of race, ethnicity, and gender biases, but I did not find the other mothers railing against the social system for its WASPishness or patriarchal domination. Many of them were baby boomers, and I sometimes heard from their children that they had indulged in the youthful rebellions of the 1960s; but as parents, they were conservative.

Despite the professional status of many of the mothers, they still assumed the primary care for their child. They arranged play times, birthday parties, and other social events for the children. The role of the fathers seemed to be limited to driving them to or from friends' houses. I did not detect any rancour among the women at having so much responsibility placed upon them, and I never heard any discussion of the males' participation or lack of it in household duties. One explanation for this may be that many had a nanny or other part-time help, and were able to buy prepared meals or eat at restaurants to reduce the stress of the double day.

Most times, it was the mothers who helped the child with schoolwork. In grade five, the students were assigned a book report on a novel of their own choosing. A parent often needed to help make the choice. The presentation of the report had to be "creative," and the children came to school with elaborately designed posters with pictures of authors, illustrations of scenes from the novel, and very well written prose. The book reports revealed the hours many a mother had devoted to the project, and one could only hope that the child had contributed to it equally.

A major event of the school was the annual parents' night, when students from grades five and six presented their science projects. I noticed that the projects often had a theme derived from one of the parents' professions. For example, a girl whose mother was a dentist presented a project on teeth, complete with pictures, charts, and plastic models of dentures. A physician's child undertook a project on dissecting a cow's tongue, while another dissected an eye, and a physics professor helped his daughter make an elaborate model of an electrical field. Nicole's project was on weather forecasting, and Tom brought her satellite pictures, instruments for measuring wind and other gadgetry that the children could touch and experiment with.

The parents spared no cost in helping their child get her or his project ready for parents' night. Each table on which a project was displayed had many elaborate posters, a variety of lavishly illustrated books and other paraphernalia. A sense of pride and happiness pervaded the school as parents celebrated their children's achievements, and no one spoiled the party by mentioning their own hard work. The children had many knowledgeable people at their beck and call, willing and anxious to help them learn. By and large, though, the students remained unconscious of their privilege, accepting it all as a matter of course.

The two stars of Nicole's class were scions of very famous, wealthy families. One was a blond, good-looking and friendly boy; the other was taciturn and prone to mischief. The antics of the two boys dominated the talk among the mothers as they stood outside the classroom, providing for me a fascinating insight into the social aspirations some of them had for their children. Some would none too subtly encourage their child to be friendly with one of the boys, or preferably both. They wanted their child to be invited to the boys' homes, and they seemed to have wholly sub-scribed to the myth that the primary purpose of a private school was to give their child a toehold in the network of the elites rather than a good education. The fact that they were nine and ten year olds and thus likely to change friendships weekly, or at least monthly, held little import for these mothers. Being assiduously courted by these aspiring mothers made life tough for the two boys.

One was a particularly difficult student and openly defied authority, but his social status intimidated the teachers, who simply did not know how to handle him. The child continuously tested the limits by openly provoking his teachers. The other students in class, awed by his defiance of the teach-ers, became his ardent followers, much to the chagrin of parents like me. The principal, however, wanted to keep the child in the school and expected the teachers to make the situation work, so they were reluctant to upset the parents by punishing him. Any other child might have been kicked out of the school, but the principal thought accommodating a celebrity's misbehaving son was a small price to pay for the bragging rights of having the kid there. The tension in the class meant that he made little academic progress; his parents wanted to withdraw him from the school, but the principal of the school, his mother told me, telephoned and "begged" her not to do so. So his mischief-making in class remained unabated and unchallenged. The only time he was completely flummoxed was when his father's uniformed chauffeur came in to get him from the class. Embarrassed by this display of family wealth, he hung his head down and, looking shamefaced, quietly slunk out of the classroom.

If some mothers seemed enamoured with the social opportunities the school provided for their children, they presented a problem for those who had enrolled their children there in hopes of gaining a good education for their child. Tanya's mother, Rose, wanted her daughter to get a good education at the school, but remain closely attached to her Italian working-class relatives. It was hard to balance these goals, but she did it with great determination and, it seemed to me, with success.

Rose had immigrated to Canada as a small child with her working-class parents. She later attended the University of Toronto and obtained a bachelor's degree. There she dated an Italian who came from a similar background, and they married soon after graduating. After finishing school, they both had a hard time finding a job, but eventually Rose's husband found a job as a driver with the Transit Commission. He supported her while she obtained certification as a teacher. Rose found a job in a Catholic school, and over the years further upgraded her qualifications. By the time we knew her she was the head of the languages department in her school. She confided in me that she had frequently offered to support her spouse through graduate school or teacher's college, but he had little interest in changing his job.

Rose was a devoted mother to Tanya, her only child. An intense and hardworking woman, she aspired to advance in her profession. Yet, like many other women at the school, she observed traditional gender norms and inculcated those in her daughter. She was the disciplinarian at home, and the rumour around school was that she imposed disproportionate punishment on Tanya for small infractions of rules. Even the teachers protected Tanya from her mother's strict discipline and never reported any of her mischief to her mother. Tanya always excelled in all the subjects.

Rose was in a difficult position in the social environment of the school, dominated as it was by professional parents. When Nicole was eight or nine, most of her friends found Tanya's father's occupation somewhat exciting, and admired his uniform when he came to get her. Occasionally, when neither of the parents could come to get Tanya, her working-class grandfather would come for her. However, by the time Nicole left the school at the age of eleven, some students, no doubt repeating the snobbish remarks they had heard in their homes, were beginning to comment on the atypical nature of Tanya's father's job. Rose's coping strategy was to eschew all social contact between Tanya and her friends after school. Tanya almost never attended any birthday parties and never visited any friend's house.

I got to know Rose because some days both of us would arrive at the school early and stand together and chat. We had much in common: we both had immigrant backgrounds and were teachers. Besides that, we were both anxious about our child's academic progress, and gossip about what was happening in the classroom brought us together. In these chit-chats I learned about Rose's family routine. Like some of the parents, Rose had a schedule of activities for Tanya outside the school, and Tanya did not have much free time. Neither, I guess, did Rose, who drove Tanya around and, she told me, also regularly cooked traditional Italian meals at home and did most of the household chores as well. She even bottled and preserved tomatoes in the fall. Rose was exceptional in having the energy and enthusiasm to spend the day making homemade preserves while most of us were scrambling to do ordinary chores.

Though many of us shared the strain of the double day, there was seldom any complaint about it—another manifestation of the reserve and restraint typical of the WASP culture that dominated the school environment. The subtle message that I got from the mothers at the school was that this was a private and individual issue, and that it would be impolite to discuss it in public, particularly since that might involve a criticism of one's spouse. The good manners observed at the school meant that one refrained from passing comment on how people managed their private household affairs. Thus, no one's sensitivity about being a full-time housewife or working woman was ruffled.

Since I was familiar with the academic debates about domestic workers, I listened attentively to the mothers when they discussed their nannies. The mothers did not seem to be suffering any guilt or anxiety about oppressing women of another nationality or race. Rather, they described their own generosity in helping with the problems the nannies encountered, either with their working visas or with their families in their countries of origin. They adopted the attitude that they needed the service and had purchased it in an open labour market at a fair price, and that was that. I politely refrained from making any comments, however oblique, that might have been construed as critical of mothers who employed nannies. I never encountered any mother at the school using a nanny to assert her status over me, and the nannies I saw at the school did not have hangdog expressions. They were cheerful and chatted with each other just like the mothers. Mothers and nannies, however, seldom chatted together.

I did find the physical strain of the double day exhausting, but my feminist politics made me wary of employing other women to cook or do other chores around the house. My routine on some days went like this: at eight-thirty in the morning I left the house with Nicole to take her to school, and after walking her up to the classroom, I went to York. There I taught my classes, attended meetings, went to the library, met with students, and took care of my correspondence. I left York at three-thirty to get Nicole from school by four o'clock. On reaching home we had a quick snack and then I drove her to piano or ballet lessons at a local community centre. Then I rushed home to get dinner started. In an hour's time I would drive back and bring her home. At home, I finished preparing dinner while talking to Nicole. At six o'clock Tom came home and we would eat, and then he would clean up the kitchen. By eight o'clock we had to be thinking about the next day. I prepared for my classes and Tom helped Nicole with her schoolwork. On particularly horrendous days, I had to return to York at quarter after six to teach an evening course. I was not trying to be a "supermom." I just wanted to keep abreast of my career and my responsibilities as a mother.

When Nicole began junior high at the University of Toronto Schools at the age of eleven, I had less interaction with the parents of her school friends, and once she could travel by public transportation on her own, I knew them only formally. I did not realize how much the memory of being called Nicole's mother had faded until a couple of years ago when she was already at university. About two weeks into a first-year course, I noticed a short, slim student with dark hair waiting quietly for me to finish talking with other students who had clustered around me after the lecture. When everyone else had left, he asked, "Are you Nicole's mother?" He explained that he had been discussing my lectures (and I guess me) with his girlfriend, who was from Toronto but attending another university. After hearing about the lectures, his girlfriend, who turned out to be a former classmate of Nicole's, said, "Oh, that's Nicole's mother." So I suppose that although I thought that the children were all absorbed in their own routines, they were noting and storing in their minds some knowledge about the diverse identities of the mothers of their friends.

Nicole accepted her family life and school environment as routine matters of fact. I can recall no incidents that might have signaled concern over her biracial identity. I have thought about stories set in the southern United States in which white Americans are shown to be outraged at the sight of a biracial couple, evoking anxiety in them and those around them. However, the social context in the 1980s in Toronto, with its immigrant population, was vastly different. There was public concern over racism and thus there were no overt comments from friends and neighbours and no incidents that made Nicole self-conscious regarding her racial identity. It was not ignored, either. Tom's sister was an ardent worshipper of the sun, and she would frequently and ruefully comment on what she described as Nicole's "ready-to-go" tanned skin. A joke in our family about my brother's children in the States, born after he moved back there, was that they were "half Indian, half Canadian, but all American."

Perhaps our network of disparate families contributed to Nicole's sense of being like everyone else. Over the years she had girlfriends whose parents were immigrants: there was Jen, with a Filipina mother and a Hungarian father; Nadine, with a Filipino father and an Iranian mother who had met each other in Japan; and Vanessa, with a Malaysian mother and a German father. But I am reluctant to read too much into this. Perhaps the girls were drawn to each other because they recognized something known and familiar, or perhaps it was mere chance, given the ethnic mix of Toronto and of the schools that they attended.

Nicole attended a summer program for high school students at Radcliffe College when she was sixteen years old and had completed grade twelve. The program's goal was to inculcate an interest in science among girls, and women in a variety of scientific fields came to meet the students. Each student was also assigned a mentor who would be a "big sister" to her. Stephanie, a post-doctorate fellow in chemistry at Harvard, was Nicole's "big sister."

Stephanie had white American parents. Her father was a professor, and she had been raised in California and studied at Berkeley. She was married to Partha, the son of an Indian engineer who had immigrated to the United States and was also a post-doctoral fellow in biochemistry. They were a perfect match for Nicole; she spent much time in their home and got to love them both. They were intending to start a family and perhaps saw in Nicole what the future might bring.

The next year, when Nicole decided to attend an American university, she sought out Stephanie's advice in choosing an essay topic to write about in her applications for admission. Stephanie recommended that she write about growing up in the two cultures of her family. Nicole enthusiastically took to the idea, but inevitably I got drawn into the project as well, and began to lecture her at every opportunity on immigration, ethnicity, race, and culture. My lectures, however, only irritated her, and losing patience with me one day, she responded angrily, "I don't really care about all that stuff." The essay that she eventually wrote described the Diwali celebrations that she had attended at my sisters' homes and the Christmases that she had spent at her grandmother's house. She talked about the decorations on these occasions, the clothes she had worn, and the food we had eaten.

Nicole concluded by saying, perhaps in response to my harping on immigration and ethnicity, that the ethnic and racial identities of her various aunts and uncles had not mattered to her because both sides of the family had loved her and that had been enough.

11

Fair Play and Safe Places

I had hoped, when I first started teaching at York, that I would be able to talk with other members of the faculty about our experiences in teaching: to share some of the trials, as well as some of the joys, to hear what they had to say about their profession and so to better inform my own approach to teaching. That wish, however, proved fanciful. I was part of the contract faculty, a status then deemed transitional and temporary. The regular faculty members tended to disregard our presence. As most of their research was best conducted independently or with individuals in their field of specialization, developing a sense of belonging and community by that route was also difficult. I came to know two or three professors as part of a teaching team in the Third World course, but had no other way of relating to the department or getting to know more about the culture of the university—how committees were run and what rules applied to them, the norms of behaviour in these committees (as well as in the classroom), where power and authority resided, whether in committees, the senate, the board of governors, designated employees or the president—and so on.

Departmental meetings should have provided an opportunity for this, but I found that almost all the people who attended them were white, tenured faculty members. None of them had any interest in me, although they always politely acknowledged my presence by saying hello. I was already conscious of being different from others as an immigrant, and now found myself sidelined as a marginally employed faculty member. Since I had little self-confidence, I never felt comfortable enough to participate in discussions, and so sitting quietly at meetings and listening to others became a disheartening and discouraging routine. Although I thought it was my immigrant status and race that had alienated me from the rest of the faculty, later I found that feelings of isolation and detachment from the department were common in the contract faculty. Many of these part-time teachers felt angry that personal circumstances or limited opportunities in their area of specialization had compelled them to accept contractual appointments. They felt exploited by the university administration.

In the 1980s I began to suspect that some contract teaching assignments in the Division of Social Science and other departments at the university were being withheld from me because of my race. The perception that I was an object of racism made me feel helpless and very unhappy. Things came to a head when I was overlooked for an assignment to teach an introductory, first-year social science course for which I was both qualified and had experience; a white woman with no PhD or prior teaching experience was hired instead. Infuriated, I decided to phone the union representing the contract faculty and ask for their advice, something I had been hesitant to do up until then, still feeling lost and insecure despite having been at York for a few years. Much to my surprise, I got a very supportive response from the people there, who invited me to come and discuss my complaints at the union office. I launched a grievance. It took a few weeks to make its way through the administrative hierarchy at the university, but eventually a decision was made, and it was in my favour.

The process brought into stark relief many interrelated issues. I realized how uninformed I was about the structure of the university, about who made decisions and how they were made. My status as immigrant and non-white contract faculty made it difficult for me to get to know other faculty members, integrate myself into the department and become knowledgeable about the university. My marginal teaching position also excluded me from informal faculty networks. Consequently, it was easy for administrators to overlook my claims. Reflecting back now, I see that my situation was similar to that of many other immigrants who lack professional networks when they first come to Canada. That makes it difficult for them to locate jobs and impedes their mobility within the job settings they do manage to find. Information, which is critical, often comes through a grapevine to which they are not connected. Immigrants may have networks within their own communities, but many, and especially non-whites, are still marginal in decision-making bodies in both the private and public sectors.

The union representing the contract faculty had only recently been certified, and the contract they had negotiated, which was somewhat rudimentary, left lots of room for "interpretation" according to the needs (or what sometimes seemed like the whims) of department chairs. Administrators frequently used two ploys to manipulate the hiring process. The first was to word an advertisement so narrowly that only their chosen candidate could possibly qualify; the second was to interpret academic qualifications in a way that would disqualify the individual they did not want to hire. In one case, the chair of a department disqualified me by adding as a requirement a "Canadian law degree." Mine, from Bombay University, did not count. Although the contract ensured some fair play in the allocation of teaching positions, its protection was minimal. This reinforcement of my feeling of vulnerability made it seem imperative that I find some way of ensuring that administrators in various departments would not casually brush aside my applications to teach courses for which I was qualified.

I was drawn to the union by the need to survive in the university system, but I also found a sympathetic community. My initial contact had been encouraging; when I expressed my disgruntlement to union officers, they listened sympathetically, and did not try to defend the administration, as regular faculty members seemed to do. I felt relief in finding myself in a supportive and responsive environment and consequently volunteered for some union committees, becoming an active participant in their meetings and discussions. As a bonus, I honed some political skills.

As an immigrant married to a white Canadian, I was free, by choice, from the constraints of my ethnic community. However, the flip side of my situation was that I had no larger group to which I could connect or relate. The values of my childhood culture eschewed individualism as selfish, and gave importance to collectives like the family and the local community. The union, for me, was like another family, and I recognized, if only subconsciously, that my well-being was linked to it. Classism, racism, and sexism directed towards other people had consequences for me, and in helping to alleviate these things for them, I was also helping myself.

At the union office and in committee meetings I met many other members of the contract faculty, most of whom, at the time, were white.

Over the years, two other Indian women became involved with the union, which was surprising since during the time I was actively involved, there were only six or seven Indian women in the whole faculty. Like me, they had no previous experience with the labour movement. Our involvement with the union had arisen out of specific, practical difficulties rather than ideological or political motivations. We all volunteered to sit on union committees (grievances and negotiations) and ran for offices such as secretary or treasurer. Many of the white activists in the union had more ideological commitments, aligning themselves, at least intellectually, with "the oppressed." It was class oppression that most interested them, followed by gender oppression, but their ideals made them sympathetic to complaints about racism as well.

At first, my value to the union lay in my willingness to occupy a spot on one of the committees, since it was invariably difficult to find people with the time to fill them. This was difficult for me as well, since Nicole was then a young child and needed me at home, but my feelings of insecurity at the university and my need to make a place for myself in an empathetic environment were strong.

A core of contract faculty members at the union set the strategy, direction, and priorities, and paid union officials aided them. By diligently attending meetings and listening intently to discussions within the union and between the union and administration, I learned about the university's structure and hierarchy. I also came to the sad realization that since our contract had yet to be fleshed out with detailed provisions, much depended on networks and contacts within the university. I felt somewhat reassured by the existence of the union, but I was now getting concrete information, as opposed to my own vague suspicions, about the workings of the university. That awareness only reinforced my feelings of vulnerability and insecurity.

Initially, I had insufficient knowledge about negotiation strategies, university politics and union priorities to insert my concerns about racism into the union agenda, but the physical presence of Indian women in meetings had an impact on the thinking of the activists in the union. Our participation in union activities made them much more amenable to including non-discrimination clauses in contract negotiations, sometimes even giving them priority. We sat across the table from senior university administrators during contract negotiations. Now, at least, they knew the names and faces of Indian women on campus.

My participation in union work meant that when I experienced some difficulty at the university, I could phone the union or senior administration and have the problem resolved quickly and informally. One summer I had just begun to teach a course when I discovered I was ill and might need to be hospitalized. At that time, the contract faculty had no provision for sick leave, so I telephoned the union and the vice-president of the university and explained my plight. The vice-president said, "Vijay, take the summer off and get well. You will be paid for the summer whether you are hospitalized or not." I was hospitalized for several weeks without having to forego my salary. Another time, a dean was investigating some hiring irregularities in one of the departments. Seeing me at one of the negotiation meetings, the lawyer for the university asked me, quite out of the blue, whether I had applied for a summer job in the department that year. I said I had, and shortly thereafter the department just happened to discover several applications, including mine, which had mysteriously gone missing when summer jobs were allocated. I was retroactively paid for a position that should have been assigned to me but had gone to someone else.

Department chairs knew that I was active in the union, so they were wary of overlooking my claims to teach courses, but surprisingly, that did not always stop them. They would usually excuse themselves by saying, "Vijay, we'd love to have you teach with us but we thought you would prefer to teach with the [such-and-such] department." My new, thorough knowledge of the contract emboldened me, and I protected myself with the grievance procedure. My experiences were shared by the other Indian women, but although we all had complaints, only some of us actually grieved. Since union officials heard complaints from all four of the Indian women who were contract faculty members on campus, they were reluctant to assign blame to us and excuse the department chairs. They were very supportive, but there was not always much else they could do. We Indian women perceived ourselves to be victims of racism and sexism, and felt that our situation was only an extreme manifestation of the precarious position of all members of the contract faculty. The situation of the Indian women prompted the union to seek ways to increase job security.

The union used one of my complaints as a test case to argue against the right of chairs to assign courses as they pleased. Eventually this complaint went to arbitration and the decision, in my favour, entrenched the principle of seniority in the contract. This clause was a boon to the contract faculty for years to come, but many administrators saw it as a nuisance, if not a curse. Winning this and many other cases helped assuage some feelings of powerlessness, and I began to feel less vulnerable and insecure.

Over the years my personal experiences influenced my academic interests, and my research came to focus more and more on racism and sexism. In the early 1990s I researched the racism and sexism experienced by Asian and black immigrants to Canada. Because I was unable to locate material on their experiences in Canada since World War II, I began to do field work among immigrant women's organizations in Toronto to collect more data. As a feminist, I was concerned not to exploit them, so I volunteered to sit on their boards of directors and various committees, and I continued to work with them long after my research was finished.

Many immigrant women's organizations, I discovered, were originally started by middle-class immigrant women from Asia, Africa, or the Caribbean in order to provide social services to working-class, non-English-speaking women in their ethnic communities. They obtained funds from government agencies to start their organizations by arguing that racism in mainstream social service agencies made it difficult for women in their communities to obtain services, alienated as they were by the WASP values and norms that dominated mainstream agencies and by the ethnocentrism of white Canadian social workers.

When I first went to these organizations in the 1970s, I found mainly immigrant women like myself. They included South Asian, Chinese, and black women from many different regions, religions and cultural backgrounds. Sometimes when meeting a South Asian, Chinese, or black woman, I would feel the familiarity of old friends, though we had known each other only very briefly and only in the context of the organization. I think this came from our shared social location as immigrants and the difficulties created by racism and sexism in our lives.

The organizations sought practical solutions to the problems of their clients. They cared much less about theoretical and ideological discussions of race, class, and gender. My training and research inclined me to think of the problems and solutions theoretically, and I wanted to apply feminist strategies, such as consensus building, developing non-hierarchical structures, and giving greater prominence to the voice of victims. They did not give my opinions any undue weight, nor were they always respectful of academic feminist or anti-racist theories and abstractions. I heard accounts, often from staff members, about horrendous experiences of classism, racism, and sexism that awed me. In comparison, mine seemed trivial.

My experiences at the union had shown me how an organization could help people overcome feelings of powerlessness. The women's organizations tried to make a "home away from home" for working-class, non-English-speaking women. They worked on behalf of women who were isolated by their lack of language skills and unfamiliarity with white Canadian culture, helping them gain greater access to social services.

There were differences between board and staff members based on a myriad of factors, including religion, education, occupation and commitment to their first culture. At York I often thought of myself as a disadvantaged woman, but the women at these organizations considered me privileged. Many of the volunteers had initially come to these agencies to seek help in resolving an immediate personal problem or difficulties encountered by someone known to them. Later, some found jobs within these organizations or became volunteer board members.

Sometimes when white Canadians representing government funding agencies visited the organizations' offices, I introduced myself as a "teacher." The staff would invariably correct me and identify me as a professor. A black board member in one organization sternly told me off. "We should let them know that not all immigrants are on welfare," she stated bluntly. "Some of us are doing quite well for ourselves." Identifying board members as professors, physicians, teachers, and managers also told the funders that "responsible people" were involved with the organization.

Most of the organizations chose conventional organizational methods rather than the collective mode espoused by feminism, from a belief that maintaining practices and norms understood and accepted by all ensured the smooth functioning of the organization. Possible contradictions between their work and long-term feminist goals such as mine were brushed aside in favour of what they considered "doable" solutions that brought immediate benefits to the women. Their confidence was not misplaced, and their decisions were validated daily by the women who came to the organizations looking for help from them. They were provided with valuable services and, in the case of abused women, life-saving help.

Many of the board members were staunch supporters of feminism and anti-racism, but diverse motivations brought them into the organizations. Some were in complementary kinds of jobs and were building networks in their professions. Some were beefing up their résumés with volunteer work, and some had aspirations of becoming spokeswomen for the organizations. Some white Canadian women (and an occasional male or two) volunteered with these organizations, and their reasons for joining—if they were lawyers, for example—were related to their jobs.

A South Asian women's organization that I came to know quite well had come into being on the initiative of an abused woman I'll call Asha. Asha told her story to the press a few times, and her situation illustrated the many difficulties that an immigrant woman encounters in trying to protect herself and gain access to social services. She had obtained funds from a government agency to study the unmet needs for social services in the South Asian community. The report she presented was viewed sympathetically, and she was given money to start an organization for abused South Asian women. Many such women, particularly those who could not speak English, came to the organization for help.

The South Asian community became less supportive of Asha when she said in a media interview that there was an "epidemic" of wife abuse in South Asian families. This remark fuelled an already simmering disagreement between Asha and the volunteer board of her organization, whose members were legally responsible for setting policy as well as being accountable financially. A power struggle between the board and Asha ensued, in which a retired Sikh teacher, a male, emerged victorious. The board fired Asha.

I joined the organization just after Asha had been fired. I liked the Sikh gentleman, who conscientiously managed the affairs of the organization. However, I had strong reservations about having a man chair a women's organization that aimed to provide services to abused women. Over time, at the behest of the chair, the focus of the organization shifted from women to families and children. These new services were valuable and much needed by the community, but they detracted from services to abused women, the organization's first mandate. Since most of the board members became committed to helping immigrants in general, and not just women, the organization lost its original feminist direction and focus.

Sometimes tensions would build up between white women and immigrant women on a board. Lynn, for instance, the paid executive director of an organization when I was the volunteer president of its board, liked to have her own way, and when she felt thwarted, her strategy was to try to put me on the defensive by making jokes about "privileged South Asian women." A white, university-educated Canadian, Lynn was about the same age as I. She was responsible for about ten full-time staff members (Chinese, black, and South Asian women). Some were refugees from Sri Lanka, some from Somalia, and some from Eastern Europe. The clients who came to the organization were all women who wanted to learn basic English or computer and accounting skills. Lynn was a good administrator, and we got along fine most of the time, but I always insisted that she implement the decisions of the board. Both of us had authority and power, she over the clients—who were all immigrants—and I over her. But while the former was acceptable to her and exercised naturally, the latter caused her anxiety.

The board was a racially and ethnically diverse group. Although there were some whites, seen as sympathetic listeners who had won their stripes by being with us in these organizations, radicalized immigrants were in the majority. Sometimes during a board meeting one of us would narrate a story about the racism she had encountered. That would set off a chain reaction, and we'd all join in, swapping stories about our experiences. This led to a bit of one-upmanship: who could recount the most horrendous experience of racism. The storytelling, however, created a bond of shared experience between us.

Often a story unlocked my own memory of a racist incident or comment I had brushed aside even though it had made me uncomfortable at the time. In retrospect, the episodes gained new meaning and import. One story I told was about the university. In 1989 I attended a conference organized by the Centre for South Asian Studies at the University of Toronto to mark the one-hundredth anniversary of the birth of Jawaharlal Nehru. I arrived early for a scheduled morning session. It was to be held in a beautiful, oak-panelled room dominated by a huge conference table. The shutters on the windows were wide open and early morning sunlight was streaming in.

When I entered the room, Milton Israel was standing at one end of the table setting up a tape recorder, and Archie Thornton was standing on the far side of the table talking to Judith Brown, a renowned British historian, as I later found out, of modern India. Thornton smiled genially at me and motioned to me to join them. I was pleased by the thought that he still recognized me, as it had been nearly fifteen years since we had last met. But it became clear after a couple of minutes that he did not know who I was and was just being polite. I said, "Professor Thornton, I am Vijay Agnew." He remembered then and apologized. He said something like: "Vijay, you must forgive me. In these last two days I have been in a sea of Indian faces and I thought you were just somebody's wife." His words ring in my ears to this day; I am still astonished by his blithe, and revealing, excuse.

What we needed and found in the women's organizations was a place to let off steam. Our feelings of outrage would give way to laughter as we chewed up the excuses—some ingenious, though still transparent—that people gave for racist behaviour. Eventually meetings would settle into brainstorming sessions to identify strategies for countering racism that could be used by the working-class women in the community. Hearing others talk about the racism they had personally encountered helped me to stop doubting myself or blaming myself for not having somehow prevented the occurrence of a racist incident in my life.

The black and Asian women whom I met were all quite forthcoming about racism and its impact on our communities and families, as well as on ourselves, but we were usually much more reticent in discussing sexism, particularly in our own ethnic communities. We tended to limit ourselves to generalizations about patriarchy and gender biases in our cultures. Even these admissions (more like confessions) were followed immediately by comparisons to "Canadian" culture, and we would turn to criticizing Canadian racist stereotypes that condemned Chinese, South Asian, and black cultures as being oppressive and discriminatory. It was easier for us to critique a society for racism than for sexism, and it was easier for us to critique Canadian society than our own.

Our feelings for the families and communities in which we had grown up made it difficult to disparage them. However, the clients of the organizations brought us clear evidence of sexism in immigrant communities and of its extreme manifestations in abuse, so we could not ignore it. We would acknowledge the biases of our cultures, but then try to exclude our own families from criticism for discriminatory attitudes and behaviours. We were prone to say, for example, that although sexism was widespread in Hindu and Muslim cultures, our own parents had eschewed such behaviour, or that although the culture was patriarchal and sexist, our families had been "progressive," "ahead of their times," and had treated sons and daughters impartially, giving them equal opportunities. I certainly thought that was true of my father, but as you have seen, he sometimes treated my sisters and me differently from my brothers, expecting us to conform to particular roles and accept certain responsibilities within the family.

Sometimes a particularly outspoken or militant woman would push for a greater or more explicit acknowledgement of sexism in our families and cultures, but others would try to interpret or explain it in more favourable terms. Many objected to feminists who seemed to say that although all societies were sexist, non-Western societies were especially so. A social worker at a mainstream social service agency who was also a board member of one of the organizations with which I was involved once gave me an hour-long lecture on the misinterpretation of her religion—Islam—by white Canadians. She argued that contrary to their misconceptions, it accorded full equality to males and females. However, even she would sometimes say, as others of us did, "Oh, you know how our men are." That was usually as far as anyone would go towards acknowledging sexism in her own culture.

Discussion of sexism in our personal relations was also muted. Women who were in ongoing relations with male partners tended either not to discuss them or to assure us that they were equal. We talked about issues like the division of housework and child care, but not about power, control, or authority exercised by a male partner. A woman might even claim that she had raised the consciousness of her partner, who was now "reformed" and had banished sexism from his personal life. Acknowledging that one still tolerated sexism might have been construed, in the company of feminists, as showing that one lacked self-respect or gumption, or that one's commitment to feminism was only skin deep.

An Indian professor, Nalini, the mother of two university-going sons, explained her outlook to me in private one day. She had come to Canada for a master's degree in science, and had met and married another Indian, also a foreign student. She finished her degree, but then became a full-time housewife and mother. Like me, she had been a volunteer with the Indian Immigrant Aid Service and other Indian immigrant women's organizations in the 1970s. When her sons were in their early teens, she had earned a PhD and found a teaching appointment at a local college. When I met her, she was the volunteer president of an immigrant women's organization. She described herself as a feminist.

Nalini said that she had tried to raise her sons in a non-sexist manner. She had expected them to help with cooking, clean their own rooms, and take turns cleaning the bathroom. She was not just being ideological, but reasoned that the young women her sons were likely to date would not be tolerant of sexism. Therefore, she felt, it behooved her to inculcate non-sexist attitudes in them and teach them some domestic skills. However, her feminism had mellowed. Now that she was in her mid-fifties, she had given up arguing with her spouse about sharing the housework. "I'm too old for all those fights," she said with resignation, but not too unhappily. Her weekend routine was to wake up early Saturday and Sunday mornings and rush around doing chores and cooking for the family. Meanwhile, her spouse relaxed and read the newspaper. From time to time he would ask whether she needed any help. This implicit acknowledgement of her housework, she said, had become sufficient for her.

Single and divorced women who sought help from the organizations did not have such a benign attitude toward patriarchy and sexism, but they too were often torn between loyalty to their family of origin and, in the case of abused women, the horrific consequences of sexism in their own lives. They were more direct, explicit, and critical of the patriarchal nature of their culture and its sexist values. Their outlooks on life were consequently ambivalent.

Roop was a staff member at a South Asian women's organization who had first come to the agency because of physical abuse by her husband. She was in her late forties, a quiet, unassuming woman who had a bachelor's degree from India and spoke English fluently; she usually dressed in Western clothes, but occasionally wore a sari. She had brought her daughter, a university student, to one of our conferences and had made a point of introducing the young woman to me. A few days later, after a board meeting, she invited me to have a coffee with her at a local restaurant. Over the next three hours she told me her story, perhaps because she knew my research at the time was on immigrant women and abuse.

Roop had been raised in a middle-class family in Ludhiana, a small town in Punjab. As her father was no longer alive, marriage to an engineer had been arranged for her by her older brothers, after which she and her husband immigrated to Canada. At first, the man had a good job with Ontario Hydro, but he became an alcoholic and was diagnosed as a manic-depressive. He began abusing her after the birth of their first child, and continued to do so for several years. Nevertheless, Roop stuck it out with this man until her daughter and two sons were in their early teens, when the abuse was extended to the children and became life-threatening. The women's organization helped her apply for welfare, secure housing, locate lawyers, and attend support groups with other women from South Asia. After a while she became a volunteer child-minder at the organization.

Eventually, she worked her way up to a full-time job, although it paid only minimum wage. Her children were all attending university with student loans, but the family was just scraping by financially.

Roop did not find fault with her arranged marriage, or blame her brothers for arranging an unsuitable match. Indeed, she had hidden the abuse from them for many years. She said that they had done their best, and her misfortune was simply a matter of bad luck. She did not want her brothers to feel guilty for how her marriage had turned out. She told me several times of the offers of help she had received from them, including a standing invitation for her and her children to return to Ludhiana and live with them. Roop did not denounce patriarchal Punjabi culture, but saw her problems in individual terms—simply her bad luck.

As a mother of young children, Roop had few options. While her spouse was working, the family had owned a townhouse and lived a middle-class life, though it had been prone to violence. She had also encountered racist name-calling at the suburban malls and even in the school her children attended. The spousal abuse had eroded her self-esteem, and she had little confidence in her ability to make it on her own. Once she left the marriage, she also became isolated and alienated from her Sikh community. Her children were ostracized by the other Sikh families because they had a violent father and were now part of a single-parent family that had fallen on hard times. Yet Roop continued to go to the gurudwara every Sunday, although she had only the most formal contact with the families at the temple.

Roop's abuse had drawn her into thinking about feminist ideas. Her experience with the disapproving Sikh families in her community had broken her ties to the culture and radicalized her. Despite that, she held on to some traditional Sikh values. Although her children dated white Canadians and she said they were free to marry whomever they wished, she harboured some traditional expectations of her sons. They were expected to help her out with the wedding expenses for their sister when they were a bit older, and she hoped to live with them and their families when she was old. She had no expectations of help, financial or otherwise, from her daughter, to whom she looked only for love and companionship.

When I was a volunteer board member at a shelter for abused women, we did not discuss racism, sexism, or classism, since their extreme consequences were staring us in the face. Rather, we discussed government funding, provision of social services, and relations among the women at the shelter. My interest in shelters had arisen in the course of researching my book *Resisting Discrimination: Women from Asia, Africa, and the Caribbean and the Women's Movement in Canada.* Although I had found that many women's organizations were helping abused women in the mainstream gain access to social services, there was little feminist literature on abused immigrants from Asia, Africa, or the Caribbean, or their experiences of living in shelters for women. I extended my research to this area.

One day I came upon an advertisement in York's Women's Studies newsletter from a shelter asking for women volunteers for its board of directors. I immediately telephoned to express my interest. They asked me to send my curriculum vitae and invited me to attend the next board meeting. The staff explained that their rules required that I attend two board meetings, after which they would determine my suitability to become a member. I remained a board member from 1995 to 1997. During that time I volunteered for several committees and consequently came to know the shelter and its staff well.

Before I joined the board, I had in mind certain images of a shelter and the kinds of women I might meet there. My expectations had arisen from reading about shelters for women, particularly a book on the formation of one of the earliest shelters in Britain. Publicly funded homes and hostels for women in need have existed for a long time, but emergency shelters are feminist-inspired spaces for women escaping violence in their homes. In Canada, shelters for women were established after feminists took the lead in making domestic violence a public policy issue. Ideally, a shelter for women is a safe and supportive environment where women cooperate with one another, live harmoniously, and eschew all social distinctions. However, the shelter I visited felt quite different.

It was located on a major thoroughfare, and looked like all the other houses in the neighbourhood, but there its similarity to a home ended. When I rang the doorbell, I had to identify myself to a staff member who scrutinized me through a one-way mirror. They were expecting me, and so I was let inside. The electronic safety system was necessary to protect residents from the possibility of an enraged partner coming to take revenge on the woman who had left him, and on the people providing her with housing.

The interior of the shelter looked like what it was—an institution crammed into a house. It was a cramped, shut-in, and depressing environment. On the main floor near the entrance was an office with the usual jumble of desks, telephones, and filing cabinets, a fax machine, and a small couch. Hanging on one wall was a poster that outlined the different stages in applying for welfare and housing.

Next to the office was a large eating area, much like a small cafeteria, with five or six tables. There were no decorations on the walls, but on one was a bulletin board with a schedule of chores and rules for using the eating area. Attached to this room was a kitchen with a commercial-style fridge, stove, coffee machine and other appliances, where a cook prepared the meals for the residents. The bedrooms were on the other side of the house and in the basement, but I was not allowed to go into them.

Whenever I entered the shelter I always became quiet and sombre. The residents, all of whom had only recently escaped violence, seemed to be in various stages of shock and mourning. Some were new immigrants, while others had been in Canada for several years. Some had been born in Canada. Some spoke English fluently, others only a very little, but almost all seemed to be poor; I guess if you were middle-class or rich you could always check into a hotel rather than go to a shelter. Board meetings were usually held around six o'clock, but when I went to them I often found many of the women sitting in the eating area in their nightgowns or walking around looking dejected and listless.

I often arrived early for meetings, and would sit and chat with the staff in the office. Residents would come into the office to get a pill for a headache or to make some inquiry. Their attitude was always very passive. They showed no inclination to prolong a conversation with the staff and seldom returned my smile or even made eye contact with me. Sometimes little children would tag along with their mothers, and they might respond to a joke or a friendly comment from one of the staff members. I found it particularly heartbreaking to see a pregnant woman living there. It was encouraging to know that she had escaped violence and was safe, but the thought of the long, tough road that lay ahead for her was very sobering.

The staff, in contrast, was usually upbeat, cheerful, and encouraging. They felt their attitude would help the women overcome their dejection and sadness. However, in the two years I went there, I only saw one happy event: a birthday party for three children. Each child received a cake and a present, and the staff, determinedly pushing along the celebration, led a singalong, played music in different languages and danced. This lasted only a brief time, and the residents soon drifted off into their rooms.

This shelter was a feminist collective—an ideological arrangement not necessarily in place in all shelters. The ideal is one of women helping each other selflessly, cooperating with one another and living harmoniously. No woman exercises power and authority over anyone else; everyone is equal and shares equal responsibility. In practice, however, shelters differ considerably from the ideals that inspire them. When I joined this shelter, it was approximately fifteen years old, and much of the original idealism had waned.

The staff at the shelter was multicultural and multiracial, and all together spoke several languages. There was a heightened consciousness at the shelter about racism, and all board members were required to attend an anti-racism sensitivity training workshop designed by the staff. The main themes of the workshop were "power relations" between English-speaking and non-English-speaking women in Canada, and the need to be sensitive to the vulnerability and feelings of powerlessness experienced by the latter. A confident and articulate immigrant who spoke Spanish and English led the workshop. She was displeased to be thrown off her script when I asked her some questions. I thought she might be stereotyping both English-speaking women, who could be non-threatening and non-intimidating, indeed friendly, and non-English-speaking women, some of whom were by no means poor or powerless in Canada (for example, immigrants who came in under the business-class category). She quite reasonably replied that members of the staff were not likely to encounter many wealthy women, and I don't think they found my points of much practical use.

Most of the staff members at the shelter were not social workers, and it was hard to determine what in their education or work experience qualified them for their jobs. However, feminists are critical of "professionalism" in fields like social work, because it is often allied with androcentric and ethnocentric values. The "power relations" between all-knowing expert social workers and their clients tend to place the clients in a subordinate position. Shelters often put their faith instead in women who have strong political and ideological commitments to eradicating violence against women or who have had personal experience of violence which may give them additional insight and empathy. One of the white staff members at this shelter was an activist in the women's movement, and one woman was a professional social worker. Most of the others seemed to have found their jobs through chance and luck. All of them had been there for several years.

Although the constitution of the shelter defined it as a collective, the only people who had equal authority, responsibility, wages, and benefits were the eight or so full-time staff members. Below them were part-time workers, student placements, volunteers, cooks, cleaning staff, and the residents. Interactions within the collective were marred by suspicion and lack of trust. Communication frequently broke down altogether amongst the staff, and then conflicts required the mediation of professional conflict-resolution consultants. Consequently, rules and regulations, committees and subcommittees, and reports by hired organizational experts absorbed much of the time and energy of the staff, wasting the scarce funds of the shelter and diverting them from providing services to the women in need.

When I joined the board, the shelter had just come through a difficult time. There had been a dispute between the board and the staff over policy (again, one of the legal responsibilities of the board), and in the ensuing power struggle, the board had resigned en masse. A new board emerged, but they too resigned—en masse—after a brief time. The board that I joined, put together by the staff, lacked cohesiveness. The new president was a white woman of European background in her early sixties, a middle manager in a provincial government agency. The other active members were an Iranian social worker, a Filipina office manager, a white South African accountant, a black former resident, and I. The president invited us to her house for dinner so we could get to know each other, but this greatly upset the staff, who had to be reassured that no coup was in progress.

Over the next little while the generous wages and benefits of the paid, full-time staff in the collective began to greatly concern me. Board members who compared them with salaries and benefits from their own places of work found them out of line. Since the members of the shelter's collective did not trust each other and jealously guarded their rights with regards to equally sharing work and responsibility, every detail had to be put in writing and brought to the board for "information sharing," discussion, and approval. Most of our time was thus wasted discussing routine matters. The staff protected themselves through elaborate personnel policies and job descriptions. They defined their jobs narrowly, so we were constantly debating the need to hire more part-time personnel and refining the budget to find ways to pay for them. Professionals were hired to write and review policies and to do fundraising. All this used up resources that should have gone to the residents.

All the board members were unhappy with the situation, and I was shocked and conscience-stricken. The president argued that despite all the problems, the staff was maintaining the shelter, and women who needed housing were able to find it. Since some good was being done, she said, it was best to let things be; complaining to the funders might lead to closing the shelter and result in some women losing their jobs and others their housing. The shelter posed too many ethical questions for me, however, and I could not abide sitting through another board meeting listening to mundane matters, instituting more rules, hiring more policy reviewers of the shelter, and managing more conflict. Eventually I despaired of the situation and resigned. In 1998, I published some of my findings on this and other shelters in my book, *In Search of a Safe Place: Abused Women and Culturally Sensitive Services*.

My association with the immigrant women's organizations brought me into contact with a wide range of women from different cultural, social, and occupational backgrounds. I learned to question the academic preoccupation with abstract theories of race, class, and gender. Although I was disappointed by the wrangling at some of the organizations, in most I felt at home and part of a community. I value the friends I made and our camaraderie in working toward similar goals for ourselves and our families in Canada. In working with other immigrants, I learned more about them and about myself.

12

Lunching with the Ladies

I have just come back from a walk. Neighbourhood dogs, running around after balls and frisbees or chasing each other, seem to have taken over the park by the ravine. Like me, they are out for their daily exercise. If one of them comes bounding up to smell me, I shrink back. The scent of my fear makes them run in circles around me, barking loudly and furiously. Petrified, I come to a standstill. The civically conscious owner, toting a "stoop and scoop" plastic bag, shouts at the dog: "Stop it!" Then, surprised at my fear, he says to me reassuringly, "He is quite safe. He won't hurt you." I feel foolish, but cannot overcome my fear of dogs.

Rob, a university student who lives with his parents around the corner from us, once observed an encounter like this between a little, white poodle and me. A dog must have traumatized me as a child, he declared. "Why else would you be so frightened?" Wanting to help me overcome my fear, he solicitously picked up the poodle, held it in his arms and encouraged me to pet the dog. To please him, I gave the dog a few tentative pats on the head. I did not explain to him that the only dogs I saw while growing up in Bombay and Delhi were the ones that rooted through garbage in the bazaars...ugly, mangy, and rabid. No one would ever have touched their flea-infested hair. Now when I go back to Bombay I sometimes see well-groomed and well-fed dogs in the park near my father's apartment, out on their walks and toddling briskly behind their well-heeled owners. I become moralistic and want to

Note to chapter 12 is on p. 283.

upbraid the owners; I have to suppress the desire to tell them to adopt a child instead.

I stay away from the dogs in the park and stick to the sidewalks instead. I follow the same route almost every day for my walk. The architectural details of the houses along the park—the shapes and styles of the windows, the textures and colours of the façades—don't interest me as much as they once did. Over the years, familiarity has made me less aware of their charms. But the flowers still draw my attention. In the summer a profusion of red, white, and pink blooms spill out of containers on the front porches and crowd the flower beds below. I especially like seeing the two houses on the street with rose bushes in their yards, weighed down now with clumps of red blossoms that lend fragrance to the air. Front doors are closed, and other than an occasional person walking a dog or pushing a baby carriage, there are few people around. It is still and quiet.

In fact it is so quiet here that sometimes I find myself crossing the street without bothering to watch for an approaching car. The chock-full pavements of Bombay, with vendors selling peanuts and bananas from ragged carts, and the chaotic, bustling roads choked with the fumes of buses and cars exert an emotional pull, but they have receded into the past. Now it is the quiet roads, drives and avenues of Rosedale that feel like home.

I am thinking of my old home in Bombay because last night my sister Rita left to go to India, where her husband Pammi had already been transferred to work. We spent the day together. In the morning we went to the St. Lawrence Market, because she said she wanted to have steak for dinner and I wanted the meal we prepared for her to be special. The market is just a huge hall with a variety of fruit, vegetable, cheese and meat stalls that look family-run, busy, and a bit messy. I suspect the market produce is no different from that of the supermarkets, but it feels special to shop there. The ambiance of the market harkens back to days gone by and lends credence to the idea that the produce is fresh and wholesome. It probably comes from the usual farms far away in California, Florida, and Mexico, but along with the ingredients for our dinner we willingly bought into the myth. At the meat store we peered through clean, glass counters at trays of neatly cut meat while the young salesman assured us of the succulence of the thick steaks, clinching the sale by giving us tips on how to barbecue them.

That evening Tom cooked the steaks, taking care to make them medium-rare, just the way Rita prefers. Later, however, as the empty plates lay in front of us with blood from the steaks congealing on them, Rita revealed that she planned to be a vegetarian for the time she was in India. "Why?" I asked, taken aback, and she launched into a long, convoluted explanation that sounded much like what any new North American or European vegetarian convert might say, except with more knowing details. She was apprehensive about the diet of the animals in India and about the hygiene at the butcher's market. "Do you think the butchers in New Delhi refrigerate their meats? In the heat, the bacteria multiply rapidly. I'm not taking a chance of getting sick." "Or maybe you are afraid to offend," I said to her, whereupon she began to quote media stories about the benefits to one's health of avoiding hormone-enriched meats. It seemed like a deal that few could resist—protecting one's health while adhering to the tenets of one's religion.

Tom was afraid that we would get into an argument, and so tried to change the topic as he began clearing the table. He served us dessert and tea and we continued to sit, nibbling at the food and refilling our cups—not because we really wanted more, but because we were reluctant to get up and start preparing to go to the airport. Rita had mixed feelings about leaving. There was, as always, the excitement of going to India, but at the same time she felt sorry to be saying goodbye to her friends and coworkers here. Over the last couple of weeks, Indian and Pakistani friends had hosted farewell parties for her, and now the time to go to New Delhi was here. Perhaps she needed to reassure herself that she would return soon, because she kept saying that when she came back we would have to go and visit so-and-so in New York or Niagara Falls and that she would have to have her house repainted—when she came back.

Tom wanted to lighten the sombre mood that was threatening to overtake us. "Rita," he offered, "your house is in Toronto. Your home is in India...in New Delhi." However, that only seemed to depress her further. "No, Tom," she replied, "New Delhi is just a city where my husband has a job. My home is here in Toronto." I know why she feels that way. There is not much of our old life left in Delhi. Many of our aunts and uncles are no more. Our cousins are busy in their own routines, and many have left the city. "There is not much left to go back to, you know, Tom," she said, echoing my thoughts.

In the last few weeks Rita and I have been talking consciously about "home," and about how our life in Canada has changed us. We have been surprised to discover how small adjustments in food, dress, and behaviour have led to deeper, more fundamental changes in who we are and where, and with whom, we now feel comfortable.

Sociology books sometimes describe immigrants as having been "uprooted" and "displaced," but I want to modify that language. Rita and I have visited India frequently, so there is no sense of having been harshly separated from the past. Nor is there a sense, as there is in, say, immigrants who come here with no facility in the English language, of being lost in an alien culture and society. We have put down new roots in Toronto. Our work, friends, and neighbours have slowly changed our values and beliefs about ourselves, and we have unconsciously adapted to new ways of being and behaving. It is hard to categorize these ways as "Indian" or "Canadian." We do not identify with a large, amorphous entity such as the "WASP" or "Indian" community, but with small, localized communities and neighbourhoods in which we spend our everyday lives. It is from these locations, and the individuals in them, that we now derive a sense of comfort and belonging.

Rita, like me, has over the years gone regularly for holidays to Bombay and New Delhi. She finds Delhi hot and dusty. When she comes back to Toronto she complains about the watered-down and sometimes contaminated food there, and the cost of living. Although she has many friends in India, her life in Canada has created a social distance between her and them, and her attitudes have become very different from theirs.

Rita dislikes housework. In Toronto, she prepares her family's meals and does other household chores, and she looked forward to having household help in New Delhi. Until, that is, she remembered how she and I had criticized our friends and relatives who were always saying, "These servants!" and complaining that they were incompetent and lazy. She did not want to become like them, nor did she want to join them in endless shopping forays or in idle chatter while they visited with each other. Since she has worked at an office for most of her life, she felt apprehensive about having a lot of free time and worried about how to fill it. I teased her by saying she could take up golf and tennis to while away her time like other rich ladies, but she was not enthusiastic about that prospect. She thought she might join other expatriate women from Western countries living in India. They could explore together and get to know Delhi and India better.

Rita's Indian and Pakistani friends had politely invited me to the farewell parties they held for her. Usually her friends only invite Tom and me to their homes when some white Canadians are going to be there. Otherwise, they seem to think having us around will spoil their fun, since Tom doesn't understand Hindi; they'd have to speak in English and wouldn't be able to tell jokes about India without first explaining the context to him, which ruins the punch line. My being an academic and a feminist doesn't help, either. They most often introduce me by saying, "Vijay is Rita's sister...the one who writes books." That puts the other women on guard, and they are usually at a loss to know how to relate to me or what topic of conversation would be a suitable. Talk of shopping, friends, and social events suddenly seems to make them feel self-conscious. They ask some polite questions about my research, but they don't have much interest in the working-class women I write about. I try to steer them back to their own topics of conversation.

One day Rita invited me to the Granite Club for lunch with four of her Indian and Pakistani friends. As we drove into the club, Rita began to berate me: "I don't know why you are being so stubborn. Why don't you join the club? All the Indian members are willing to sponsor you. Besides, the club is looking for new members, and they are making it easy for people to join." Since Rita has been a member for over ten years, we have had this discussion many times. I did not want to start an argument by pointing out that there were less than a dozen Indian members; I satisfied myself instead by saying, once more, that I had no desire to spend time lounging around at the club. "Anyway," I said, "it is much too expensive and snobbish for me." Rita, however, thinks I am being shortsighted and pig-headed. She says that joining this club—and others like it— is regarded by many Indians and Pakistanis in Toronto as a symbol of success and assimilation into white Canadian society. "Why not join?" she scolded. "Other Indians are doing it."

Until very recently, the Granite Club was the exclusive preserve of privileged WASPs in Toronto. Rumour has it that they did not even allow Jewish people to become members. Now, however, the club is eagerly seeking new members of any race or ethnicity who are willing to pay the substantial membership dues. This change of heart by the club does not reflect a belated attempt to be progressive and fair-minded; I suspect it has also been driven to adopt this stance by sheer financial necessity. The club's membership base is declining as current members age and so the rules are being changed to attract middle-aged and younger people; they have even made changes in programs to accommodate children and nannies. The club also relaxed the regulations as to who can sponsor new members and introduced easier ways of paying membership initiation fees, such as in installments. Some South Asians are using this opportunity to become members, and they are sponsoring their friends for membership as well.

Rita's friends love to meet with each other at the club, which among its features has tennis and squash courts, lawn bowling, exercise rooms and saunas. It also has facilities for formal and informal dining. The men arrange to play tennis or squash and the women use the exercise rooms. They have dinner and drinks together and entertain their visitors from India and Pakistan. In many ways their routine is no different from that of the WASPs who belong to the club. However, there is some sense of disappointment as well, because only separate, parallel social groups have tended to emerge. One of the conventional advantages of membership in a social club is the opportunity it provides for networking with other people, but here, the South Asians network with each other and the white members with each other. There is little evidence of cross-cultural social intermingling.

On the day of our visit, the driveway leading into the club was lined on either side with huge flower pots trimmed with lush English ivy and overflowing with pink, white, and red impatiens and begonias. A wood-panelled reception area at the entrance to the club was decorated with several huge paintings of Canadian landscapes. In the centre of this room stood a round, polished-walnut table holding a large vase filled with silk flowers. There were comfortable leather chairs near the fireplace, where we sat to wait for Rita's friends, who soon arrived, dressed in lightweight linen pants and jackets. That surprised me, since often on warm summer days Indian and Pakistani women wear saris for social events. But Rita and I had dressed in light cotton dresses, too.

Rita rushed over to greet her friends and give each one of them a hug. There was no decorous joining of hands or greetings of "*Namaste.*" Each of the women found a way to compliment another by remarking that her clothes made her look younger, or thinner, or more attractive. As we sat down to chat, they turned to admiring each other's earrings, rings and bracelets. For middle-aged, upper-middle-class women in India and Pakistan, it is *de rigueur* to wear pearl and diamond jewellery, and although they complimented each other on their good taste, I suspect that, much like their grandmothers in India and Pakistan, they were also silently appraising value.

After a few minutes of this we stood up to walk towards the dining room. Rita and her friends continued to stand chatting animatedly, so I pulled my camera out of my purse and tried to take a picture of them. We were in a lighthearted mood, and it was hard to get them to stop joking and laughing when I asked them all to stand together for the camera. Absorbed in my task, I was startled when a man in a pinstriped suit suddenly appeared beside me, tapping on my shoulder to get my attention. "Here, let me do this for you," he said. "You go and join your friends." He seemed in no hurry, and spent a few minutes taking a variety of shots of us with my camera. We thanked him as he went on his way. The graciousness of members like this makes Rita and her friends feel at home and comfortable at the club. Members are unfailingly polite and friendly, and seem to regard the presence of South Asians as normal and routine. The club, my sister and her friends seem to be saying, belongs equally to all of us.

We walked through a hallway lined on each side with polished tables, vases full of fresh flowers, large paintings on the walls, and sofas upholstered in blue and gray. The subdued atmosphere of the décor made us lower our voices and speak in hushed tones. We decided to have a buffet lunch rather than go to the formal dining room. The buffet was being served from tables laden with food in a casually decorated room. Adjoining this room was a verandah with white garden tables and umbrellas, where a chef in a huge white hat and apron was barbecuing steaks and ribs. The verandah overlooked tennis courts on one side and a ravine on the other. We picked a table in full sunshine. It was a warm, pleasant afternoon, and there were many middle-aged women at the club in large summer hats, along with a few children and men in business suits.

I noticed that we were the only non-whites there. Even the serving staff was white. The women with me did not seem to notice, or perhaps did not care. Four of them were members, so possibly they were used to the situation and did not feel self-conscious. I have been going to the club with Rita a few times a year for the last ten years or so, and it is always like this. Sometimes we come across another South Asian friend and, invariably, we all sit at the same table and have our meal together.

I found myself sitting next to Mehroo, a middle-aged mother with two daughters going to university. Mehroo wore a white linen jacket and dark brown pants, and her hair was loosely tied up with a black silk bow.

Mehroo's appearance and manner of speaking were reminiscent of the rich Parsi women amongst whom she had grown up in Bombay, although here in Toronto her life has followed the pattern of many other middle-class women. Mehroo had married a chartered accountant and immigrated to Canada soon after graduating from university with a bachelor's degree. At first she stayed home to take care of her children, but then started working part-time. As soon as her children became teenagers, she started to work full-time as an underwriter in an insurance company.

Mehroo is an active participant in the Parsi community organizations in Toronto and celebrates Zoroastrian religious days with them, so I asked her if she had ever met the writer Rohinton Mistry at any of these gatherings. To my surprise, she looked distinctly pained at my question, and replied in a disgusted tone, "What does he get by making fun of people? Can he not find something else to write about?"

Rohinton Mistry is a Parsi from Bombay who now lives in Toronto. He won the Governor General's award for his novel *Such a Long Journey,* and a few years after that was short-listed for the prestigious Booker prize for *A Fine Balance.* In Bombay, there's a widely held belief that intermarriages among the small Parsi community makes them extremely eccentric, and when Mistry writes about the poor and lower-middle-class Parsis in Bombay, he gently pokes fun at their many eccentricities. Mistry is sensitive to the fact that other Parsis resent his depictions of them. In a story entitled "Swimming Lessons," he describes his father's reaction to reading his first collection of short stories:

> In the stories that he's read so far, Father said that all the Parsi families were poor or middle-class, but that was okay; nor did he mind that the seeds for the stories were picked from the sufferings of their own lives; but there should also have been something positive about Parsis, there was so much to be proud of: the great Tatas and their contribution to the steel industry, or Sir Dinshaw Petit in the textile industry who made Bombay the Manchester of the East, or Dadabhai Naoroji in the freedom movement where he was the first to use the word swaraj [a sovereign nation], and the first to be elected to the British Parliament where he carried on his campaign; he should have found some way to bring some of these wonderful facts into his stories, what would people reading these stories think, those who did not know about Parsis—that the whole community was full of cranky, bigoted people; and in reality it was the richest, most advanced and philanthropic community in India, and he did not need to

tell his own son that Parsis had a reputation for being generous and family-oriented.[1]

Mehroo thought it was sheer cussedness on Mistry's part to write about poor Parsis for the edification of the reading public of the Western world. Like the author's father, she worried that all Parsis would be cast in the same light. Sociologists, particularly in the past, would sometimes discuss an ethnic group in terms of the characteristics of its majority population. The differences within the group were neglected or mentioned only briefly. Consequently, newly arrived immigrant groups were often thought of as poor or working-class individuals attached to the religion, language or dress of their countries of origin.

People like Mehroo resented being stereotyped as working-class, traditional "Indians," and were angry that white Canadians were not sensitive enough to clue in to the differences of dress and behaviour that distinguished them from their working-class compatriots. Mistry's writings, she thought, would just give white Canadians additional grist for their mill. Nowadays sociologists are careful to note the diversity within groups, both in terms of socio-economic characteristics and beliefs about ethnic identity. Nevertheless, the emphasis in discussions of immigrants—and multiculturalism—remains by and large on the working class. The image of "poor immigrants" is so ingrained in people's minds that even though over the years the reality has changed, to a great extent the perception of most Canadians may not have caught up with the facts.

Mehroo would like to cultivate an image of the Parsis that mirrors her own life. She reflects her own upper-class Parsi upbringing in Bombay, and enjoys the advantages that flow to individuals who become Westernized. In the eyes of her kin, those who obtain an English education, do graduate studies in the West and find jobs in multinational corporations have achieved success, even though these experiences often alienate them from the rest of the community.

However, people's everyday lives are lived in the context of localized and specific communities. An English education, residence in Western countries, or even the cultural norms of a profession can also provide commonality and form a core from which a sense of community is created. Mehroo is not alienated from the culture of the smaller, more cohesive community of individuals who share experiences, education and work similar to hers and have developed a network among themselves based on their shared values.

Mehroo and her friends do not reject the culture of their families and the larger community in favour of anglophone WASP culture. They would like to bridge the distance that separates immigrants like them from it socially, but they are not aiming at full assimilation or integration. They'd like to maintain a hybrid culture incorporating different elements of South Asian and WASP cultures. They practise Zoroastrianism and speak Gujarati, but their local community also comprises Indians and Pakistanis with different languages and religions. The ethnic group is diverse and people socialize with each other across religious and linguistic lines. More important, they socialize with each other across national lines—India and Pakistan—which historically have had acrimonious relations. Their professional success also gives them the confidence to pick and choose among the norms of WASP culture that serve their personal and professional needs. Mehroo prides herself on her facility in moving back and forth between her South Asian and Canadian friends.

On my other side sat Tazmeen, a warm and friendly Muslim woman in her early forties, the youngest amongst us. A smile always seems to be hovering around Tazmeen's lips, and she easily breaks into laughter. That day she was dressed in very loose-fitting green linen pants with a matching short-sleeved blouse. She wore vivid red lipstick and long, dangling earrings, and her thick, black, curly hair hung loose around her shoulders. I had met Tazmeen several times before and knew a little bit about her from Rita. She and her husband, who had been educated in Britain, had emigrated from Pakistan about fifteen years earlier and lived in Toronto ever since. Over lunch, she reminisced about her life in Pakistan.

Tazmeen told me that she came from a conventional Muslim family that had arranged a marriage for her when she was only eighteen years of age. Her husband, in his early twenties, came from a wealthy, landed and entrepreneurial family. Soon after the marriage, she said, his family had "sent" them to live in a small town and manage the family-owned factories, which employed a thousand or more people. In this small town their employees' wives and children would call her "*Begum*" (an Urdu honorific for a married woman of high social status) and ask her advice on a variety of issues relating to their families and children. Tazmeen said that when she was first referred to in that manner, she would look over her shoulders for an older woman. She did not feel like a begum at all, but just like any other young teenaged girl.

Tazmeen observed the rules of purdah in this town and in Karachi, where she grew up, since her parents and in-laws were very religious, but had discarded them since immigrating to Canada. I have met her sometimes at social events in the homes of her Indian and Pakistani friends. At these events she wears vivid silk salwar kamiz delicately embroidered with silver and gold threads. She usually has a dupatta with which she is supposed to cover her head, but Tazmeen simply slings it around her neck. (In Pakistan, and in most Islamic countries, covering one's hair is a sign of female modesty and is required of women of all ages.) Once I met Tazmeen and her husband at a prenuptial dinner and he was wearing, apparently at her insistence, *pyjama*† *kurta* (similar in style to the salwar kamiz) with a silk vest. She had joked about her husband's embarrassment, and his reluctance to leave the house dressed in the pyjama kurta. He had put on a trench coat to hide his clothes and only removed it when he was safely inside their friends' home. When Tazmeen goes shopping or to other public places, she dresses in pants, blouse and jacket, but considers short dresses a bit risqué for her.

I was having a hard time reconciling what Tazmeen was telling me about her life in Pakistan with what I knew about her life here in Toronto. In Toronto, Tazmeen leads a privileged and leisurely life. She has no children. She does not do any paid work. In truth, what could she do? She has had only a limited education and has no marketable skills. It is fortunate that her husband can provide for her. On occasion she has done some volunteer work with South Asian women's organizations, but her main interest, along with socializing with her Indian and Pakistani friends, is sports. In the summer she plays golf and in the winter she skis; she also attends the yoga classes now being offered at the club. She and her husband have bought a boat and in recent years have become avid sailors. She even wears a sailor's cap on the boat.

Tazmeen was enjoying the rapt attention with which I was listening to her life story. She was conscious that she was talking to a woman who "writes books" about immigrants, and she was conscious of all the white Canadians around us on the verandah. Her eyes glided casually to the other people lunching on the verandah and then with a glint of mischief in her eyes she said, "Even now I observe the purdah when I go back to

---

† Many Hindi words, such as *pyjama*, *kismet*, *bazaar and bungalow*, along with the Hindustani-derived *shampoo*, have been freely assimilated into English language.

Karachi. I do not want to upset my mother. It is only for a short time any-way." Perhaps she thought this would provoke me into repeating some well-worn Western feminist clichés about purdah and Islam. However, I wasn't about to reiterate the standard tale of how Islam oppresses women and how liberal values give them an opportunity to overcome the burdens of their cultural heritage.

Had I taken Tazmeen's bait, she would no doubt have given me the standard reply. She, like other Muslim women of her social standing, argue that the Koran, if "properly" read, does not assign women an inferior place. Rather, it accords them dignity, honour, and respect. Purdah may be a symbol of conventional gender roles, but women voluntarily observe it. Politely, and in deference to my beliefs, she would have acknowledged the right of women to equal opportunity at the work place. Had I pressed the issue, she could have pointed out flaws in white Canadian culture: "Com-pare the strength of our families with the problems besetting white Cana-dian families—the high rate of divorce, dysfunctional family lives, alien-ated youth, and mistreatment of the elderly! We are much better off."

Tazmeen's sense of who she is is fluid, and it changes in different social contexts. When Tazmeen is in Karachi, she takes on traditional roles, per-ceiving herself as a begum and a married daughter of her parents. This sta-tus guides her behaviour and makes it appropriate for her to observe pur-dah. Surrounded by her extended family and friends, following Islamic values seems normal and natural, and provides her with emotional and psychological security. Refusing to observe purdah in Karachi would be interpreted by her family and community as a significant deviation from Islamic values. However, purdah symbolizes a wholly different set of meanings in Toronto. Whereas in Pakistan it symbolizes female modesty and decorum, here it is a symbol of patriarchal domination and gender oppression.

In Toronto, Tazmeen is an immigrant woman who lives under the shadow of various stereotypes. Not observing purdah here is a pragmatic response to her environment; it does not connote her disavowal of the norms of her faith. Here, Tazmeen lacks the cultural infrastructure pro-vided by her family (and paid help) in Karachi. She has a variety of chores to do—buying groceries, shopping, banking—often in freezing weather that would make it extremely hard to observe purdah.

Tazmeen, like Mehroo, prides herself on being able to traverse cultures and customs easily. In a way, going back and forth between cultures gives her a sense of freedom and provides her with choices. It may be that over time her family and social life in Toronto will transform her sense of self. Over time she may decide to assert herself and realize her human potential in different ways. For now, however, Islamic values form her reference points and guide most of her behaviour towards her spouse, his family, and her relatives.

After we had chatted for a while over a glass of wine—and a soft drink for Tazmeen—we went to get some food. There was a large selection: hot chicken soup or gazpacho, a variety of pasta and green salads, cheese, and cold cuts. There were lots of different kinds of bread. "Good food!" Tazmeen said as we returned to our table, and the rest of us all nodded in polite agreement. After a few moments, Mehroo said, "A bit bland though, eh?" and we all burst out laughing. Rita then summoned the waiter and asked him if he could bring us a bottle of Tabasco sauce. He looked through the condiment trays on the verandah and inside the dining room, but came back empty-handed. Rita is not one to give up easily, so she then asked him to go and ask the bartender for his bottle of Tabasco (sometimes added to a Bloody Mary). Mystified, the waiter returned with the Tabasco and then stood back and watched in wide-eyed horror as each of us in turn liberally sprinkled it on the food piled on our plates. "They should make different kinds of food," Mehroo said discontentedly. (The club has since introduced "theme weeks," during which popular Chinese, Thai, and Mexican foods are served.)

I was sitting across from Suraksha. Suraksha grew up in a middle-class home in a small town in the Punjab. She had an arranged marriage soon after she finished her bachelor's degree. She and her husband lived in New Delhi and Bombay and had a daughter. About five years later, however, her husband died in a road accident, and Suraksha found she had no means of supporting herself and her child. According to the cultural norms of her region and social class, she was expected to remain a widow, eking out an existence in some relative's home. However, a friend of her husband who lived in Britain had recently divorced his British wife and was keen on marrying an Indian woman. He proposed the idea to Suraksha's mother, who passed the message on to her daughter. Suraksha, with her mother's approval, defied tradition, married this man and moved to Britain. Their family there comprised the two of them, her daughter, and his son.

Suraksha's husband worked for a multinational corporation, and he was posted to several countries in Europe and the Far East. His employers brought him to Toronto and the family applied for landed immigration. The children are now grown and have left home. Like many of her friends, Suraksha does not do any paid work. However, she got another bachelor's degree studying Sanskrit, Hinduism, and Indian art at the University of Toronto. Having had some difficulty just previous to our luncheon in explaining some aspects of Hinduism to my students at York, I asked Suraksha how she would explain the soul in Hinduism. How is it different from the person whose soul it is? Is it different from the person's self or personality?

Before she could say a word, the other women intercepted. "Who cares about these things?" they asked. They were all religious women, but they dismissed the discussion as merely "book knowledge." The philosophical principles of Hinduism weren't well known to them and had little significance in guiding their everyday behaviour. Religion to them meant, in the first instance, practising the rituals of their faith: frequently attending prayers at temples and mosques, refraining from eating certain kinds of foods, and fasting on holy days. Religious prayers solemnized weddings and funerals. With the exception of Tazmeen, they didn't have much commitment to religion as a source of values or norms to guide their everyday lives.

These professional, middle-class Indians and Pakistanis are in many ways similar to their white counterparts. They strongly endorse the Protestant work ethic and drill it into their children, as do many European immigrants. They value education as a means to social mobility for their daughters and sons. They are committed to gender equality in the public sphere. They are struggling to overcome gender stereotypes in raising their children. They put the needs of their nuclear families first. In their everyday routines, practical matters supersede spiritual ones.

I was the first to head for the dessert table. Along with pie and chocolate cake, there was cheesecake, trifle, baked Alaska, fruit and cheese. I was trying to make a choice when a blond-haired man in a light business suit came up. He engaged me in some casual banter about the tempting desserts and recommended several of them. I took one or two small servings, but he dropped a big helping of trifle on my plate. Seeing my shocked expression, he laughed and said, "Oh, be decadent! It's good for you!" and then walked off. I went back to our table, where Poonam had ordered a pot of tea.

Poonam is tall, and with her broad shoulders looks much like her foremothers in Punjab. She has long, black hair, tightly pulled back that day and done up in a round knot at her neck. She was wearing light-blue linen pants and a white jacket, and was heavily made up with bright red lipstick. Poonam is forceful and direct; she has some "edges" to her personality. Although she herself is a Hindu, she is married to a Sikh. There were no strong social distinctions between Hindus and Sikhs up to very recent times, and intermarriage between them was not unusual. It is only now, with the politicization of the Sikh religion and demands for a separate homeland, that there is some social distance between the Hindus and the Sikhs. The political differences have spilled over in Toronto, and Hindus and Sikhs do not mingle as freely here as they once did.

Poonam has two sons who are being raised as Sikhs. The major issues for the boys are the Sikh practices of never cutting one's hair and wearing a turban. When some Canadian rules prohibited Sikhs from wearing turbans on duty as RCMP officers or while attending functions in some Legion halls, they successfully challenged them in the courts. However, other Sikhs have cut their hair and do not wear turbans. Poonam's spouse wore a turban when he first immigrated to Canada, but over the years he has stopped wearing one in public. He still has long hair, but wears it in a braid, which gives him an unusual and attractive appearance. When they were young, their sons stuffed their hair in baseball caps, but as it became longer, it became more and more difficult to do that. The private school they attended had strict restrictions about hair length, but they were given permission to keep theirs long. One of their sons is now six feet tall and is a handsome young man, but his waist-length black hair sometimes makes him look like a cross-dresser! He has enjoyed the consequent attention, but now that he is finishing university, the problem of appearing for job interviews with this long hair is beginning to concern the family.

All of us at the table were raised in families that observed religious norms. Tazmeen continues to pray several times daily, and Poonam goes regularly to the gurudwara on Sundays, but the rest of us are more lax in our religious observances. We perceive ourselves as cosmopolitan and progressive respecting the religion of our friends and as not discriminating against people on the basis of their religion. We socialize with friends of other religions, we visit and eat together, and our children are friends with each other, but any questions from me, however obliquely phrased, about their feelings on the others' religions would have offended my sister's friends. They would have construed them as insults or put-downs arising from a misunderstanding of people's daily lives, and giving too much significance to "book knowledge," particularly as it is presented by Western scholars and sensationalizing journalists. They would have lectured me on the religious tolerance practised by their families for several generations. Nevertheless, there is still a bias against intermarriage between caste Hindus and Muslims which has only been aggravated by religious conflicts in the subcontinent. And the rise of fundamentalism among Hindus, Muslims, and Sikhs in India has reverberated here in Toronto. We continue to socialize with each other, but we usually tiptoe around each other's religious loyalties and sensibilities, and avoid discussing the political minefield of the subcontinent.

Poonam has an MBA, and worked for a bank for several years before starting her own business. She is now a successful businesswoman who is proud of her success and not empathetic towards those who are having a more difficult time in their lives. She managed, as usual, to bring the conversation around to all the status symbols acquired by her family and their friends, and the conversation took an unseemly turn as the other women joined in, noting all their recent endeavours to keep up with the Joneses and outdo one another. I was beginning to find their one-upmanship tiresome, but I tried to be understanding. Their goals in immigrating to Canada included finding the good life: fine food, expensive cars, and big homes. They wanted to have access to education and opportunities for their children. They have a right to feel proud of achieving these goals, regardless of what I think. Sometimes I think they place so much emphasis on material success because they are afraid that if they do not assert it they will be lumped in with working-class South Asians and be further ill-treated. They are caught up in creating and perpetuating an image of themselves as cosmopolitan citizens of the world who are equally at home everywhere. That attitude sometimes comes across to me as pretentious.

We were barely aware as we talked that the verandah had slowly emptied and most of the other guests had departed. We looked at our watches and bemoaned the need to break up the party and get back home to prepare dinner, do the laundry or catch up on missed professional work. Poonam recalled the old days in India, when women in her family could spend a whole day with their friends without feeling rushed. We promised each other that we too would try to live less by the clock. Then we made our way back through the club to our cars.

13

A Canadian in New Delhi

Now that I have lived in Canada for some thirty years, I feel comfortable with its culture and with my social environment. White Canadians frequently see me as an Indian woman (never as simply "Canadian") and an immigrant, and I lug around with me the burden of the preconceptions of others about who I am and what my values are. Over the years their perception of me has become an integral part of my mindset, and I am now emotionally committed to being an Indian. I am sensitive to racist stereotypes that see Indians as "traditional" and "oppressed," and I have become an ardent anti-racist activist.

However, when I am in India, even my relatives and friends see me as a Westerner. My skin colour, which defines who I am in Canada, does not seem to allow me to merge with the population there. In India, other aspects of my person, such as dress, speech, accent, language and behaviour, take precedence. These identify me as a Canadian.

There might be some validity in Indians' calling me a Canadian, for on reflection I realize that I now see India though "Canadian eyes." When I am in India I am always making mental notes about people and events that might be interesting to my students at York or provide useful illustrations in my writings. I want to fill in the picture of India for white Canadians by showing the history and the cosmopolitan character of its cities. India also has a vibrant and dynamic women's movement, and when I come across an interesting woman there, I want

Canadians to know about her so that they can revise their views about the country and its women.

While most local people take the environment as a matter of routine, in India I am standing back mentally and observing and recording. I try to evaluate things in their own context, but my interest is piqued when events are in marked contrast to Canadian social situations.

An immigrant's life in the twentieth century provides relatively easy and frequent access to the homeland, and that raises a number of questions that defy simple, straightforward answers: Where is an immigrant's physical and emotional home? Immigrants, like most others, belong to several communities. What are the reference points that guide their values and norms? Is the sense of belonging to a group or community a mutable experience, or is there something more constant and stable despite change of physical circumstance?

Immigrants are sometimes torn between their own and others' perceptions of their identities, and these diverging opinions have been occasions for conflict and social tension amongst individuals, their communities, and the society at large in their chosen countries. Over a period of years, the experience of being an immigrant changes the individual. What then comes to define individuals is not just skin colour or social context, but also their evolving values and norms. Indeed, my response to people and events reveals who I am more than mere abstract analysis of my person and temperament—that is, identity.

My ambivalence over being Indian or Canadian is not unique; it is shared by other non-white people who live in the West. A poignant example from Canadian history is of Japanese-Canadians during World War II. Identified by white Canadians as the "enemy," they were not allowed to join the Canadian armed forces. They then challenged this exclusion in the courts and won the right to join up. However, when some of them were sent to Japan, people there looked upon them as Canadian. Later, in a bumbling effort to compensate Japanese-Canadians for the wrongs done to them during the war, the Canadian government initiated a program to repatriate individuals wishing to go back and live in Japan. The few who accepted the offer found themselves to be foreigners in Japan, and some came back to live in Canada.

Despite my confusion over identity, India still exerts a pull on me. When I hear Indian classical music, for instance, it resonates in me quite differently from Western music: it stirs my emotions. Yet, when I am in

India I feel overwhelmed by the traffic, the noise, and the pollution, and constrained by the once unquestioned norms of the members of my family who live there.

In the winter of 2001, I began to plan a visit to New Delhi to do research on Indira Gandhi and the women's movement in India at the Nehru Memorial Library. Questions arose in my mind about the nature of the visit: was I an Indian returning home, or a Canadian academic on a research trip? This time I wanted to live on my own, away from my relatives, and rely on myself to "smooth the way" during my time there. My life in Canada had put some distance between me and my family. I felt detached from their concerns and somewhat out of place when I was with them. I wanted to locate myself with academics, hoping to find a community with shared interests. Perhaps I also wanted, subconsciously, to transcend the issue of skin colour within the context of work and find relief from it with like-minded people.

Other questions haunted me as I planned my trip. I was apprehensive of being construed by Indian feminists and academics as a woman of privilege. They might perceive me as a Western woman who was appropriating their material for my own academic purposes. As a citizen of the "Imperial West," I might seem to be exploiting them.

With the help of some American friends, I had chosen the India International Centre, a kind of social club for academics, as a suitable place to stay. When I phoned from Toronto to make reservations, the first question the clerk asked me was, "Are you an Indian national?" There was a good reason for him to ask, because as an Indian national I would pay only about 750 rupees ($25 Canadian) for a single room for a day, but as a Canadian I would have to pay four times that much. (Rate differences like this are common in India for both accommodation and travel). I answered the clerk in Hindi to assert my Indianness, and he accepted my answer. However, when I actually arrived at the centre, the manager looked at me skeptically and asked, "Are you an Indian?" At first, I was amazed at her question, since I am only accustomed to people giving significance to my skin colour outside India. Could the manager not see that I was Indian? What personal aspect had signalled my Western identity?

My decision to stay at the centre put me in the midst of people from all around the world who were visiting India to do research for books, write articles, give talks or merely enjoy the warm weather and the local ambiance. There were about eighty people living at the centre. Some were non-resident Indians like me; others were from various cities in India or from the West. I met people from the United States, Spain, France, Norway, Sweden, Britain, South Africa, and Canada.

The centre is located in Jor Bagh, an upper-class neighbourhood in New Delhi. It is a sprawling, two-storey building surrounded by large gardens with lily ponds. Hundreds of terra cotta pots filled with flowers and ferns line the driveway, footpaths and walls of the property. In February and March, when I was there, there was a profusion everywhere of dahlias, roses, and gladiola. Bougainvillea draped the brick walls that encircled the centre. There were many rose bushes, clustered together according to colour. Some even had nameplates; a cluster of white bushes at the back of the building was called "Mother Teresa."

The area around the centre reflects India's long history of invasions by foreign powers. Directly behind the building is a twenty-acre park with mausoleums and a mosque, all of which were built in the fifteenth and early-sixteenth centuries by one of India's earliest invaders, the Lodis, who had originally come from Afghanistan and controlled what was then referred to as the Delhi Sultanate. The Lodis laid the foundations for the next invaders, the Mughuls, who also established a dynasty in India. It was the Mughuls the British overthrew, ruling India thereafter for about two hundred years. Although the park, created in 1936, was named Lady Wellingdon (also spelled Wellington) Park, that seems never to have caught on and it continues to be popularly referred to as the Lodi Estate or Lodi Garden. Adjacent to the centre are the offices of the Ford Foundation, which finances several development and research projects in India, and another building surrounded by fountain-filled gardens that houses the United Nations Development Program building.

The mausoleums combine features of Hindu, Tulghluq (also spelled Tuglaq), and Muslim architecture. People sometimes describe them as stern and heavy-faced, but I found their simple grey, pink and black exteriors charming. The structures were constructed to appear double-domed, and are square or octagonal in shape. The mausoleum called "Shish-Gumbad" (meaning "a dome of glass") was built in Sikander Lodi's reign (1489-1517), and its exterior wall still displays a few traces of the blue-tile friezes that originally decorated it. Inside there are eight tombs laid in plain concrete that has blackened over the years. They are devoid of any decoration and, since the names of those buried there are not known, there are no identifying nameplates.

The "Bara Gumbad," built between 1451 and 1526, is square-shaped and has stucco and painted ornamentation inside, but no tombs. The mosque attached to the mausoleum combines the architectural features of the Tulghluq and Mughal periods. Inside, it is richly decorated with floral and geometrical designs, and has inscriptions from the Koran in white stucco that has now grayed. With the destruction by the Taliban of Buddhist statues in Afghanistan in mind, I was happy to see signs at the entrances of the mosque and mausoleums that read "Protected Monument" and "Site of National Importance." The signs warned of fines and imprisonment under the Archeological Sites and Remains Act of 1958 for anyone who "destroys, injures, alters, defaces, imperils, or misuses" the monuments. The hundreds of people who walked around the mausoleums every day, however, took the presence of these historical buildings for granted. By early spring, I too was more attracted by the huge bougainvillea trees with their lush magenta blossoms.

I took a one-hour walk in the morning, and sometimes in the evening, in the Lodi garden. Hundreds of people walked along its well-designed stone pathways every day at sunrise and sunset. I was struck by the clean, well-kept appearance of the gardens and the absence of vendors and beggars, perhaps because of the contrast this provided to what I had experienced in previous visits to India. Around the grand monuments people nonchalantly practised yoga, played ball with their children or lounged on the grass gazing up at the clear blue sky. The only unpleasant elements were a few mangy dogs that sometimes stood blocking the walkways. I made a wide circle around them.

I would often stop to watch gardeners at work. Their tools and techniques fascinated me. I saw males and females sitting on their haunches and sweeping the grass with brooms made of thin bamboo twigs. Sometimes I saw women sitting in a corner making these brooms. To cut the grass, the men wielded eighteen-inch steel scythes. One man carrying a stick led a bullock drawing a three-foot blade behind it, along with a bin for gathering the clippings. Another kept the bin aligned with the bullock as the two walked back and forth to mow each portion of the park. (At the centre, an electric mower was used; one man pushed it while another carried the cord.)

I never saw anyone else watching the gardeners while they worked. However, I was looking at them with "Canadian eyes," comparing their tools and methods with what I was familiar with in Toronto. The rakes and the electric lawn mower in my garage at home made the tools and practices of these gardeners seem quaint.

In the mornings I sometimes saw couples through the open archways of the mausoleums. They obviously wanted some privacy. Others walked and talked beside the flowers. At times I saw two men or two women holding hands as they walked around. As a young woman in India, I had been accustomed to seeing such hand-holdings, and thought them unremarkable. My assumption then had been that they were just friends, but after years of living in Canada and learning more about same-sex relationships, I was skeptical of my earlier assumptions.

The centre combined features of a small convention centre and a private club. Since the government of India had declared 2001 the year of Women's Empowerment, I had the opportunity to attend conferences on world literacy, women's writings, gender and racism, and the "girl child." Topics of talks that I attended ranged from the Middle East in India's foreign policy to the female form in Indian art. I noticed two things. First, many Indian feminists were engaged in development projects that had immediate consequences for the most disadvantaged women in India—for example, access to water for farming and drinking. Many of these projects were funded by agencies such as the Ford Foundation. Secondly, the women were absorbed in the problems of their own societies, and seldom compared themselves with their Western counterparts. This did not mean that they were uncaring of other women. On March 8—International Women's Day—I saw Indian women outside the United Nations building alongside some hijab-wearing women protesting against the sanctions imposed on Iraq.

Participants often came to the centre in cars driven by chauffeurs and were let off at a platform at the end of the driveway inside the compound. When they were ready to leave, they called for their cars from a stand marked "Car Hailer," where a hidden microphone connected them to the parking lot where the drivers were waiting. Often a dignitary, such as a former prime minister or a current minister, would come to address a gathering. Then, a number of rifle-toting guards could be seen standing conspicuously at various points around the centre.

Sometimes I sat on the verandah in the mid-morning sun and watched the elegantly dressed Indian men and women who were members of the centre casually joining each other at the tables and talking animatedly with their companions. I became curious about their professional and social identities. When I asked some long-standing members of the centre about the membership, they described them as the Indian intelligentsia. Indeed, I had met Indian journalists, authors, publishers, editors, and academics at the centre. I envied what seemed to me their sense of belonging and their comfort with each other. At such times I would have to remind myself that in many other ways—access to books, libraries, research assistance—I was much better off than most academics in India.

The food at the centre was very inexpensive compared to similar restaurants in New Delhi, and I began to wonder who was underwriting it. My queries met with looks of puzzlement from members, eliciting the simple response that it was membership dues—dues that turned out, on enquiry, to be nominal as well. Some funds must have been realized by renting out the auditorium, but it all did not quite add up for me. A few Westerners cautioned me in hushed tones to be discreet in asking people about it. I wondered if an international agency or foreign government had endowed the centre. I recalled the case of *Imprint* magazine in the 1960s, with its CIA funding. However, no one was interested in pursuing this line, and I eventually dropped the issue.

The academic in me noticed the dress worn by the white people at the centre and attached importance to it. It was an index by which to measure changes in attitudes towards Indians and India over the twentieth century. Many of the white men and women had taken to dressing in Indian clothes—a kurta with a woollen or raw silk vest with a high collar for the men and salwar kamiz for the women. A former American ambassador to South Asia dressed in a skirt and jacket but, like many local women, wore a woollen shawl against the morning cold. A Norwegian woman I met who attended an Indian wedding had an intricate pattern of the henna drawn on her palms along with the rest of the wedding party.

When the British came to India in the seventeenth century, some of the men adopted Indian clothes, but later the colonial elite frowned upon such a practice. As the British Raj became more established, dress codes became rigid, and the British style of dress was strictly adhered to for official and social gatherings. I remembered seeing pictures of British men dressed in heavy suit coats and trousers in what must have been sweltering heat. Cartoons sometimes ridiculed the British practice of wearing woollen suits and bowler hats and carrying umbrellas in the burning heat of the midday sun (giving rise to the phrase "mad dogs and Englishmen"). British women clung steadfastly to dresses, eschewing any

Indianization of their dress or appearance and strictly maintaining British mores in India.

The rigid dress norms symbolized the British sense of racial and cultural superiority. Dress was a means of maintaining social distance from the "natives." Indian males with ambitions to rise in the colonial bureaucracy adopted British dress, but the colonial elites heaped scorn on them for their efforts. During the nationalist struggle led by Nehru and Gandhi, Indians discarded western dress as a symbol of their rejection of the British Raj. Simple, homespun cotton clothing that conformed to regional Indian culture became the norm among patriotic men and women. Now, some fifty years later, whites were trying to close the gap between themselves and Indians.

Deciding whether to wear Indian clothes or Western was complicated for me. Although being considered an outsider annoyed me, I wanted to assert my difference in India by dressing in Western clothes. Yet I was drawn to the bright and colourful saris and salwar kamiz. One day, I went to the library dressed in an old salwar kamiz and Sushma, the librarian, complimented me on my appearance. Her compliments were far more lavish than my dated clothes deserved, but wearing the salwar kamiz seemed to have created a new familiarity that reduced the distance between us. We became merely two Punjabi women of Hindu culture who lived in different parts of the world. Sushma, who was about my age and, like me, a wife and a mother, knew that I came to the library to use the Internet to check for e-mails from Tom and Nicole. She bent the rules to give me priority in using the computer. She must have apprised the two young male technicians of my situation as well, for when I showed up at ten on the dot, when the Internet facilities became available, I was greeted with big, genial smiles.

When I visited my relatives and showed up in my dated Indian clothes, my nieces and nephews and their spouses were disappointed. In a sari or salwar kamiz, I was just one of their middle-aged aunts. They much preferred it when I wore jeans and jackets, for then I exuded an aura of Westernness that they liked. When they introduced me to their friends, they emphasized that I was married to a white man, was living on my own in New Delhi, and was gathering material for a book. These characteristics made me unconventional and interesting. For my part, I liked wearing Western clothes while I was with them. My clothes signalled that I was not bound by the local norms and was free to behave in whatever manner I chose. I appreciated the sense of freedom that the clothes provided me with my relatives.

Regardless of how I dressed, in Indian or in Western clothes, my identity was constantly queried. When I spoke in Hindi, waiters, taxi drivers and service personnel were taken aback and asked, "Are you an Indian?" I always presented myself in formal and informal gatherings as an Indian, but I was usually met with skepticism. I went to one conference held at the centre dressed in black jeans and a cotton shirt. Thirty other women and I, seated in a circle, introduced ourselves by name. Throughout the morning I sat quietly and inconspicuously in the outer circle, but after lunch one of the organizers pointed to me and said, "Everyone here wants to know who you are." I stood up and introduced myself as an Indian who had been raised in Delhi. That bit of information only met with puzzled looks. I added that I had lived in Canada for thirty years. There was a sudden sense of understanding before the women quickly lost interest in me.

I had not done research in India for some twenty-five years, so I had had little contact with feminist academics or activists in India. While preparing for my trip, I called acquaintances in Canadian universities for some leads. A professor at York—a white American woman who does research on India—suggested that Douglas Verney, a former political science professor from York University, might provide some useful information. As luck would have it, he told me he would be staying at the India International Centre during the time of my planned trip; he promised to help with introductions and provide guidance. I met Douglas and his wife Francine the day after I arrived, and through them I met many other academics staying at the centre. They introduced me, for instance, to Alice Thorner, an elderly American who was well known to Indian feminists in New Delhi.

Douglas, Francine and Alice were all very familiar with India, having visited it annually for the previous twenty years. The stream of Indian visitors who came to see the three of them during meals showed me that they were well liked and respected. I was happy to be with people who shared my academic interests. Yet, being with them also made me rethink the feminist idea that only people belonging to a particular group are best located to speak for them.

Francine has written books on India's political economy that are widely referenced by other scholars. She is the director of the Center for the Advanced Study of India at the University of Pennsylvania and has founded a similar institute in New Delhi. Douglas, too, is a well-respected academic. He told me that he was swamped with papers and research proposals that Indian academics had requested he read and comment upon.

Alice had collaborated with Indian feminists and had written on urban architecture as well as on the women's movement. I had not had much success in meeting feminist academics by simply calling them on the phone and introducing myself, so I solicited Alice's help in gaining introductions. She took me with her to a conference taking place at Jamia Millia Islamia University to celebrate twenty-five years of Women's Studies and there introduced me to several women. She seemed to be popular and well liked. Subsequently, on three separate occasions and in different locations, women came up to me and said, "Weren't you at the conference with Alice?" Alice provided me with an entry into the academic feminist community, and the start of a chain of interviews that facilitated my research.

Although my observation of Francine, Alice, and Douglas raised questions for me, their attitude was simple and straightforward: they were academics studying India. The Indians who met with them at the centre did not evince any hostility to them as Americans or whites. Although some post-colonial academics and feminists in India and elsewhere might be critical of their doing research on India, these issues were not considered significant there.

When I went to the Centre for Women's Development Studies in New Delhi to consult its library, as a courtesy I sent in my business card to introduce myself to its founding director, the pre-eminent feminist Vina Mazumdar. I had hoped that we might have a quick, five-minute chat. I was pleasantly surprised when someone came out to escort me to her office, where she settled into a chair to have what turned out to be a long talk with me. I regretted that I had not prepared questions for her. As it turned out, though, that would have made no difference. Vina had very definite ideas of what she wanted to say to me, and right away she launched into a long discussion on some of her favourite topics.

Vina is a Bengali, but she has lived in many cities of India. She was an academic who worked as a civil servant in a government research institute before joining the Centre for Women's Development Studies. She was a veteran of many international women's conferences, having represented both the Indian government and non-governmental organizations. Although she is in her early seventies and retired, she is still in great demand to address women's meetings in New Delhi. Other feminists refer to her as "Vinadi." The suffix "di" means older sister; they add it to her name to mark their respect for her age and position.

Vina was dressed in a cotton sari and had cropped, gray hair. She chain-smoked through the entire three hours I spent with her. When I first sat down, she tapped my business card on her desk and asked me what my research subject was. I replied hesitantly, "Women and politics in India," whereupon she said immediately, "You Western feminists should stop counting heads!" It was not important, she insisted, how many women were members of parliament or ministers. There were other, more urgent and interesting questions for feminists to pursue. She then proceeded to tell me what topics were important; these included family planning, female education, and work.

Vina co-authored a government-sponsored report called *Equality Now* in 1974. She narrated in detail the politics that had been involved in setting up the committee on the Status of Women appointed to write the report by the government of Indira Gandhi. Only prodding by the United Nations convinced the government to bring this committee together to conduct research studies on women in rural and urban India. Its report documented that everywhere in India, despite a constitutional guarantee of equality and non-discrimination, women's situations had worsened since independence in 1947.

Hours went by as Vina animatedly recounted events since the 1970s. Occasionally she interrupted her talk to call out loudly to her male assistant to bring us some tea or photocopy some article she wanted me to read. Eventually, at six o'clock, the offices emptied, and Vina's daughter arrived to accompany her home. Vina handed her purse to her daughter, who rummaged around in it for some money and then sent the assistant out for more cigarettes. After these were delivered, she stood patiently in the doorway, also chain-smoking, and looking indulgently at her mother. Later, when Vina left the room for a few minutes, her daughter whispered to me, "When Mummy starts talking, you can't stop her!"

On another day, I was talking with a Syrian Christian historian at the centre. She said that she thought my "distance" from the subject of my research—public policy regarding women under Indira Gandhi's government—might give me the advantage of being more "objective" than feminists who had lived through Indira Gandhi's government in India and might be "biased." She assumed a distinction between the research I might undertake and that which might be done by a woman in India.

Such incidents made me feel uneasy. Who was I? Where did my loyalties lie? Clearly, many of the local women did not see me as one of them, although I had lived in India for many years and knew at least as much about it as many of the women I met. But I realized there was a difference as well. My knowledge was now increasingly derived from academic sources; they had the advantage of experience and everyday life in India as well.

I attended a conference held at the centre on Dalit women. It was billed as a "National consultation of gender and racial discrimination examining issues of racism and racial discrimination, xenophobia and related intolerance." The conference was in preparation for the world conference on racism to be held in South Africa in the fall of 2001, and was scheduled just prior to an international conference on Dalit Human Rights to be held the following week in New Delhi. Dalit literally means "broken people" and refers to those who are at the bottom of the Hindu caste hierarchy—the "untouchables." The word was originally coined by Dr. B. R. Ambedkar, himself an untouchable, who was one of the architects of India's constitution of 1950. Gandhi's term for the untouchables was "Harijan," meaning "children of God," but people resist this name because of its Hindu connotations. Rights activists struggling on their behalf now commonly use the term Dalit.

Thirty years before in India, I had been oblivious of the socio-economic conditions of the untouchables, and had been amazed to learn later about their oppression deriving from caste and class. Now, at last, even the most disadvantaged women in India were struggling against this oppression, and were representing themselves in international conferences. They had "come to voice."

The conference made me see some parallels between the second-wave women's movement in Canada and that in India. The women's movement in India was at first dominated by elite, upper-class, educated, urban women, but their leadership was soon challenged by others. In the thirty years since, hundreds of women's organizations had emerged in India with different ideologies and memberships.

I also saw that as a caste Hindu, I was implicated in racism against the Dalits. So the tables had been effectively turned on me. In Canada, I was one of the victims of racism, but in India I belonged to the caste and class of the perpetrators. There are, of course, enormous differences between the subtle racism that I experience in Canada and what is experienced by the Dalits in India. Fortunately, I had the good sense not to express any solidarity as a fellow victim with the Dalit women, thus saving myself from the humiliation of being laughed at.

I got to the conference a bit late and when I entered, the hallway was empty except for a woman standing at the registration desk. She turned out to be the chair of the National Federation of Dalit Women. She looked at me quizzically when I approached the desk, but when I handed her my business card and explained that I was an academic interested in racism, she gave me permission to participate.

I stood with her for a while outside the meeting room, taking the opportunity to ask about the classification of caste discrimination as racism. She explained that the United Nations Convention on the elimination of all forms of discrimination defines racism very broadly. I knew that caste violence was a major political issue in contemporary India, but I wondered what grievances Dalit women specifically had. Were they organizing with Dalit men, or with other Indian women on the basis of gender? She sidestepped some of these questions, asserting only that Dalit women were lobbying the government of India for affirmative action. Dalits already have constitutional guarantees of affirmative action in educational institutions and government bureaucracies, but gender discrimination has especially minimized the opportunities for women of this caste and class.

When I entered the conference room, about thirty women were seated around a table. During introductions, some women identified themselves as Dalits, while others did not reveal their caste identity. Since no one was making an issue of the omission, I too declined to say anything on that score. A strikingly good-looking tribal woman who appeared to be in her early thirties caught my eye; having grown up in cities, I had never seen an Indian tribal woman in traditional dress before. Her forehead and cheeks were tattooed with vertical, linear markings and her earlobe was completely covered with small silver hoops. She wore a sarong-like skirt. There was little in the physical appearance of the other women to distinguish them. I was told they were "grassroots women"—Dalit activists and other academics and reporters. One woman, whom I had met while doing research at the Nehru library, had a PhD in sociology and taught at the Law Faculty in Hyderabad, a city in southern India. She had helped to write a report on violations of Dalit women's human rights that the meeting was going to discuss further and finalize for presentation at the conference in the fall.

Three of the women had come to present testimonies about discrimination. The tribal woman spoke passionately, but in a language I did not understand. I wondered how many of the others were at the same disadvantage, as the languages of the conference were Hindi and English. Academic papers followed these testimonials. One woman presented a paper in English that gave an overview of racism; another gave a comprehensive description of various international treaties and conventions on racism and human rights. During discussions, a woman complained that "racism" was a "Western and value-loaded term that was being imposed on the Dalits." There was a need, she argued, for an "Indian term." Another countered that "racism" could be defined to include the experience of Dalits, asserting vehemently, "We will fill the definition with our own pain and suffering."

I had wanted to attend the world conference on Dalit human rights, but somehow got the dates and meeting places mixed up and missed it. One evening, I decided to walk to the local market to order some books. Few residents walked in this upper-class neighbourhood, so I was somewhat startled when a well-dressed man caught up with me and asked when the stores at the market closed. At first, I was somewhat brusque with him, but I decided that although the man appeared to be an Indian, his accent was "foreign" and so perhaps his enquiry was genuine. I slowed down and let him catch up with me again. He introduced himself as Jody, in New Delhi from South Africa to attend the Human Rights Conference and staying at the centre. Now I was full of questions, but we reached the market in a few minutes and he wanted to pick up a few souvenirs for his family, while I wanted to go on to attend a rally protesting the Taliban's destruction of the Buddhist statues. We agreed to meet for dinner at the centre that evening.

Jody was a Hindu in his early fifties. He had dark skin and eyes and black hair, but his speech had an inflection that was unlike the English spoken in any region of India. I asked him if the local population thought of him as an Indian and he grimaced, "Yes, all the time, but only until I speak." Jody spoke Tamil, but knew no Hindi or Punjabi, the two dominant languages in New Delhi, so he encountered the same difficulties as many other visitors to the city.

Jody and I found much to talk about as two immigrants with experiences of racism. I became more aware that evening that the Indians in Canada were just one part of the larger diaspora of Indian people spread all over the world. Although we are almost all brown-skinned and of Indian origin, our histories differ markedly from each other and are informed by local conditions. There are very few parallels between the histories of Indians in South Africa and Canada, for example, and the subtle racism in Canada is vastly different from that legislated in South Africa, particularly during apartheid.

Jody's Tamil ancestors had left South India in the late-nineteenth century to work in South Africa. Large proportions of Indian emigrants had gone to work on the railways there, or on plantations. Jody's ancestors were store owners. He had grown up in a mixed neighbourhood in Pretoria with what are referred to in South Africa as coloureds, or biracial people, but in the 1960s his parents were forcibly moved out of the city by the government and resettled with other Indians. They received no compensation for their loss of property and had to rebuild their lives from scratch. Even in post-apartheid South Africa, Indians have received no compensation from the government, though demands for it are occasionally voiced.

Jody's personal life has centred primarily on other Indians. He grew up in an Indian neighbourhood and all his social interactions are with people there. Not surprisingly, he married a Hindu woman of Indian descent. In post-apartheid South Africa, he considered leaving his neighbourhood and moving elsewhere, but he was beset with doubts. He worried that he would only be moving away physically, that this neighbourhood would continue to be the hub of his social life and that he would constantly be returning to visit his parents and in-laws or to go to the temple where he regularly prayed with his family. There seemed to be no compelling reason to move. Thus, although Jody is now legally free to live anywhere he chooses in South Africa, he continues to live in his old, Indian neighbourhood. As we ate he fretted over where he could go to buy salwar kamiz for his teenaged daughters, who liked to wear them when they went to the temple and to family events.

Jody attended the conference as one of the seven full-time members of the Human Rights Commission in South Africa. He confessed, in a somewhat embarrassed way, that he knew little about the Dalits, but had been reluctant to turn down the opportunity to visit India, which he had visited once before with his wife. He had done some reading in preparation for the conference, and offered to give me a copy of a book published by the Human Rights Watch on the Dalits in India.

There are some parallels between the situation of the Dalits and that of Indians and blacks in South Africa. No legislation in India forced Dalits to live in a "Dalit only" colony, yet the traditional hierarchy and norms of caste Hindus, as well as class distinctions, do segregate the Dalits in specific communities. Dalits who try to breach this norm and integrate themselves with the rest of the population have in recent times been victims of severe violence perpetrated on them by caste Hindus, particularly in small towns and villages. In the state of Bihar, politically motivated incidents of violence had led to death in some cases.

We were nearly finished eating, and Jody was still fretting about the clothes he had to buy for his daughters the next morning. We became nostalgic for our homes and families, and started swapping stories about daughters. Jody shamefacedly confessed that occasionally he talks in stereotypes about others and his daughters pull him up, crying, "You, a human rights commissioner, say that!" However, he confidently predicted that his daughters would marry men of Indian descent, much like themselves, primarily because that is the identity of the people in their social groups.

I hesitated to make any predictions of my own.

14

Life among the WASPs

If I had stayed in India, I would probably have become an upper-class housewife whose main occupation was looking after her children and household. I would have fluttered anxiously over the children while they studied and nagged them endlessly to eat something. My sense of self would have been dependent on their success, and I would have derived vicarious pleasure from their achievements. Perhaps by the time I reached forty my arteries would have been clogged from rich, fatty food and I would have suffered from heart disease brought about by an idle life. I would have led a carefree, sedentary life—without the media pressure forever exhorting me to stay in shape. I would have gossiped endlessly over tea brought by the household help, at the same time bemoaning my fate of being burdened with responsibility for everyone and everything in my house. I would have contrasted myself with lucky Western women who have all kinds of appliances to take care of household tasks automatically and without complaint. I would have repeated over and over, "It is my karma," and devotedly bribed the gods with offerings as I prayed to them to grant me better luck in my next life.

Instead, I rush around between classes and meetings at the university, and between "the three C's"—computer, cooking, and cleaning—at home. I rail against the tyranny of a cycle of chores all needing to be done right away. I feel compelled to work obsessively, having taken to heart the Western maxim that an idle mind is the devil's workshop. I think about

258

the oppressiveness of patriarchy, keeping me in this never-ending cycle of work. In particularly grumpy moments, I blame feminism for adding to my woes by sensitizing me to the ills of womankind and the need to resist patriarchy. "But what to do?" I ask myself as I slump down on a couch in front of the television. Within a few minutes, guilt once again overwhelms me, and I am reminded that I must exercise—go for a walk or at least get down to the basement and count to two hundred on my skipping rope. While getting ready for bed, I pray to some beneficent god that she grant me better luck in my next life.

Immigrants like me often romanticize about what could have been. The present seems harsh and full of difficulties. I contrast Canada's values with India's: the materialism of the West and the otherworldliness and spirituality of the East; the individualism of Westerners and Easterners' orientation to family. Westerners, being too polite to say "backward," call Eastern society traditional and their own progressive. In everyday life, however, our values shift and change. We are pragmatic, and we need to get by from day to day.

Perhaps if I had stayed in India I would have met only people like myself, and never had the opportunity to examine my values. I would have thought my cultural norms were superior, and the values of others would not have been a significant factor in my life. Here in Canada, however, self-interest has compelled me to try to understand the values of "Canadians," so I can handle many different situations here. Many white Canadians have no opportunity, or perhaps never care, to get to know people of another race and culture. They do not feel obliged to familiarize themselves with the norms of other people or cultures, since they have little impact on their well-being. This is true even in a city like Toronto, where it is impossible not to encounter people of different races and cultures. Seeing such people in one's social landscape is different from learning about them or their cultures. That requires an effort.

At first, immigrants like myself see values and norms in very broad strokes as "Canadian," not knowing what makes it so. When I first came to Canada in the 1970s, for instance, the charisma and charm of Prime Minister Pierre Trudeau seemed to have mesmerized some sections of the Canadian population. I quickly learned that my fellow students were proud of their handsome, somewhat philosophical prime minister. I did not try at the time to analyze their particular "Canadian" values or examine any more of them. However, over time we new immigrants pick up clues that suggest to us that there are differences in values. Some people are regarded as proper and conventional, while others are radicals, hippies, Marxists, feminists, and so on. There was some concern over Trudeau's marriage to a "flower child." Immigrants have little choice but to make this effort once they are in Canada. The onus is on them to understand Canadian values—despite a great deal of media and academic rhetoric to the contrary.

I had choices then. I could hold on strongly to my Indian values, attitudes, and behaviour, adopt some Canadian norms, or submerge myself in a group identified by its politics or ideology. In retrospect, I see that what I then identified as "proper" values, attitudes, and behaviour were those of people I would now call WASPs—roughly speaking, the norms of middle- or upper-class white Canadians, typically of Anglo-Saxon (British), Protestant descent. Sometimes the term is restricted to the privileged and powerful upper class, but WASP values are emulated by many middle-class and even working class people.

Of course, I got to know one "Canadian" family very well in the 1970s. They were later to become my in-laws. Lettie, Tom's mother, had been born in Canada to Scottish parents, and his father Albert was the son of Protestants who had emigrated from Ireland. Neither had ever had much contact with people from different cultures. They had always lived in Ontario and had never travelled outside the province. When I met them, Lettie worked as a clerk at an Eaton's store and Albert, who had Parkinson's disease, was on a disability pension. They lived in a small, semi-detached home on a street which was all white in the early 70s but over the years was to attract many immigrant families from Third World countries until by the 1980s it had become quite multiracial and multicultural.

Lettie was a plump woman with a happy disposition who liked to make jokes and giggle delightedly at them. Sometimes, caught up with laughing and joking, she would clap her hands in excitement and happy satisfaction. She was a woman of few pretensions who seldom envied others for their means or social position. She was more likely to make self-deprecating jokes about her own limited resources.

When I was first introduced to the family, we had little in common. What could we talk about? I had no knowledge or understanding of their culture, and having never met anyone from a Third World country; they knew little or nothing of mine. The same was true of most of their friends and relatives. Their idea of a different culture was Catholics! They did not mix with any families from eastern or southern Europe, either. When their children had friends whose parents were immigrants from Italy, they invariably referred to them, not by their names, but as "the Italians." Despite the wide social gulf of culture and education between us, however, my in-laws and I tried valiantly to find topics to chat about when I visited.

I never talked to Lettie and Albert about how I was raised or any other aspect of my family background, except to mention the number of siblings I had, and I never discussed any aspect of my culture with them; they never asked or showed any curiosity about it. In the twenty-five years that I knew them, I never cooked an Indian meal or even a single Indian dish for them. Over the years they did figure out that I liked spicy food, and when I ate at their house, Lettie would sometimes ask if I wanted to add a dash of pepper! But most of the time she forgot about it and we ate the seemingly bland food to which they were accustomed. My Indian connections were not a secret, but the two sides of the family were kept apart. My in-laws always knew when I visited India or when some of my Indian relatives were staying with me. Tom and I had Indian pictures hanging on the walls of our home. It was easier when we were with his parents, however, just to follow their way of doing things and talk about things that were familiar to them.

Given the already ample social distance between us, it required a great deal of goodwill to keep communication pleasant and open between us. I am sure it would have taken only a picture of a snake charmer in a colourful turban playing his flute and enticing a delicately poised snake out of a basket to bewilder Lettie and Albert. Pictures of scruffily bearded, saffron-smeared gurus and mendicants lying naked on beds of nails would have freaked them out completely. But Lettie and Albert were unaware of even the most clichéd images of India. They knew little about it besides the fact that people there had "different" (their polite word for weird and outlandish) names and ways of dressing. I thought I was in a better position to understand them, so I assumed responsibility for keeping things seeming as normal to them as possible. In turn, they accepted me as one of the family and gave me their love and affection.

When Tom, her eldest child, turned sixteen, Lettie asked him to quit school and find a job. As he was not so inclined and she was, fortunately, an indulgent mother, she let him be and he continued going to high school. When he graduated, though, she again expected him to leave school and find a job. She could not comprehend why he would want to continue with his education; the children of her friends and relatives routinely quit school at the age of sixteen, or if not then, certainly by eighteen. Tom's sister and brother both quit school at sixteen.

Lettie was probably not worried about the social distance that education might create between Tom and the rest of the family. University was simply an unknown and alien world to her. She did not know whether going to university was good or bad, whether it would improve Tom's job prospects or just be a waste of time and money. However, it was the choice Tom made, and as a loving and supportive mother, she helped him as best as she could while he was a student at the University of Toronto. Over the years, as she saw us leading an increasingly comfortable life, she would jokingly say of a new car or house or some other acquisition, "It must be all that education!" But she remained skeptical of its value.

The attitude of many of Lettie and Albert's relatives and friends towards education changed. Our economically secure and comfortable life became an example in the family network. Children were exhorted to get a university education and their parents helped them finance it. If any of them feared that higher education might mean another marriage to a "foreigner," they never let on to me. They came to see university education as a way to a secure, well-paying job for their children, and gave little thought to the social consequences for themselves and their families. They expected no dramatic changes in the values and norms of their children and, as it turned out, their confidence was not misplaced.

Lettie and Albert and their network of family and friends were Canadians, but even as a relatively new immigrant, I knew they did not fit middle-class Canadian norms. Like me, they were conscious that there were "proper" ways of doing things, but they did what best suited their own temperaments and means. They were also conscious of their limited circumstances and of being at the lower end of the scale, so to speak. One consequence of their being at the bottom was that they did not look down on people of other cultures and races.

Lettie was a devoted grandmother to our daughter Nicole. When Nicole was seven, we bought a piano for her, and no one was more delighted than her grandmother, who had always wanted her children to take music lessons. A piano had been beyond her reach, and she had been content to buy guitars for Tom and his brother. For Lettie, a piano in our house symbolized Tom's success in becoming middle-class. Her reaction was somewhat different when we bought the house in Rosedale, which has the reputation of being an old, established neighbourhood and the home of very wealthy people. She kidded us about it in her usual manner, but over the first couple of months I could sense some underlying anxiety in her. She feared that living there might change us and increase our social distance from her.

Buying a house in Rosedale had been an audacious investment for Tom and me. The banter amongst our friends when the topic of our new house came up revolved around the snobbery of Rosedale residents. So I was pleasantly surprised during the first week when our next-door neighbours, seeing me in our new front yard, came over and introduced themselves and welcomed us to the neighbourhood.

Margaret conformed in some ways to the stereotypical idea of a Rosedale matron. A tall, blonde woman of about fifty, she was a stay-at-home wife and mother. She was always dressed in casually chic Ralph Lauren clothes, but she was not snobbish and she was respectful of my profession. Like many wives and mothers, she often fretted about the well-being of her children and was preoccupied with the chores that needed to be done around the house and in the garden.

Since Margaret was a friendly and frank woman, I soon got to know the basic facts of her life and family. She had grown up in Rosedale, and took pride in being a long-term resident of the neighbourhood. As a university student and later when first married she had lived elsewhere, but she was glad to have returned to the area. She remembered a time when milk was delivered daily and placed in specially constructed little milk boxes at the backs of the houses.

Margaret had worked as a teacher for a few years, but had quit her job when her second child was born to become a full-time housewife. Her life seemed to have followed a pattern similar to that of many housewives in the neighbourhood. When her children were young, she was always busy taking care of them and chauffeuring them to their hockey, ballet, and piano lessons. Her husband Ian was a successful lawyer who worked long hours six or seven days a week and seldom helped at home. Since two of Margaret's three children had grown up and left home, she had more spare time when I met her and worked out with a personal trainer as well as participating in volunteer work, raising money for charities and helping out on some afternoons at a museum.

During our first year in Rosedale, I usually spoke to our new neighbours outside, in front of our houses or in the driveway. I was familiar, by then, with the "Canadian" sense of privacy and formality. A few months after we moved in, though, Margaret phoned to say that she wanted to have a neighbourhood party to welcome Tom and me to the street. Responding to my surprise, she explained that this was an old custom of the neighbourhood. I was taken aback, but quickly agreed to go along with whatever she had in mind.

As the date for the party approached, I became apprehensive. I did not know what to expect and did not want to reveal my ignorance by asking Margaret for details—who would be there, how we were expected to dress, and so on. I decided that since we were just an ordinary young couple employed in mundane jobs, there would be little incentive for most neighbours to come and meet us. (I had heard stories about the networking and deal-making that goes on in private parties in neighbourhoods such as these.) I imagined this would be a casual affair with a handful of people. And so, on the appointed day, Tom and I dressed in our very best woollen pants and sweaters and jokingly reminded each other as we walked across the yard to Margaret and Ian's house to be on our best behaviour and "mind our manners."

Margaret had asked us to arrive half an hour before the other guests, perhaps to give Tom and Ian a chance to get better acquainted, or maybe just to "teach us the ropes" of the big event. We rang the bell and Ian, dressed in a suit, opened the door. Right behind him was Margaret, wearing a simple but elegant black dress. They were standing in a spacious front hall with an Oriental rug on the floor and a console table topped with an arrangement of fresh flowers against one of the walls. We gingerly handed over our coats to Ian and walked with Margaret into the living room. It was softly lit with chandeliers, and a fireplace with burning logs created a warm and welcoming environment. There was a painting hung above the marble mantelpiece, where some silver and porcelain were also on display.

I felt quite overwhelmed by the elegant surroundings, and yet found the voice to compliment Margaret on the décor, admiring some pieces of furniture in particular. She told me she loved to collect antiques and that she had also been fortunate to inherit some antique furniture, paintings, and silver. My compliments drew the offhand comment, "Oh! Those belonged to my grandmother!" When I admired a painting, she said casually, "That has been in the family for generations." I gathered that she came from a family that for at least a generation or two had shown the culture and taste necessary to appreciate craftsmanship and beauty—and the means to acquire and keep valuable things.

Soon the other residents on our street started arriving—all of them, it seemed to me—and they too were formally dressed. Margaret and Ian had hired a caterer for the food and help to serve the wine. (Later I was to discover that this is the norm in Rosedale.) All the guests made a point of speaking to Tom and me, trying to put us at ease by talking about the university, making jokes with Tom about the weather, and giving us information about activities available for young children in the neighbourhood. No one gave any indication, though, of noticing that I was Indian; nor was there any mention of the few other Indian families who lived in the neighbourhood at that time or word on any Indian professional associates they may have had.

I got the impression that this group was bound together by their sense of being part of a community and a neighbourhood. Their general attitude towards me seemed to be that since I was going to be living amongst them, I was on some level just one of them. "Who I was" beyond that was not relevant. I suspected that their sense of community did not reflect any particular religion or political party, for instance, but I did detect conservatism and a strong family orientation. Yet they were all members of the same social class and race.

Over the next twenty years, I came to see that the stereotypes about Rosedale and its residents have a few grains of truth. The owners are predominantly white, but they are not necessarily of British origin. I have met several second-generation European immigrant families. Some are Protestant; others are Catholic and Jewish. There are a very few South Asian and Chinese families. Given that the majority of the homes in the neighbourhood cost a million dollars and more, of course, most of the owners are people of considerable means. But it is predominantly "new money" that buys in Rosedale today.

The large majority of residents are self-made people who have been successful in their professions. Some own their own businesses, and others are former politicians or senior bureaucrats. In the early 1980s, on my stretch of the street, there were six other professors (four males and two females, one of the latter married to an architect) and many lawyers, accountants, and physicians. Over the years, however, people who work in the financial industry or consultants have increasingly replaced them. Some of the women are lawyers, accountants, or physicians. There are also many females who choose not to be employed and are now full-time housewives.

The physical appearance of Rosedale reinforces the view that it is the home of wealthy white Canadians in Toronto. The streets are lined with hundred-year-old oak and maple trees that lend an aura of permanence and stability to the neighbourhood. These mammoth trees and their thick, leafy branches provide shade from the sun (although I still long for the feel of its direct rays on my face). The area is bordered on all sides by ravines and has several small parks that create peaceful and idyllic settings where children can play and adults can walk.

Houses in Rosedale—some of which are better described as mansions— were built mostly at the turn of the last century in Georgian and Victorian architectural styles with pillars, porticos, and verandahs. Their façades are brick or stone, cleaned and restored over the years. The norm in Rosedale is to maintain the external façade and the original interior structure of a house, but modernize the rest—plumbing, heating, air conditioning, doors and windows, etc. When a house is replaced, the new one usually replicates the English architectural features common to the neighbourhood.

A handful of houses in Rosedale are contemporary, with clean, straight lines and no adornments, but they are sniffed at by the neighbours, who predict erosion of property values. You can imagine what they would say if anyone had the gumption to introduce Muslim or Hindu architecture into the neighbourhood. Conformity to existing styles and designs seem to establish the class and status of an individual and provides an entrée into the world of the social elites who live in Rosedale.

The design and décor of the houses speak of "old money." The main floors frequently have a library with a fireplace and walnut or cherry panelling that lend dignity and charm—a genteelness—to the rooms. Owners often add a contemporary family room at the back of the house. There's usually a separate staircase connecting the kitchen with bedrooms on the second and third floors, wiring for a bell from the main rooms of the house to the kitchen, and a serving pantry beside the kitchen. Many owners have gone to a great deal of expense to maintain these features, which hark back to the time when Irish and English girls worked as maids in these homes.

The sense of belonging that a white man in loafers and tweed exudes while walking his dog on these streets could easily lead one to mistake him for a British country squire. The exigencies of contemporary life, however, make it more common to see a woman briskly walking a dog or, more frequently, a paid dog-walker leading a pack.

My neighbours would be aghast if I compared their homes to what are derogatorily referred to as "monster homes," but there is some similarity between them. Rosedale mansions are built on small lots, considered appropriate for homes in the city, but residents frequently obtain special permission from the city to add more rooms, exceeding what zoning regulations permit. "Monster homes" are large homes built on similarly small lots in some of the new suburbs around Toronto. They also often reproduce English architectural features, although their owners may not feel as reverent towards them as the owners of Rosedale mansions. The critical difference between the "monster homes" and Rosedale mansions, however, is what they symbolize.

Rosedale homes are thought to belong to WASPs, "monster homes" to immigrants from places such as Hong Kong and Italy. Rosedale is perceived to be the home of old money; "monster homes" the embodiment of new money. WASP snobbery prefers houses that suggest lineage, status, and class. "Monster homes" symbolize crass materialism and conspicuous consumption in their lavish use of marble, glass, and chrome. The WASP norm is to display wealth in an understated way through antiques or reproductions of English and French furniture and fabrics. However, renovations to maintain the aura of old money can frequently be extravagant in Rosedale mansions. New owners may replace a one-year-old kitchen with something more to their liking or have their house painted two or three times in rapid succession until they are satisfied with the colour. I regard the excessive spending on renovation and re-renovation as immoral, but it does create jobs for a slew of building contractors and skilled workers.

What establishes class and status in one culture and environment may have no meaning in another. A woman in Punjab could signal her social status by wearing a finely embroidered, antique pashmina shawl or a piece of traditional, museum-quality Kundan or Meena jewellery, a Canadian in Rosedale by wearing a mink coat or jewels by Cartier. However, a vintage pashmina shawl can look like an old rag to someone unfamiliar with Punjabi culture, and a mink coat is coming to symbolize cruel, cold-hearted attitudes towards animals and contempt or ignorance of contemporary politics.

Rosedale homes bestow upon their owners a social, cultural, and class identity which is often at variance with the facts. The owners come and go, and by no means do all of them represent old money; however, by the social norms of elite, white Canadian society, they seem to belong and are realizing their aspirations of being considered part of the Establishment. On the other hand, people do not often flaunt their immigrant or non-upper-class backgrounds. The norm in that case is to merge by conforming to existing codes of dress, home furnishing, and social behaviour.

Very occasionally, owners will turn up their noses at the Establishment and "do their own thing." A Marxist professor walks around the neighbourhood in dirty jeans and an old jacket. His gray hair is tied in a ponytail and he wears a mud-coloured hat with a wide brim and heavy, ankle-length boots. New residents may wonder whether he is a vagrant they should warn their children about, a potential robber they should report to the police, or a homeless man living in one of the parks in the area. Could he be an owner? No way! Rosedale residents who know him avert their eyes and refuse to condemn unseemly behaviour by one of their own.

Margie is a tall brunette who lives on a neighbouring street. A vivacious woman who has a great deal of self-confidence, she is assertive and outspoken about her views on any number of things. She loves to talk with her neighbours when she sees them out on the street, and is always full of stories about one of her four young children. She often goes by my house walking her dog, and if she sees me working in the garden, will stop for a chat. Over the ten years she has lived in the neighbourhood, I have gotten to know her and have learned about her family life.

Margie's Hungarian-born father was a blue-collar worker and her mother a secretary. The family was able to buy a nice home in North York and a "cottage" outside Toronto, and Margie and her two siblings had many of the comforts and privileges of middle-class children while growing up. Margie's father died in middle-age, but by that time Margie had obtained a bachelor's degree and a teaching certificate; she taught at a public school for several years.

Margie met Ramon, her future husband, when she left university. Ramon is an immigrant from Brazil who came to Canada in his late teens and started university right away. He completed his bachelor's degree in commerce and then qualified as a chartered accountant. After working with a major accounting firm for several years, he launched his own business. It has grown and expanded and he is now well established.

Margie and Ramon lived in several homes in North York before buying a house in Rosedale and spending a small fortune renovating and furnishing. Margie took on this work with enthusiasm. This was going to be her dream home and set her up as a full member of the Establishment. She wanted to make her home look "more stately" by adding pillars and a portico to the front, but she also wanted it "to blend into the neighbourhood as if no one had touched it," to make it look old and "authentic."

The interior of Margie and Ramon's home is interchangeable with many others in the neighbourhood: polished wood floors, Oriental carpets, stained or leaded glass windows, gilded mirrors, antique chandeliers, marble bathrooms and kitchens, paintings (some by Canadian artists), and silver and porcelain accessories. There is nothing in their house, or in their appearance or behaviour, that speaks of their ethnic and immigrant background. Their taste has been nurtured by mainstream home-furnishing magazines and stores that emphasize English, French, and Italian décor. Ethnic furnishings are found in cheaper stores, and adding such elements does not appeal to individuals trying to be part of the old-money Establishment.

Margie and Ramon's ethnic backgrounds are not relevant to their everyday life. Margie grew up in North York on a street that had no specific ethnic character. My conversations with her indicate that her ethnicity is not an important factor in her sense of self and identity. It does not figure in any critical way, negatively or positively, in her social and economic aspirations for herself and her family. If she were Jewish, it might be important for her to observe some norms of Jewish culture. White ethnic groups that have had a history of persecution or have been stigmatized in the past may resist the temptation to "pass," while others may forget about their background and feel no nostalgia for their roots.

A very few people in the neighbourhood have inherited their homes. Others, who were born into the Establishment but did not inherit a house in Rosedale, are easy to identify if one has a sharp enough ear to catch the tone in a voice mentioning their name when they buy in the neighbourhood. When I hear this deference towards the name of a new owner, I sometimes use my status as an immigrant and an outsider to bluntly ask a knowing neighbour who they are. Neighbours are usually happy enough to fill me in with the details; their knowledge distinguishes class-conscious "Canadians" from immigrants like me.

An old-money family lived briefly in one of the homes on my street. The man, let's call him Charles, was in his late thirties, an enthusiastic sportsman and ardent polo player, and consequently, the family was usually at their country estate during the weekends. His wife, Phyllis, was from a middle-class family. She had met and married Charles while they were both attending university. The news that Charles and Phyllis were moving into a house on the street was received by the neighbours with quite a sense of satisfaction. They conveyed the feeling that the presence of this well-known, old family would enhance the quality of the street and the value of their homes.

Phyllis was an outdoorswoman who loved riding. I almost always saw her dressed in jeans and sweater, and there was nothing in her appearance that would have identified her social class or status. She drove a large Jeep—not a luxury sports utility van, but the type of utilitarian vehicle a construction worker might drive, except that hers was equipped with a television set to entertain her children on long rides.

Charles and Phyllis had a neighbourhood party to which we were invited. It was a lavish, professionally decorated and catered affair. At the party, a friend of the polo-playing Charles tried to make small talk with me by asking, "So, what do you hunt?" Since I do not come from a tiger-hunting Maharaja's family, as he may have thought, I tried to steer the conversation in another direction. The man obviously had no clue how to converse with a relative plebeian like me.

Myth would have it that parties and gatherings such as this are important venues for networking and making deals among the WASPs. That may be, but for a professor like me they are only occasions for a pleasant evening, good food, and some interesting conversation. I am included because I live on the street, am married to a white Canadian, and have over the years acquired the status of an "honorary white" with the neighbours. They are polite and friendly and although on many levels I am not quite one of them, they are unfailingly courteous towards me. I interact with them on their turf by observing their values and not trying to impose my "foreign" ways on them.

Most of the people I have met in Rosedale are well educated and successful, but they are not much interested in other cultures and ways of life, and few show any interest in topics outside the range of ordinary North American or European experience. At social events or coffee parties held for candidates running for political office, or at the annual "Mayfair" (an outdoor fair held to raise money for the local community centre), the food is invariably North American and the conversation about local or national events.

Nevertheless, things are slowly beginning to change. Last year some women got together and started a book club. Most of us are married and have adult children, but all, except for me, are white. Some are Protestant and others are Catholic. We held an introductory meeting in my house to discuss our choice of books. Some suggested reading classical English literature; others wanted to read only contemporary novels. One woman, however, who had recently returned from a holiday in South Africa, suggested that whether we chose contemporary or classical literature, we should include books "on other countries" as well.

One of our meetings centred on John Irving's *Widow for a Year,* which had recently been published. The novel is set in New Hampshire and the main characters are upper-class, white Americans. The story revolves around the death of two teenaged boys in a car accident. After their death, the mother is overcome by grief and disappears from the life of her husband and baby daughter. To cope with the tragedy, she absorbs herself in a writing career. I asked the group what would be some of the most common ways for a "Western" woman (I meant white and Christian and was understood that way) to cope with such a personal tragedy. There was surprise at my question, but the women quickly listed drugs, alcohol, therapy, and shopping!

I then told them that a Hindu woman would cope with a similar tragedy very differently. An upper-class Hindu woman was more likely to become very religious, forsake all pleasure, devote herself to frequent visits to gurus and adopt an ascetic way of life. At other meetings I have pointed out to them that the values and norms underlying some of our discussions are often specific to middle-class North American culture, but such suggestions may just reinforce their view of me as being different from them...a Hindu, I suppose.

I am sure that most residents of Rosedale would staunchly support the right of "ethnic" people to practise the norms and values of their culture, but they certainly do not think of themselves as being "ethnic" as well. They would describe themselves as "just Canadians." Occasionally, to my great disappointment, I have heard racist and sexist comments from some very distinguished people who forgot for a moment my race and gender or who were simply unaware of my presence. For example, when I was out taking a walk and stopped to chat with a member of the legal profession who lives in the neighbourhood, he said to me, "All the black men who come to my court are pimps." I do not have the confidence to chastise such people.

A substantial population of Filipina women live in the neighbour-hood, but mostly they work as nannies or housekeepers. As a feminist social scientist, I have studied the conditions under which nannies work, and I know that not much insight comes from simply seeing them walk-ing young children in the neighbourhood. Most are well dressed; many of them drive their employers' cars. Gossip in the neighbourhood is that most can charge whatever groceries they need at the small, local super-market. Such expense is small change to most of their employers; it ensures the smooth functioning of their home, and they feel secure in knowing that they have left their children in the care of happy or at least not depressed or angry women. However, there is some racism here as well: a Filipina walking in the neighbourhood is assumed not to be an owner of a house.

One day, a year after we had moved into this house, the doorbell rang. Dressed in jeans and a sweater, I opened the door to a well-heeled white woman in a business suit holding a leather folder. She opened the con-versation by remarking on the pleasant fall day we were having, adding ruefully that we could soon expect much colder weather. She said she was collecting money for a charity and asked, "May I speak to the lady of the house?" When I responded that she was speaking to the lady of the house, she was embarrassed by her mistake and clearly wanted to make a quick getaway. But, much to her chagrin, I insisted on chatting with her for a few more minutes before I would say goodbye. Over the years, however, most salespeople have become cagey. Now when I open the door, they ask somewhat less presumptuously, "Am I speaking to the lady of the house?" or "Are you the lady of the house?" before they give me their sales pitch.

I have never had any discussions about race or ethnicity with any of my white Canadian neighbours, not even with some of the Jewish families who live there, who may have been subjected to more discrimination than most European immigrants. The dominant practice I have encountered in Rosedale among the white liberal residents, even at the present time, is to pretend not to notice differences of race and culture. The norm they observe is that in polite company one never comments on someone's skin colour—other than to admire a nice tan acquired in the Caribbean during the winter. Sometimes our neighbours even say that they have never noticed my skin colour. Yet if someone coming to visit us has forgotten our house number, they can knock on any of the neighbours' doors and ask where "the Indian woman" lives. They are invariably directed to our house.

Since many of my neighbours think it is impolite to refer to the colour of a person's skin, I seldom use the word "white" to describe anyone in their presence. I suspect that they would find such a description too "in your face" and offensive. In my experience, if someone of another race or culture is present when the topic of race comes up, people tend to become wary and feel uncomfortable. They are apprehensive of saying the wrong thing or of giving offence, and so would much rather not have such discussions. Non-white people, on the other hand, talk about their experiences of racism all the time amongst themselves, and some might like to have a face-to-face dialogue with some friendly white people as well. Unfortunately, when such discussions take place in academic conferences, they sometimes deteriorate quickly into guilt-tripping, accusations, and tears on both sides.

I am sure that all the white Canadians I have met in Rosedale believe that it is wrong to discriminate on the basis of skin colour. If I were to raise a question of race and ethnicity with the neighbours, some might patiently point out how Canada is different from the United States. The more knowing neighbours might talk to me about how immigrants are expected to become American through the "melting pot" or assimilationist experience of everyday life there, and distinguish it from the "salad bowl" or "mosaic" approach that characterizes the contemporary expectations of immigrants by white Canadians. I might hear the standard story about the old days when people were expected to assimilate here as well and conform to the norms of an Establishment dominated by immigrants and their descendants from Britain. "But that is history," they would say. At the present time, they contend, all immigrants are free to do their own thing, and there is no compulsion for them to adopt the ways particular to any other group. They are aware of the disadvantages of having black or brown skin in a white society, but they seem to feel quite complacently that things are getting better all the time, and they are not so conscious of how much being "white" has provided the privileges that accrue to them.

A summer or two ago I became enthusiastic about the notion of hosting a barbecue for the neighbours on the street. I reasoned that over the years I had enjoyed the hospitality of many of them and it was time for us to reciprocate. Tom, however, resisted the idea and began to feel insecure about our house. We were still making do with an old kitchen, he said, so at least we should wait until it was renovated. "What will the neighbours think?" he asked me repeatedly. But I was unconcerned. "They know you are a civil servant and I am a professor," I replied.

My nonchalance in the face of Tom's concern stemmed from my having gotten to know the neighbours better through casually chatting with them. I knew that Mary liked to talk about her children, that Jane grumbled about the cost of home repairs and escalating house prices. Meg was always rushed, but if she was in a good mood, she would stop and have a long conversation. I knew that Stacey attended the local church regularly and participated in its activities. Andrea was aloof and would speak only if we happened to come face to face on the street. Noreen, the wife of a former ambassador, would look right through me, as she did with all the neighbours. Tom's interaction with the neighbouring families was limited though, and that made him unsure.

We compromised by buying a new barbecue. Most of our neighbours came to the party, despite some spitting rain. Much to my surprise, some who usually did not attend such events came. I served the usual barbecue fare—no tandoori chicken, kebabs or samosas—just hamburgers and salads. Many of the guests brought wine and appetizers, and some helped serve. I was pleased that, despite the threat of rain, things seemed to move along smoothly and people had a pleasant evening together.

Later, as I tidied up the backyard, memories of "home" came flooding back to me, even though I was in my own house. I had been happy and at ease with most of the guests at the barbecue. I recalled the lost and lonely student I had been that first year in Waterloo, and thoughts about that time made me nostalgic for my life as a young girl in Bombay. At moments like these I begin to regret having lived my life as an outsider and a foreigner. I cheered myself, by thinking of the different people I have been able to meet here and the varied experiences I have had.

I have now lived most of my adult life in Canada. I remain emotionally attached to India, and although I no longer want to return to it, I feel a bond of sentiment and nostalgia for it that will always resonate in me. Yet I am a different Indian from the one who came to Canada some thirty years ago, and my sense of self—"who I am"—has been changed forever.

Afterword

I did not set out to reminisce about my life in India and Canada, or to document my reflections on Canadian society. This book began quite differently, in a conversation with an editor who suggested that we meet at a pub around the corner from his office to discuss another book of mine, which was about to be published, on women's shelters in Canada. He said he liked the clear writing in that book, and expressed his frustration with the complex language and dense theorization that often appear in the work of other contemporary academic feminists. There was a need, he said, for a book that would explain feminism to general readers—for example, to his working-class mother. I wasn't immediately compelled by this idea, but over the next few days it began to preoccupy me, and I decided I would see if I could write such a book—a kind of "Feminism for Dummies."

I anticipated that an easy-to-read book on feminism would give people a clearer idea of its fundamental principles, and that trying to write it would help me to understand them better, too. I could use anecdotes from my own experiences at work and at home to illustrate feminism in the context of women's everyday lives. However, as I began writing, I kept slipping into academic language and losing direction. I persisted over the next two years, but in that time the focus of the book shifted from theories of feminism to my personal story. It seemed egocentric to be writing about myself, but I felt that my story could provide insight not only into

Note to afterword is on p. 283.

275

an immigrant woman's life, but also into a feminist academic's perspective on Canadian society. An account of some aspects of my life would still be sufficiently multilayered to reveal the complex ways in which race, class, and gender intersect in an immigrant woman's life, and I could engage my readers in a conversation that would narrow the distance between us and show how we differ and what we share.

I felt a strong obligation to communicate to my readers the values, norms, and attitudes that underlie my perspective—to tell them "where I was coming from." Feminists have disputed the claim that knowledge is unbiased and neutral, arguing that an individual's race, class, and gender determine what and how they think about things. My experiences have shaped my interests and guided them in certain directions. For example, my personal experience as a victim of racism enraged me; it made me willing to commit time and energy to understanding such bigotry. I became an anti-racist activist. However, it was impossible to describe my perspective simply, for instance by saying that I was a non-white immigrant woman. For one thing, my perspective has changed over the years as my "location" has changed, and has no doubt changed again in the process of writing this book. For another thing, there are conventional images associated with these terms that make them almost useless in classifying my perspective.

Think, for instance, of the misbegotten clichés of hordes of welfare-grabbing immigrants from Third World countries straining Canadian resources, particularly its social services. Think of the images of women from these countries, denigrated for adhering to traditional and oppressive cultures and for not participating in the public life of either their old society or their new one. (Of course, there are also stereotypes on the other side, of white villains in Canada with discriminatory and oppressive attitudes who delight in making the lives of Third World people a misery.)

My perspective is further complicated by my personal loyalties: I am an Indian-Canadian; my spouse of twenty-five years is a white Canadian, and together we have a child. As a teenager attending school in Toronto, our daughter identified herself as a South Asian, but now that she has graduated from an American university, she perceives herself more distinctly as a Canadian. In narrating some of the incidents in this book, I too have had to struggle with a sense of hybrid identity.

Feminists have also argued that what were deemed in various academic disciplines to be universal values were specific to white, university-educated males primarily in Western nations; they were "androcentric" and "ethnocentric." People in general tend to see their own values not as peculiar to their own locations but as universal standards for evaluating and interpreting other cultures and societies. They judge from the vantage point of their own culture and find "the other" to be not only different but also deficient, or pernicious and oppressive. My description of growing up in New Delhi and Bombay reveals how, socialized by my family in a specific time, culture, and class, I absorbed their values.

A fundamental feminist principle that underlies much of this book is that a person's identity is socially constructed. The characteristics that a society associates with a person's race, class, and gender are seen as defining her or him. The terms society applies shape people's identities. In Canada, I have been termed a "foreign student," an "Indian woman," an "immigrant," an "Indian feminist," and a "Third World woman." Each of these designations has affected my relationships with other people and contributed to making me the woman I now am. Part of my motivation in writing about my experiences in Canada is to fight attempts to define who I am in terms such as these.

My experiences as a foreign student illustrate the feminist slogan that the personal is political. The white, male professors with whom I studied were gracious and kind men—comfortable with who they were, but unaware of the biases in their perspectives. Their understanding of history was informed by the power of the affluent, technologically developed West over poor, "underdeveloped" India, and of whites over non-whites, and of men over women. Much of this power was invisible, however, and because my relationship with them as a student seemed so normal, natural, and routine to me, I remained unconscious of it.

The gender-centred feminism of the 1970s and early 1980s alienated Asian and black women like me, and eventually more feminists came to see that it is not just gender bias that oppresses women from Asia, Africa, and the Caribbean, but race and class biases, too. However, my discussion of volunteer work with immigrant women's organizations shows that a gap remains between the theory and practice of feminism, even though the theory has expanded to recognize the integrated nature of race, class, and gender discrimination. Discussing sexism was difficult for us in the immigrant organizations; it meant criticizing our families and cultures, and we became defensive. However, in the lives of working-class, non-English-speaking women from our communities, we constantly saw evidence of sexism's extreme manifestation in abuse. Their lack of personal resources (itself a consequence of sexism), their alienation from white Canadian society, its exercise of racism and classism against them, and a myriad of other factors made it difficult for us to be "theoretically pure." Attacking the patriarchal structure of Western or non-Western families or taking political action against the systemic sexism of Western or non-Western governments would not have helped the women involved. Instead, the organizations chose to focus on providing for the safety and survival of women above everything else.

"Coming to voice" is a metaphor often used in feminist literature to describe one stage in the process of resisting the oppression of women. Sometimes the power exercised in race, class, and gender relations kept me silent in classrooms and faculty meetings. I came to voice in the company of women, who like me, had been victimized by racism. The attempt by some feminists to include women from Asia, Africa, and the Caribbean by chanting the mantra "race, class, and gender" had little effect on me. Instead, I worked with other groups to help working-class, non-English-speaking women secure social services. My books, *Resisting Discrimination* and *In Search of a Safe Place*, along with articles written from the perspective of marginalized women, attempted to let the voices of women who had previously been silent be heard.

Racist and sexist incidents have been a part of my life in Canada, but I have also experienced friendship and graciousness in white Canadians. The opportunities I have had for intellectual and emotional growth and development at Canadian universities and in the communities where I have lived weaken the arguments that racism and sexism are endemic to Canadian society. My story may disappoint readers looking for a portrayal of an unhappy immigrant woman's life, but I speak in a more layered voice.

The self-reflection that was necessary to write this book has also changed me. In exploring the past, looking at "where I come from" and the people and places that have shaped who I am, I have discovered how much my experiences in the 1970s differ from those of people who now immigrate to Canada from Third World countries. The revelation that there have been some improvements makes me happy, but I am also saddened to realize that some of the racism I encountered in the past persists even today, expressed in subtler and more indirect ways.

I recall people and places from a perspective that they, in part, created. What I remember (including my feelings at the time) reflects my feelings now. At the time of their occurrence, many of the events I describe were merely part of the hustle and bustle of everyday living, but now they have an import I was unaware of at the time. Finding the right words to convey my perspectives on events when they occurred and my view of them now is difficult. Of necessity, I see my past perspectives through my present ones, and the very process of writing about them changes them as much as my present perspective and the distortions of memory alter the past. Perhaps, in the end, my book is the best expression of the perspective from which I wrote it. I recall the words of Montaigne, who also recognized that writing about oneself alters oneself. He said: "Painting myself for others, I have painted my inward self with colours clearer than my original ones. I have no more made my book than my book has made me."[1]

I am sitting with my husband amongst thousands of parents assembled in Harvard Yard to watch our daughter, Nicole, graduate with the class of 1999. The day is warm and bright, but huge, profusely leafed trees in the Yard provide soothing shade from the sun. We're facing Memorial Church, where the commencement ceremonies will be held. Yesterday a service was conducted for the class by Reverend Peter Gomes, the black, gay minister of the church, and broadcast to the parents sitting outside. I listened solemnly while a male student and a female student read some passages in Sanskrit from the *Bhagavad-gita* and sang the "Gayatri Mantar," a prayer sung by Hindus on all significant occasions. That was a very emotional experience for me, and I—a non-practising, non-religious Hindu woman— was surprised to feel so stirred by it. Readings from the Torah, the Koran, and the Bible had probably touched the other parents as well.

Today we are to hear speeches by dignitaries assembled for the graduation ceremonies. The class speech is to be given by Sharmil Modi, a small, thin-boned, bespectacled student whose Gujarati parents came originally from Surat, a small town near Bombay. I had met him on one of my earlier visits to the campus and was pleased and proud when I heard that he had won this honour. Absorbed in watching the other parents, I am waiting, a little impatiently, for things to begin.

Suddenly I hear Sharmil over the loudspeaker. "*Bhul bhale biju(n) badhu(n), paN tu(n) kyaa(n) thi aavyo chhe e bhuli na jaish,*" he says. I am startled to hear Gujarati spoken, and I sit up to listen intently. "Forget all else," he translates, "but do not forget where you have come from."

This first sentence leads me to expect that Sharmil will talk about his Gujarati heritage and the struggle of his immigrant parents to raise him in an alien, American environment. Instead, he describes the communities in which he spent his childhood and youth, and the people in both the United States and India who nurtured him and taught him the values and beliefs that now define him. His parents, other family members in India, his neighbours, his school teachers, and of course all the students and professors he met at Harvard are cited as contributing to his achievements.

Success, he reminds his classmates, may be variously defined, but it must "include a loyalty to where you came from, to those who came before you, and to those who will follow." He ends by promising "*Hu(n) bhuli nahi(n) jaau(n)...*"

"I will not forget."

Notes

INTRODUCTION

1 Salman Rushdie, "Unfunny Valentine," The *Globe and Mail*, February 5, 1999, p. A13.

CHAPTER 1: BEGINNING IN CANADA

1 Salman Rushdie, *The Satanic Verses*, 1992, Dover, DE: The Consortium, p. 131.
2 Rushdie, *The Satanic Verses*, orig. Amer. ed. 1988, New York: Viking, p. 145.
3 Salman Rushdie, "Damme, This Is the Oriental Scene for You!" in *Step across This Line: Collected Non-Fiction 1992-2002*. Toronto: Alfred Knopf, 2002, p. 148.
4 Peter Nadas, *A Book of Memories*, New York: Penguin, pp. 8-9.

CHAPTER 2: AN IMMIGRANT STUDENT IN TORONTO

1 Robert Harney, *Toronto: Canada's New Cosmopolite*. Toronto: The Multicultural History Society of Ontario, 1981, pp. 10-20.
2 R. K. Narayan, "Vedanta Plaza," in *From the Outer World: Perspectives on People and Places, Manners and Customs in the United States, as Reported by Travelers from Asia, Africa, Australia and Latin America*, ed. Oscar Handlin and Lilian Handlin. Cambridge: Harvard University Press, 1997, pp. 269-270.
3 Rabindranath Tagore, "A Monotony of Multitudes," in *From the Outer World*, ed. O. and L. Handlin, p. 57.
4 Gloria Wade-Gayles, "Pushed Back to Strength: A Black Woman's Journey Home," in *Written by Herself: Women's Memoirs from Britain, Africa, Asia, and the United States*, ed. J. K. Conway. New York: Vintage, 1996, p. 595.

CHAPTER 4: BOMBAY

1 Salman Rushdie, *The Ground Beneath Her Feet*, New York: Henry, Holt and Company, 1999, p. 7.
2 Norma Evenson, "An Architectural Hybrid," in *Bombay: Mosaic of Modern Culture,* ed. S. Patel and A. Thorner. Bombay: Oxford University Press, 1995, p. 170.
3 Evenson, "An Architectural Hybrid," p. 165 ff.

CHAPTER 5: HISTORY AND HERSTORY

1 Mulk Raj Anand, *Conversations in Bloomsbury.* New Delhi: Arnold-Heine-mann, 1981, pp. 11-12.
2 Ranajit Guha, *Dominance without Hegemony: History and Power in Colonial India.* Cambridge: Harvard University Press, 1997, pp. 2-3.
3 Amartya Sen, "India and the West." *The New Republic,* June 7, 1993, pp. 29-30.

CHAPTER 6: IN SEARCH OF A COMMUNITY

1 Meena Alexander, "Fault Lines," in *Written by Herself,* ed. J. K. Conway. New York: Vintage, 1996, pp. 502-503.
2 Rushdie, *The Ground beneath Her Feet*, p. 177.
3 Anita Rau Badami, *The Hero's Walk.* Toronto: Alfred A. Knopf Canada, 2000.

CHAPTER 7: BEING AND BECOMING

1 Salman Rushdie, *Midnight's Children.* London: Picador, 1982, p. 351.
2 Carlos Fuentes, "How I Started to Write," in *The Art of the Personal Essay: An Anthology from the Classical Era to the Present,* ed. P. Lopate. New York: Anchor-Doubleday, 1994, p. 436.
3 James Joyce, *Portrait of the Artist as a Young Man.* New York: Viking Press, 1916, p. 253.

CHAPTER 8: RETURNING TO BOMBAY

1 Rushdie, *The Ground beneath Her Feet*, p. 43.
2 Handlin, O. and L., eds., *From the Outer World*, p. 27.
3 Rushdie, *Midnight's Children*, p. 81.
4 Evenson, "An Architectural Hybrid," p. 172.
5 Dom Moraes, *Bombay.* Amsterdam: Time-Life International, 1979, p. 158.

CHAPTER 9: A THIRD WORLD ACADEMIC

1 Jack Granatstein, *Who Killed Canadian History?* Toronto: Harper Collins, 1998, p. 84.

2 Christopher Lasch, *The Revolt of the Elites and the Betrayal of Democracy.* New York: W. W. Norton, 1995, p. 12.

3 Donald Kennedy, *Academic Duty.* Cambridge: Harvard University Press, 1997, p. 9. [Quote originally attributed to NAACP leader Jesse Jackson.]

4 Granatstein, *Who Killed Canadian History?* p. 85.

5 Leslie Sanders, "White Teacher, Black Teacher," in *Talking about Difference.* C. James and A. Shadd, eds. Toronto: Between the Lines, 1994, pp. 141-142.

6 bell hooks, *Teaching to Transgress: Education as the Practice of Freedom.* New York: Routledge, 1994, p. 90.

7 *Gandhi* [motion picture]. Directed and produced by Richard Attenborough, 1982.

8 Kennedy, *Academic Duty*, p. 66.

9 hooks, *Teaching to Transgress*, p. 19.

CHAPTER 10: IN THE COMPANY OF MOTHERS

1 V. S. Naipaul, "I Am the Sum of My Books." The *Globe and Mail*, December 10, 2001, R3.

CHAPTER 12: LUNCHING WITH THE LADIES

1 Rohinton Mistry, *Tales from Firozsha Baag.* Toronto: McClelland and Stewart, 1987, p. 245.

AFTERWORD

1 Phillip Lopate, ed. Introduction to *The Art of the Personal Essay: An Anthology from the Classical Era to the Present.* New York: Anchor-Doubleday, 1994, p. xliv.

Glossary

Hindi Words and Expressions

ashram: an ascetic environment where daily routines are devoted to prayers, meditation, and spiritual learning

atman: soul

ayah: nanny

bai: maid

begum: an Urdu honorific for a married woman of high social status

bhangan: a female untouchable

bhangi: a male untouchable

bindi: the red dot that women in India paint on their foreheads

bhai-bhai: brothers

biradari: caste, social grouping

channa: chickpeas

chunnis: scarves

churidars: leggings

Dalit: "broken ones," the untouchables

dhoti: a cotton loincloth reaching below the knee

dupatta: a long scarf

fakir: a poor man

guru: a spiritual teacher

gurudwara: temple

Harijan: "children of God," Gandhi's term for untouchables

hijab: a head scarf

khansamas: cooks

karma: actions in previous incarnations having a bearing on an individual's present life

katoris: bowls

kismet: fate

kurta: a long, loose shirt

mantras: prayers

maya: illusion

masala-chai, tea leaves boiled in water and milk with spices and sugar added

moksha: liberation from earthly human desires

namaste: hello

nokar: servant

purdah: gender segregation

pyjama: loose-fitting pants

pyjama kurta: an ensemble similar in style to the salwar kamiz

roti: flat, unleavened bread

sadhu: a holy man

sahib: master

salwar kamiz: an outfit comprising a long, loose shirt and baggy pants

samosas and *pakoras:* Indian savouries

satsang: literally, a truth association, or an assembly of devotees chanting and praying

satyagraha: a term coined by Mahatma Gandhi for non-violent civil disobedience

Swayambar: a royal ceremony in which a princess chooses a mate from assembled guests by placing a garland on the suitor of her choice

tabla: a small set of drums

thalis: large dinner plates

tobah: for heavens's sake!

yogi: a holy man

Bibliography

Agnew, Vijay. *In Search of a Safe Place: Abused Women and Culturally Sensitive Services.* Toronto: University of Toronto Press, 1998.

_____. *Resisting Discrimination: Women from Asia, Africa, and the Caribbean and the Women's Movement in Canada.* Toronto: University of Toronto Press, 1996.

_____. *Elite Women in Indian Politics.* New Delhi: Vikas, 1979.

Ahmed, Leila. *A Border Passage.* New York: Farrar, Straus, and Giroux, 1999.

Anand, Mulk Raj. *Conversations in Bloomsbury.* New Delhi: Arnold-Heinemann, 1981.

Badami, Rau Anita. *The Hero's Walk.* Toronto: Alfred A. Knopf Canada, 2000.

Bissoondath, Neil. *Digging up the Mountains.* Toronto: Macmillan, 1985.

_____. *Selling Illusions: The Cult of Multiculturalism in Canada.* Toronto: Penguin, 1994.

Bloom, Allan. *The Closing of the American Mind: How Higher Education Has Failed Democracy and Impoverished the Souls of American Students.* New York: Simon and Schuster, 1987.

Butalia, Urvashi. *The Other Side of Silence: Voices from the Partition of India.* New Delhi: Penguin, 1998.

Conway, J. K., ed. *Written by Herself: Women's Memoirs from Britain, Africa, Asia, and the United States.* New York: Vintage, 1996.

D'Souza, Dinesh. *Illiberal Education: The Politics of Race and Sex on Campus.* New York: Free Press, 1991.

Evenson, Norma. "An Architectural Hybrid." In *Bombay: Mosaic of Modern Culture*, S. Patel and A. Thorner, eds. Bombay: Oxford University Press, 1995.

Fuentes, Carlos. "How I Started to Write." In *The Art of the Personal Essay: An Anthology from the Classical Era to the Present*, P. Lopate, ed. New York: Anchor-Doubleday, 1994.

Gandhi [motion picture]. Directed and produced by Richard Attenborough, 1982. In colour, 188 minutes running time.

Granatstein, J. L. *Who Killed Canadian History?* Toronto: Harper Collins, 1998.

Guha, Ranajit. *Dominance without Hegemony: History and Power in Colonial India*. Cambridge: Harvard University Press, 1997.

Handlin, Oscar and Lilian Handlin,. eds. *From the Outer World: Perspectives on People and Places, Manners and Customs in the United States, as Reported by Travelers from Asia, Africa, Australia, and Latin America*. Cambridge: Harvard University Press, 1997.

Harney, Robert. *Toronto: Canada's New Cosmopolite*. Toronto: The Multicultural History Society of Ontario, 1981.

hooks, bell. *Teaching to Transgress: Education as the Practice of Freedom*. New York: Routledge, 1994.

Irving, John. *A Widow for a Year*. Toronto: A. Knopf, 1998.

Joyce, James. *Portrait of the Artist as a Young Man*. New York: Viking Press, 1916.

Kennedy, Donald. *Academic Duty*. Cambridge: Harvard University Press, 1997.

Lasch, Christopher. *The Revolt of the Elites and the Betrayal of Democracy*. New York: W. W. Norton, 1995.

Lopate, Phillip, ed. Introduction to *The Art of the Personal Essay: An Anthology from the Classical Era to the Present*. New York: Anchor-Doubleday, 1994.

Mistry, Rohinton. *Tales from Firozsha Baag*. Toronto: McClelland and Stewart, 1987.

Moraes, Dom. *Bombay*. Amsterdam: Time-Life International, 1979.

Nadas, Peter. *A Book of Memories*. New York: Penguin, 1997.

Naipaul, V. S. "I am the Sum of My Books." The *Globe and Mail*, December 10, 2001, R3.

Narayan, R. K. "Vedanta Plaza." In *From the Outer World: Perspectives on People and Places, Manners and Customs in the United States*, O. Handlin and L. Handlin, eds. pp. 260-270. Cambridge: Harvard University Press, 1997.

Patterson, Orlando. *The Ordeal of Integration: Progress and Resentment in America's "Racial" Crisis*. Washington: Counterpoint, 1997.

Rushdie, Salman. *The Ground beneath Her Feet*. New York: Henry, Holt and Company, 1999.

_____. *Midnight's Children*. London: Picador, 1981.

_____. *The Satanic Verses*. The Consortium, 1992.

_____. *Step across This Line: Collected Non-Fiction 1992-2002*. Toronto: Alfred Knopf, 2002.

_____. "Unfunny Valentine." The *Globe and Mail*, February 5, 1999, p. A13.

Sanders, Leslie. "White Teacher, Black Literature." In *Talking about Difference*, C. James and A. Shadd, eds. Toronto: Between the Lines, 1994.

Sen, Amartya. "India and the West." *The New Republic*, June 7, 1993.

Sommers, Christina. *Who Stole Feminism: How Women Have Betrayed Women.* New York: Simon and Schuster, 1994.

Syal, Meera. *Anita and Me.* New York: The New Press, 1996.

Tagore, Rabindranath. "A Monotony of Multitudes." In *From the Outer World: Perspectives on People and Places, Manners and Customs in the United States*, O. Handlin and L. Handlin, eds. Cambridge: Harvard University Press, 1997.

Tharoor, Shashi. *India: From Midnight to the Millennium.* New York: Arcade, 1997.

William, A. Henry III. *In Defense of Elitism.* New York: Doubleday, 1994.

Suggested Readings

NON-FICTION

IMMIGRANTS TO CANADA

Adelman, Howard, Allan Borowski, Meyer Burstein, and Lois Foster, eds. *Immigration and Refugee Policy: Australia and Canada Compared.* 2 vols. Toronto: University of Toronto Press, 1994.

Burnet, Jean, and Howard Palmer. *"Coming Canadians." An Introduction to a History of Canada's People.* Toronto: McClelland and Stewart, 1988.

Nakhaie, Reza, M., ed. *Debates on Social Inequality: Class, Gender and Ethnicity in Canada.* Toronto: Harcourt Brace and Company, 1999.

Troper, Harold, and Morton Weinfeld, eds. *Ethnicity, Politics and Public Policy: Case Studies in Canadian Diversity.* Toronto: University of Toronto Press, 1999.

Tulchinsky, Gerald, ed. *Immigration in Canada: Historical Perspectives.* Toronto: Copp-Clark, 1994.

SOUTH ASIANS IN CANADA

Buchignani, Norman, and Doreen M. Indra. *Continuous Journey: A Social History of South Asians in Canada.* Toronto: McClelland and Stewart, 1985.

Israel, Milton, and N. K. Wagle. *Ethnicity, Identity, Migration: The South Asian Context.* Toronto: University of Toronto, Centre for South Asian Studies, 1993.

INDIA

Chandra, Bipin, Mridula Mukherjee, and Aditya Mukherjee. *India after Independence 1947-2000.* New Delhi: Penguin, 1999.

289

Khilnani, Sunil. *The Idea of India.* Delhi: Penguin, 1997.

Mendelsohn, Oliver, and Marika Viciziany. *The Untouchables: Subordination, Poverty and the State in Modern India.* Cambridge: Cambridge University Press, 1998.

Naipaul, V. S. *India: A Million Mutinies.* London: Minerva, 1990.

Varma, Pavan. *The Great Indian Middle-Class.* Delhi: Penguin, 1998.

WOMEN IN INDIA

Menon, Nivedita, ed. *Gender and Politics in India.* New Delhi: Oxford University Press, 1999.

Rajan, Rajeswari Sunder, ed. *Signposts: Gender Issues in Post-independence India.* Delhi: Kali For Women, 1999.

Sathyamurthy, T. V., ed. *Region, Religion, Caste, Gender and Culture in Contemporary India.* Delhi: Oxford University Press, 1996.

FEMINISM

Alexander, Meena. *Fault Lines: A Memoir.* New York: Feminist Press, 1993.

Conway, J. K., ed. *Written by Herself: Women's Memoirs from Britain, Africa, Asia, and the United States.* New York: Vintage, 1996.

Crow, Barbara, and Lise Gotell. *Open Boundaries: A Canadian Women's Studies Reader.* Toronto: Prentice-Hall, 2000.

Heitlinger, Alena, ed. *Émigré Feminism: Transnational Perspectives.* Toronto: University of Toronto Press, 1999.

Nussbaum, Martha. *Sex and Social Justice.* Oxford: Oxford University Press, 1999.

Roman, Leslie, and Linda Eyre, eds. *Dangerous Territories: Struggles for Difference and Equality in Education.* New York: Routledge, 1997.

Wade-Gayles, Gloria. *Pushed Back to Strength: A Black Woman's Journey Home.* Boston: Beacon Press, 1993.

RACISM IN CANADA

Cannon, Margaret. *The Invisible Empire: Racism in Canada.* Toronto: Random House, 1995.

Henry, Francis, Carol Tator, Winston Mattis, and Tim Rees. *The Colour of Democracy: Racism in Canadian Society.* Toronto: Harcourt Brace, 1995.

James, Carl, ed. *Perspectives on Racism and the Human Service Sector: A Case for Change.* Toronto: University of Toronto, 1996.

Strong-Boag, Veronica, Sherrill Grace, Avigail Eisenberg, and Joan Anderson, eds. *Painting the Maple: Essays on Race, Gender, and the Construction of Canada.* Vancouver: University of British Columbia Press, 1998.

FICTION

South Asians in North America

Jhabwala, Ruth Prawer. *East into Upper East: Plain Tales from New York and New Delhi*. Washington: Counterpoint, 1998.

Lahiri, Jhumpa. *Interpreter of Maladies*. Boston: Houghton Mifflin, 1999.

Mukherjee, Bharati. *The Middleman and Other Stories*. Markham: Viking, 1986.

Narayan, Kirin. *Love, Stars and All That*. New York: Washington Square Press, 1994.

Vassanji, M. G. *Amriika*. Toronto: McClelland and Stewart, 1999.

India

Desai, Anita. *Diamond Dust: Stories*. Boston: Houghton Mifflin, 2000.

Hospital, Turner Janette. *The Ivory Swing*. Toronto: Seal Books, 1983.

Mistry, Rohinton. *A Fine Balance*. Toronto: McClelland and Stewart, 1995; and *Family Matters*. Toronto: McClelland and Stewart, 2002.

Roy, Arundhati. *The God of Small Things*. New Delhi: India Ink, 1997.

Rushdie, Salman. *Midnight's Children*. London: Picador, 1982.

Seth, Vikram. *A Suitable Boy*. Boston: Little, Brown, 1993.

Women in India

Baldwin, Shauna Singh. *What the Body Remembers*. Toronto: Alfred A. Knopf, 1999.

Desai, Anita. *Fasting, Feasting*. London: Chatto and Windus, 1999.

Divakaruni, Chitra Banerjee. *Arranged Marriage*. New York: Doubleday, 1995.

Racism in Canada

Alexis, Andre. *Childhood*. Toronto: McClelland and Stewart, 1998.

Bissoondath, Neil. *The Innocence of Age*. Toronto: Alfred A. Knopf, 1992.

Brand, Dionne. *In Another Place, Not Here*. Toronto: Vintage, 1997.

Chong, Denise. *The Concubine's Children*. Toronto: Penguin, 1995.

Hutcheon, Linda, and Marion Richmond, eds. *Other Solitudes: Canadian Multicultural Fictions*. Toronto: Oxford University Press, 1990.

Life Writing Series

In the **Life Writing Series**, Wilfrid Laurier University Press publishes life writing and new life-writing criticism in order to promote autobiographical accounts, diaries, letters, and testimonials written and/or told by women and men whose political, literary, or philosophical purposes are central to their lives. **Life Writing** features the accounts of ordinary people, written in English, or translated into English from French or the languages of the First Nations or from any of the languages of immigration to Canada. Life Writing will also publish original theoretical investigations about life writing, as long as they are not limited to one author or text.

Priority is given to manuscripts that provide access to those voices that have not traditionally had access to the publication process.

Manuscripts of social, cultural, and historical interest that are considered for the series, but are not published, are maintained in the **Life Writing Archive** of Wilfrid Laurier University Library.

Series Editor
Marlene Kadar
Humanities Division, York University

Manuscripts to be sent to
Brian Henderson, Director
Wilfrid Laurier University Press
75 University Avenue West
Waterloo, Ontario, Canada N2L 3C5

Books in the Life Writing Series Published by Wilfrid Laurier University Press

Haven't Any News: Ruby's Letters from the Fifties
edited by Edna Staebler with an Afterword by Marlene Kadar
1995 / x + 165 pp. / ISBN 0-88920-248-6

"I Want to Join Your Club": Letters from Rural Children, 1900-1920
edited by Norah L. Lewis with a Preface by Neil Sutherland
1996 / xii + 250 pp. (30 b&w photos) / ISBN 0-88920-260-5

And Peace Never Came by Elisabeth M. Raab with Historical Notes by Marlene Kadar
1996 / x + 196 pp. (12 b&w photos, map) / ISBN 0-88920-281-8

Dear Editor and Friends: Letters from Rural Women of the North-West,
1900-1920 edited by Norah L. Lewis
1998 / xvi + 166 pp. (20 b&w photos) / ISBN 0-88920-287-7

The Surprise of My Life: An Autobiography by Claire Drainie Taylor
with a Foreword by Marlene Kadar
1998 / xii + 268 pp. (+ 8 colour photos and 92 b&w photos) / ISBN 0-88920-302-4

Memoirs from Away: A New Found Land Girlhood by Helen M. Buss / Margaret Clarke
1998 / xvi + 153 pp. / ISBN 0-88920-350-4

The Life and Letters of Annie Leake Tuttle: Working for the Best
by Marilyn Färdig Whiteley
1999 / xviii + 150 pp. / ISBN 0-88920-330-X

Marian Engel's Notebooks: "Ah, mon cahier, écoute" edited by Christl Verduyn
1999 / viii + 576 pp. / ISBN 0-88920-333-4 cloth / ISBN 0-88920-349-0 paper

Be Good Sweet Maid: The Trials of Dorothy Joudrie by Audrey Andrews
1999 / vi + 276 pp. / ISBN 0-88920-334-2

Working in Women's Archives: Researching Women's Private Literature
and Archival Documents edited by Helen M. Buss and Marlene Kadar
2001 / vi + 120 pp. / ISBN 0-88920-341-5

Repossessing the World: Reading Memoirs by Contemporary Women
by Helen M. Buss
2002 / xxvi + 206 pp. / ISBN 0-88920-408-x cloth / ISBN 0-88920-410-1 paper

Chasing the Comet: A Scottish-Canadian Life by Patricia Koretchuk
2002 / xx + 244 pp. / ISBN 0-88920-407-1

The Queen of Peace Room by Magie Dominic
2002 / xii + 115 pp. / ISBN 0-88920-417-9

China Diary: The Life of Mary Austin Endicott by Shirley Jane Endicott
2002 / xvi + 251 pp. / ISBN 0-88920-412-8

The Curtain: Witness and Memory in Wartime Holland by Henry G. Schogt
2003 / xii + 132 pp. / ISBN 0-88920-396-2

Teaching Places by Audrey J. Whitson
2003 / xiii + 178 pp. / ISBN 0-88920-425-X

Through the Hitler Line by Laurence F. Wilmot, M.C.
2003 / xvi + 152 pp. / ISBN 0-88920-426-8

Where I Come From by Vijay Agnew
2003 / xiv + 298 pp. / ISBN 0-88920-414-4